# WORLDS TO KNOW

*A Philosophy of Cosmic Perspectives*

# *Worlds to know*

## A PHILOSOPHY OF COSMIC PERSPECTIVES

*By*

### RADOSLAV A. TSANOFF

*Professor Emeritus of Philosophy*
*Professor of Humanities*
*Rice University*

HUMANITIES PRESS
NEW YORK

Type set at The Polyglot Press

Printed in the United States of America
by Noble Offset Printers, Inc.

DEDICATED TO

RICE UNIVERSITY

SEMI-CENTENNIAL, 1912-1962

# TABLE OF CONTENTS

# PART III. THE REALITY OF VALUES

# Part I.

# REALITY AS SUBSTANCE

# CHAPTER I.

# THE TRADITIONAL WORLD OF BODIES AND MINDS

## 1. Introduction

We speak commonly of our world in the singular, but as our general title indicates, there are several worlds to know. The scientist, the historian, the artist, the business man or the industrialist, the religious worshipper, each of these shares with the others some aspects of the world which engage us all, but also concentrates on his own characteristic perspective or slant on nature. We are all in the same world, but it is not the same for all of us. These radical differences of cosmic outlook are familiar to us in our daily experience and social converse. There are group opinions or professional viewpoints that find expression in the various kinds of shop talk to which the outsider may listen, perhaps with some interest, but in which he can scarcely participate. A newspaperman who may have to report in turn on a business men's convention, a scientific meeting, an art exhibit, or a religious assembly must feel like a traveler in different worlds. I belong to a university staff, and daily around the luncheon tables at the Faculty Club the course of conversation has carried my colleagues and me through the various worlds of different professional interests.

In this variety of world outlooks the specialist in each field, in his own work, naturally follows his particular bent. But he also can and does learn from others, for every man is sure to spend a part of his life of thought across the borderlands which separate him from his sundry neighbors. Here, for instance, is an unusually wide-ranging physical scientist who is distinguished in his specialty but also takes an active interest in public problems, has a cultivated musical ear and keen appreciation of poetry, and some religious sympathies. How does he manage to see his way through, in what variety of orderly thought? In our conversations he holds firmly to his scientific view of the world, but how does he then allow for his other outlooks which make his life so richly significant?

This situation in our daily experience raises a problem of intellectual synthesis which cannot be set aside. Contemporary thought records this need of correlation in many fields. Modern atomic research has imposed on our minds a radical revision of fundamental principles of cosmological outlook. Evolutionary biology has settled quite definitely certain traditional issues about life processes, but it has also raised new problems of philosophical interpretation. And likewise we find that psychology, the social sciences, and the humanities, with their contributions to a theory and an appraisal of civilization — all of them raise problems of cosmic import.

These world perspectives, as we may call them, are sometimes contending alternatives between which we have to choose. But they may be also complementary: they may indicate an available expansion of understanding, a deepening of insight. In some degree all of these fundamental slants of thought have engaged philosophical inquiry from its earliest beginnings in Greece: but the history of ideas manifests a shifting emphasis on one or on another of these approaches to nature. Some interesting problems of interpretation are thus brought to our attention. The examination of them will be the purpose of this study.

In trying to understand nature and human nature we may consider mainly things and substances, the various kinds of beings, their essential qualities, their relations to each other. A plain survey of the data of experience leads us to recognize, beyond all detailed kinships or differences in nature, the deep-lying duality of material and mental existence. Thus arises the agelong problem of body and mind, with its various proposed solutions, which will be examined in this chapter.

The many baffling difficulties of explaining the relations of mind and body when regarded as substances have led to the modern emphasis on a dynamic conception of reality, to which scientific and philosophical thought has proceeded also on other grounds. Nature has been conceived not so much as a system of things but rather as a cosmos of processes. From this dynamic

4

point of view the main alternative interpretations of nature present themselves in a new contending array. Now we ask: What sort of plot or action is the course of nature? Is it ultimately mechanical, and are all kinds of activity in the world basically reducible to physical processes? Or do the purposive character and the productive initiative of our intelligent experience manifest a type of activity which no thorough interpretation of nature can ignore or explain away in mechanical terms? Surely it is not necessary to point out that we have here the old mind-body problem, expanded and deepened in a cosmic perspective.

The dynamic outlook of the theory of activism is confronted with the problem of purposive activity or teleology. The straightforward recognition of the purposive character of intelligent activity has led many minds to consider the values with which purposive intelligence is concerned. Philosophical inquiry has thus acknowledged another ultimate aspect of reality, the world of values. This is surely a fundamental involvement of all the activities of our higher life. How are we to relate it to our other basic phases? How are we to consider the reality of our spiritual values: truth, beauty, virtue, justice? How are we to interpret Plato's conviction that the highest type of reality is "the Idea of Good," the Principle of Value?

Even in this brief introductory statement we may note some of the fundamental outlooks on reality as they confront philosophical inquiry. A glance at our Table of Contents will show that there are still other cosmic perspectives which we shall have to explore. And it should be stated clearly here at the outset that no list of such aspects or phases can be regarded as exhaustive. Whether or not nature has top or bottom, it is unlikely that we shall ever grasp the strict measure of either of them in a neat final formula. This reflection is not sceptical, nor does it express a romantic dispraise of formulated thinking. Knowledge advances step by step through the persistent examination and analysis of some one chosen aspect of nature, and this involves abstract procedure. In his concentration on his own set of postulates, the specialist may adapt to his use the words of the Apostle: "This one thing I know." But while knowledge is yielded by specialized inquiry and abstract procedure, wisdom awaits the insight that comes from integrated thinking. This integrated thinking has not always marked the speculations of philosophers, but it is the true purpose of philosophy. Be it noted that it must be the integration of real thinking, of what has been clearly and thoroughly thought out in detail. Goethe may teach us wisdom here, in his two lines packed with meaning:

> To reach unto the Infinite,
> Distinguish first, but then, unite! [1]

Prior to clear distinction or adequate synthesis, the early Greek theories of nature combined vaguely Substance and Process as fundamental principles of explanation. We should note the varied and also somewhat indefinite connotation of the Greek word for nature, *physis*, from which we get our terms physics, physical. *Physis* meant origin or birth and growth, the source and process of activity in a thing, how it comes to be what it is, how it arises and realizes its character and constitution. When this active principle was regarded as the basic or essential element, *physis* signified the primary stuff or matter, the substance or matrix of which things are made. *Physis* also connoted the power of growth or vital agency in living things. Or the essence of things was viewed in terms of their form and system, and then *physis* was considered as the cosmic order, and by extension the universe.

The Latin word *natura* had a similar flexibility of meaning. It was derived from the verb *nascor*, meaning "to be born." "The nature of things" signified their birth and original production, their heart and core, their essential substance and constitution. It came to mean the orderly source and course, the generation and pattern of things. May we use the term "bearing" to express this various meaning? "The bearing of things" should then signify their characteristic production, their essential structure, and their orderly relations to other things. In this brief verbal analysis the student of ancient thought may recognize hints of leading ideas in contending philosophical theories. Later reflection has carried on this interplay of the phases of substance and process, of things and activities.

The first of these views of nature, which is here called Substance, is concerned mainly with the objects of experience. It regards the world as a sum or system of existent things or substances. It recognizes their teeming variety and seeks to describe their characteristic differences, but it does not accept multiplicity and variety as the last word of understanding. It explores the relations of different things and their likely explanation as forms of some basic substance or substances. The first chapter of ancient science and philosophy, in Ionian Greece, began with the supposition which philosophers call monistic, namely, that the many various things we know are reducible in their basic nature to some primary stuff or elemental being.

The initial proposal to reduce the immense variety of things to a single primary stuff did not remain unchallenged, for the early explorers of nature were versatile in their cosmological speculations. The monistic view itself, that the observable multiplicity of things could be explained as a variety of forms of some basic substance, implied continually shifting forms in the manifestation of this substance, and so raised directly the problem of change. The controversies between the advocates of change and permanence, which were baffling when argued on a monistic basis, turned Greek minds towards a pluralistic outlook. Change and permanence could be reconciled by considering the world as a system in which a plurality of unchanging elementary substances operated in a system of everchanging combinations.

The basic view of Substance has emphasized a spatial outlook on nature. The world has been conceived as a world of things located and related to each other in space: expanding or condensing, joined or separated, above or below or alongside one another. The problem of change also tended to assume a spatial form and focused on the recognition and explanation of motion.

We shall have occasion to note the radical revision of this ancient view of nature in the developing course of modern science. But even in our age of thoroughgoing reconstruction of physics and chemistry, the traditional view of the world as an immense system of substances still characterizes much of our general unprofessional thinking. And, of course, for many purposes of description and explanation, this outlook on nature has served very well. This desk on which I am writing in the library, these chairs, doors, walls, the rows of book stacks along the long corridors, my colleagues working in their studies, all of them exist in their substantial identity and respective location. Our knowledge of things involves precise and reliable accounts of their qualities and relations: of their shape, texture, color, sound, heat, motion or rest, and of the ways in which the perceived stability or change in any of these and other qualities and conditions affect other bodies. This

7

may be taken as a rough statement of our ordinary ideas of the world in which we live.

While this cosmology has seemed obvious to common sense, its final adequacy was questioned by some critical minds in classical antiquity and by many more in modern science and philosophy. In its way it is correct, but is it a thoroughly true version of nature and of human nature?

A serious objection to the cosmology of substance has been that it yields a defective account of mind and rational activity. Socrates, to be sure, was an object in space, with his bones and muscles and the rest of him inside his skin, walking in a street of Athens or sitting on his bench in the prison cell. But this sort of account missed the main points of Socrates' character and career: his inquiring mind, his power to stimulate and enlighten other minds, his unyielding loyalty to his convictions but also his respect for the laws of his native city, his resolution to remain in prison and await his death rather than to escape, though the jailer had been bribed to open the gates. If we should try to evade these important and really relevant characteristics of Socrates in terms of whirling clusters of atoms in space, it would be, as Plato called it, "an idle mode of speaking." [2]

## 2. The Relation of Minds and Bodies: Main Alternative Theories

The history of philosophy records that the thinkers of the seventeth and early eighteenth centuries were especially engrossed by the problem of mind and body, but scarcely any period of philosophy has been indifferent to it. In considering the contending theories, we shall note their principal advocates, but shall concentrate on plain discussion rather than on detailed historical exposition.

### Causal Interaction of Mental and Material Substances

Since Descartes's dualistic cosmology drove the problem of mind and body into the center of scientific and philosophical controversy, we should start with it. It is of advantage to keep the Cartesian perspective clearly before us. Descartes did not entertain

8

a vague idea of the nature of mind and of body, the causal inter-action of which could thus be viewed somehow without definite contradiction. He insisted on a rigorously mechanical explanation of all material existence, even of the human body. But he also acknowledged the reality of rational mind. Physical science on the one hand, logic on the other: these two revealed a dualism of ul-timate and irreducible substances, material and mental, which should on no account be confused. Bodies are in space and do not think; minds are immaterial thinking substances and are not in space. As the undergraduate wit summed it up, "What is mind? - No matter! What is Matter? Never mind!" Causal interaction between them was inconceivable. Now, however, as Descartes noted, although inconceivable, interaction between minds and bodies is an observed fact. And right here is the systematic dif-ficulty of dualistic cosmologies on the Cartesian pattern, which proceed from the initial theory that bodies and minds are ulti-mate and radically different substances.

In a cosmological dualism of substances, our sense-perceptions and our voluntary actions would seem to be, as we may say, unten-able actualities. How could an idea, a mental act, be the effect of a physical process; and how could it in its turn cause and produce a bodily, physical effect? Let it be understood clearly that we are considering here, not our ability to perceive or to act voluntarily, but our perplexity in explaining these daily experiences in terms of a dualism of substances.

Imagine ourselves discussing this problem. Suppose I should request you to raise your right hands whenever you find my ex-position obscure or unconvincing. Now, how could we explain the hand-raising? You might say, it is quite simple, until you try to account for it without messing up your physical science. Simple are the facts of experience, but the explanation of them is not at all simple. Let us follow these processes step by step. I had the idea of using this example to illustrate the difficulties in our problem. No trouble so far on a dualistic basis: all this is simply thinking, the activity of my mental substance. But now we say that my mind's having this idea caused my tongue to speak out: "Will you please raise your right hands whenever you do not understand clearly what I am saying, or whenever you disagree with it." When my tongue actually speaks these words, or else when my hand writes them down, do we not have physiological, bodily processes?

9

But how could they be the effect of thinking, if thinking is a purely mental, non-physical activity?

On your side, in raising your hands, you would be embarrassing physical science in the reverse order. Let us say that we were speaking together. You heard and you understood my request and then started your hand-raising. The sound of my voice, for you, was a physical process in the air. Your auditory response to it was a physiological reaction of your organism. But note, your understanding of my words, that was purely mental, according to the dualistic comology of substances. How could this understanding, - not the stirring of your ear tissues by the air vibrations produced by my voice, but your perception of this auditory sensation and its meaning, - how could this be the effect of strictly physical and physiological processes? And furthermore, how could your ideas, perceiving and understanding my request, cause you, not always but at some specific points in our discussion, to raise your hands? How can an idea move a hand?

If we hold strictly to the dualism of substances, then every sense perception, every voluntary action would seem to violate the mechanical system of nature to which physical science is committed. In sense perception a physical cause would be regarded as having a non-physical effect; in voluntary action, a non-physical cause would be regarded as having a physical effect. In one case there would be an alleged loss of physical energy, and in the other, an alleged gain: both of them unthinkable in physical science.

### Materialistic Denial of Mental Substances

The confusion in the interactionist psychology have led many thinkers to question the analysis of nature into two radically different substances. Surely these two must be ultimately related, or one of them should be reducible to the other, and we should view nature as basically one. Dualism must finally yield to monism. This monistic revision followed several different lines of interpretation, leading to fundamentally alternative views of nature and human nature. Each of them continues to have its advocates to this day.

One of these monistic theories was the materialism of Thomas Hobbes, who disposed of Descartes's entire problem by recognizing only one kind of reality, material. What is commonly called mind is simply another variety of body. Sense perceptions are merely physiological operations of bodily substances. Voluntary actions are just as mechanical as any other physical and chemical reactions. This doctrine was neither original nor exclusive with Hobbes. It had been advocated by the atomists of Greece and Rome - Democritus, Epicurus, Lucretius - and during the three centuries since Hobbes' *Leviathan* it has had many vigorous champions. So LaMettrie wrote a treatise on *Man a Machine*; Holbach regarded consciousness as a merely physiological process, like digestion; Feuerbach proclaimed boldly: "Man is what he eats"; and Moleschott proposed a chemical analysis of reason in his formula: "No thought without phosphorus."[3] Materialists have often expressed their doctrine in the language of some prevailing scientific tendency of their times. So in the seventeenth century they followed mainly the line of mechanics; during the eighteenth century they preferred a physiological statement; and since then, chemistry, evolutionary biology, and behaviorist psychology have provided the newer versions of materialism.

Materialism claims the merit of seeking to integrate mind with the rest of nature in one continuous physical account. So even psychologists who are not prepared to go the whole length with behaviorism seem to regard it as a scientific gain if they can write their accounts of mental activities in physiological terms. What the psychologist can study scientifically is behavior, the cerebro-neural and other physiological changes of the bodily organism and the observable actions taking place when, as we say, we remember or think or will. The presumption, then, is that we gain scientific grasp of mind when we have ascertained its anatomical structure and its physiological concomitants.

The defect of materialism is basic. It is advanced as a true theory, yet in reducing mind and the meaning and value of its ideas to bodily-physical terms, it rules out any recognition of validity or truth or any other value. Ideas true or false may be entertained *about* bodies *by* minds, but not *by* bodies. How could the materialistic reduction of mind to bodily substance be proved? On his own statement, the materialist is himself merely a body, and bodies do not prove or disprove. This embarrassment would affect all science, if it were explicitly committed to an ultimate materialism. Can we really believe, how could we prove, that Newton's advance from his observing the fall of an apple to his formulation of the universal law of gravitation was itself nothing but an instance of that law? Surely we are bound to recognize that physical science itself is not merely physical. It deals with physical facts, but as a science it is a rational system. It must use and must rely on laws of logical order and necessity. If nature were exclusively reducible to material substances, the expressions "therefore," "conclusion," and "theory" would not be available, for no mere mechanics can supply their meanings, or any meaning.

The materialistic monism of substance has not provided an adequate solution of the mind-body problem because it has not really considered mind for what it is. It has not acknowledged the mind's capacity to entertain meanings, to pursue understanding, to attain and to prove truth values. Mind must quite unsay and negate itself before it can be utterly reduced to body.

Another essential disparity between the structure and behavior of bodies and the constitution of minds is the integral and interpretative character of mind, its normal concern with the meaning of the whole situation which confronts it. We may observe even in biological processes various degrees of integral reactions, for instance in the repair of tissues; but the integrity of mind expresses a response to meanings and problems. The extent of the significant relations which are thus brought into play are themselves tests of mental power. They are superlatively evident in the intelligence of scientific or poetic genius. Can a materialistic account of the causal effect of a physical stimulus on the behavior of an organism explain the difference between Newton's response and that of his gardener to the fall of the apple in the orchard, or of Wordsworth and the average tourist at Tintern Abbey?

### Epiphenomenalism

Even while claiming the merit of resting squarely on physical science, the materialistic account of mind as simply a kind of body rules out the recognition of scientific logical activity and of the other distinguishing characteristics of mind as we know it in our experience. The most careful exploration of the brain and the nervous system would still come short of revealing to us mental experience in its *full* significance. And yet we are bound to recognize the cerebro-neural concomitants of mind. There is a physiological reaction when the mind reaches a conclusion and proceeds to a decision, even though conclusion and decision are not simply neural discharges. How are we to hold together in one true statement this twofold report of our experience?

One proposed answer to this question has been to recognize the series of distinctively mental activities, and also their correspondence to the series of conditions and reactions of the organism, but to regard only the latter, the bodily-physical series, as causally determined. The actuality of sense perceptions, ideas, volitions, and mind generally, cannot be gainsaid. But now we are told: nothing mental ever operates causally in the organic-bodily system. The mental series is a causally ineffectual bypath in nature. All the causal traffic moves on the physical highway. To express this view of mind as a collateral sideglow, the term "epiphenomenalism" has been used. The theory that mind is an epiphenomenon, then, would avoid the defect of the materialistic reduction of mind to body, by acknowledging the characteristic mental experiences. But it rejects the belief that in voluntary action our minds react productively on nature. Epiphenomenalism reaffirms the strict correspondence of the mental to the physical, and then denies any causal determination of matter by mind. In the business of nature mind may not be an altogether silent partner, but at any rate it has no vote.

The doctrine of causal interaction of mind and body has been criticized as conflicting with the principle of conservation of energy. Epiphenomenalism intends to avoid this embarrassment. As its noted advocate, T. H. Huxley, put it, "the phenomena of consciousness which arise along with certain transformations of energy, cannot be interpolated in the series of these transformations inasmuch as they are not motions to which the doctrine of the conservation of energy applies."[4]

We should consider more clearly and definitely the epiphenomenalist account of the relation of mental states to physical-physiological factors. Let me use a concrete example from my direct experience at this moment. I am writing this page in my study in the Library, and, glancing at my watch, I note that it is quarter to twelve. I reflect that the warning bell will be sounding presently and that I should gather up my notes, for I want to leave by the front entrance of the Library which closes today, Saturday, at noon. I should like to finish this little discussion but realize that I lack the time for it. So even now, after writing this sentence, my hands will be clearing my desk. The five minute bell sounds; I lock up my desk, snap lock my door, and am off.

Now that I am back here again, on Monday, let us see how we are to explain the causal and collateral, epiphenomenal connectedness of all the details of my experience. The visual stimulus of the watch marking quarter to twelve was followed by some brief pencil-scratching and shuffling and gathering of notes. The ringing of the bell was followed by a quick exit. That is what a physiologist looking through my door window would have recorded. But would his account be sufficient; would it not be missing the real point? If I had not had the idea that it was Saturday, and that on Saturday the front door of the Library closes at twelve, none of the above reactions would have followed. Both in my sense perceptions and in voluntary actions, an essential factor in my response to my stimulus was my interpretation of it. The epiphenomenalist correctly remarks that ideas are not motions. But my ideas about my stimuli do somehow affect the choice of motions with which I respond to them.

## Mentalism: The Denial of Material Substances

The sharp alternative to materialistic monism has not stopped with the acknowledgment of effective mental activity. It has proceeded the whole length to the denial of any material substance. This view may be called Mentalism. Its chief advocate was the eighteenth century Irish philosopher, George Berkeley.

Berkeley was an empiricist and insisted on sticking to the direct evidence of experience. According to him, we really know only the sense perceptions and ideas of our minds. The so-called material objects are merely combinations of sense data in our experience. "Thus, for example," as he writes, "a certain colour, taste, smell, figure and consistence having been observed to go together, are accounted one distinct thing, signified by the name *apple*." Existence is so much perceptual content on which our

14

mind can reflect. "To be is to be perceived." [5] Berkeley regarded the real world as a world of our minds and their ideas.

Experience informs us that we share our ideas with other minds, yet not exactly and not altogether. The experience of various minds agree in part and in part differ. Our minds are thus finite, but they operate in a boundless range, and there is no assignable limit to their expansion. Berkeley inferred that our finite and imperfect minds are all sharers in the infinite experience of a perfect Divine Mind. God's mind is absolutely rational; of this, Berkeley was assured by the order and connection of the data of experience which our minds can share and attest.

Berkeley regarded this doctrine as adequate to provide the basis for a thoroughly consistent experimental science. Scientific knowledge does not require for its theoretical formulation the assumption of any ultimate material substance. In place of the materialist's dogmatically asserted ground of objectivity Berkeley held firmly to the course of experience itself. Experimental science is systematic knowledge of the evidence supplied by experience. The conclusions drawn from experimental inquiry, the scientific laws of nature, are the careful reports of the uniform ways in which our perceptions and ideas are connected.

This theory aroused much criticism, for surely the recognition of physical realities is fudamental to science and cannot be explained away. The materialist's denial of mental substance and his reduction of our perceptions, ideas, and volitions to physical-physiological processes give rise to serious difficulties of explanation. But the description of material objects as simply compounds of sense qualities of our minds has not carried conviction.

One disturbing result of Berkeley's theory was promptly brought out by David Hume. In good empiricist fashion Berkeley had insisted on recognizing only the data of our experience, and had therefore rejected the traditional doctrine of material substance. The only real apple is the compound of experienced qualities. But on that empiricist procedure, what grounds do we have for a doctrine of mental substances, to which Berkeley continued to adhere? If an apple is only so much roundness and redness and tartness and so forth all experienced together, then what can mind be but so many perceptions and memories and reflections and volitions all experienced together? In his stricter empiricism Hume rejected all doctrines of substances, mental as well as material.

**15**

### *Psychophysical Parallelism*

Our examination has shown us that we should not try to reduce mind to body, or body to mind. If we are to do justice to the plain facts of our experience, we are bound to recognize both material and mental elements in our complex existence. Are we thus brought back to the Cartesian dualism of minds and bodies? An offhand answer, yes or no, would scarcely suffice at this stage of our discussion. If we return to the view of material and mental substances, we shall again be embroiled in the confusing problem of their causal interaction. But may we not regard both mind and body as different phases of one ultimate reality? This double aspect theory, advanced by Spinoza, has aroused much discussion during the past three centuries. It is faced with grave objections, but in some revised form it can be the starting point towards new significant perspectives in dealing with the relation of the physical and the psychical.

The philosophy of Spinoza was a thoroughly monistic rationalism. That is to say, he relied on rational analysis but demanded its rigorous application. Cosmological dualism, he concluded, is inadmissible; it cannot be reasoned out without contradiction. There cannot be two ultimate realities, for they would have to be in some relation to each other, or one of them would be a form of the other, or both would be aspects of a really ultimate being. Substance, self-dependent reality, can be only one, infinite and eternal. Spinoza called it "God or Nature." But this universal ultimate substance manifests its essence in a variety of attributes, of which we know fundamentally two: body and mind. These are two essential aspects or phases of nature. Spinoza regarded them as universally corresponding to each other. This is the doctrine of psychophysical parallelism.

Nature, we are told, must be regarded both materially and mentally. On its material side or aspect, it is a system of extended bodies in states of motion and rest. On its mental side, nature is a rational system of thought, expressed in states of intellect and will.

The next step is crucial. According to Spinoza, these two, the material and the mental, always correspond to each other. The parallelism is universal, in detail, and in both directions. As Spinoza put it, "the order and connection of ideas is the same as the order and connection of things." [6] Consider what is taking place

16

right now as you are reading this discussion. On the one hand, it is a series of physical and physiological processes, optical, visual, stimulation or fatigue of bodily tissue. But it also demands a mental account, as your acceptance or criticism or rejection of my reasoned exposition of ideas. The mental and the material phases of nature are both ordered, each in its appropriate way. Thus there can be no question of any causal interaction between bodies and minds, for causality concerns only bodily states. But our minds and ideas have their own order of necessity, which is logical.

This doctrine in various forms is spread extensively across the pages of modern philosophy and psychology. It is not a mere compromise; it seeks a real reconciliation and synthesis of our basic views of nature. But it cannot be said to close the discussion; it raises radical problems in its turn. Of course, it may without much dispute be adopted as a convenient principle of procedure. That is to say, generally speaking, we should recognize both the physical and the mental and should not confuse them. Each has its province or perspective, and each has its appropriate order admitting of systematic inquiry. But difficulties arise as soon as we proceed to more definite and rigorous statement.

Considered as an inductive inference, the conclusion of universal parallelism in *both* directions is not impressively convincing. Psychologists would insist that all mental activities have their parallels and counterparts in certain brain changes or other bodily conditions. Surely no examples are needed: physiological psychology provides an abundant, detailed, and experimentally ascertained ground for this general conviction. But how could we assert confidently the converse proposition, that every physical state has its parallel in some mental state? All my sense data and ideas of the last Gulf hurricane had, and my memories of it still have, definite physico-physiological parallels. And there surely are some parts of that storm that did have their parallel mental states. But am I bound to go further, and can I really believe that the entire course of the hurricane — high seas, furious gales, flooded fields, ravaged forests — that it all had its mental counterpart in detail?

Parallelism leads to some odd reflections when it is applied in detail. Consider Coleridge's composition of his poem "Kubla Khan" under the influence of a narcotic. What sort of parallelism may be traced here? Of course, we say, there is the physiological counterpart of the poet's creative mental activity: the intoxication and the composition, each paralleling the other. But should we not in thorough parallelism recognize also another correlation here, namely, of the drug and its psychical "double"? Thus we might be saying that while the narcotic acted on Coleridge's body, the mental counterpart of the drug inspired the poet's mind to compose "Kubla Khan." Driesch, who quotes a similar example, regards it as rendering parallelism a laughable theory. [7]

Notwithstanding its inductively debatable character, parallelists may uphold their doctrine as an *a priori* conclusion, but some objections have to be met. The infinite Substance, according to Spinoza, must have an infinite number of essential attributes, of which we know two. It should be noted here that Spinoza had quite reinterpreted the old doctrine of Substance. The dualist, the materialist, the mentalist, each in his own way, expounded a doctrine in which ultimate reality is described as this or that kind of substance. Spinoza proceeded differently. In his theory Substance is not *a* substance, a particular variety of being. It has ultimate reality, and it is all that ultimate reality connotes, with its infinitude of attributes. It is God *or Nature*.

Psychophysical parallelism, thus considered, would mean that we should recognize some correspondence which the various aspects of nature bear to one another. But may we not here raise the question whether all these aspects are as it were on a par cosmologically? Nature manifests itself in many ways; some of them may be more or less extensive, more or less significant than others. And actually we find that philosophers and psychologists have differed in their estimate of the relative extent and importance of the basic aspects of nature. Physical scientists who do not go the whole length of materialism have generally agreed in emphasizing material existence as the more basic and fundamental attribute of nature. Descartes recognized the far more extensive range of that phase as compared with the mental; but he did not draw the inference that bodily substances manifest the nature of reality more adequately and more fundamentally than minds do. Idealists ever since Plato have emphasized in their accounts of nature the dominant role of mind. Thus some parallelists, who set out from the pre-eminence of physical science, emphasize the real character of nature as material and describe the system of conscious processes as merely the mental aspect. On the other hand, the parallelists of idealistic slant consider material existence as the external staging or framework of a reality whose inner essential character is expressed in mental terms.

Without definitely exalting one of the two parallel versions as more basic than the other, and without regarding them both as forms of appearance and turning a sceptical glance at ultimate reality, may we not proceed from parallelism to what may be called a correspondence of perspectives? In any field of our experience we may center our attention on specific description and explanation, on ascertaining the antecedent conditions which determine certain effects. We shall then be concerned with mainly physical-physiological investigations. But on the other hand, instead of dealing with the factual connection of parts with parts, we may become interested in the character and meaning of the whole experience. In this latter case, some of our inquiries will definitely require our recognition of psychical, mental existence. Furthermore, while in many other inquiries even our comprehensive study would still be the study of physical existence, the study itself, the meaning of what we are doing, would require the self-recognition of mind.

Such a view of the vast and various fields of our experience is not entirely alien to parallelism. It recognizes definite correspondence of details, as of ideas to brain changes, but it is not committed to any rigid parallelism in both directions. The two perspectives, the material and the mental, need not be coextensive throughout. Indeed, the importance of recognizing them both is in part due to the fact that, while they are in many respects parallel, each of them manifests in its own way some characteristics of reality which the other one does not disclose.


## 3. Deficiency of the Cosmology of Substances

The history of modern science records the gradual obsolescence of substantialism. In fact, a physical scientist is apt to take the transition to a dynamical view of nature as so thoroughly settled that he may regard the examination of the traditional doctrines of material and mental substances as having only a historical or even an antiquarian interest. This radical shift in basic outlook may be quite clear to the scientist, but the old view still persists in our general untechnical thinking. And it has not been in fact completely outgrown even by expert minds. Though abandoned technically in the revision of physical scientific theory, it still colors our general outlook on nature.

The relation of minds and bodies poses a problem which is fundamental and crucially important. And the problem itself, while it raises the most profound scientific and philosophical issues, is directly present to the least technical reflection. No amount of learned subtlety and mathematical equations can set it aside. Whatever the most expert science and philosophy may conclude regarding the nature and constitution of the world, we are justified in expecting that they should somehow include and reveal us, ourselves and no other, recognize us somewhere in their portrayal of our world. A world-view which rules us out is no world-view for us. We rightly demand that the scientist and the philosopher should not forget us — or themselves. A specialized science may not raise this problem directly, though even a scientist cannot ignore it finally. But for a philosopher the issue is inescapable. It is a cardinal test of a philosophical system that it must be capable of accounting for itself, and for the thinking that produced it. That is why the problem of mind and of man's place in nature is central. It therefore provides a decisive trial of the basic adequacy of the traditional world-view of substantialism.

Our test has exposed essential defects in the cosmological perspective of substances. So long as we maintain that standpoint in our view of nature, neither dualism nor monism of whatever sort, materialistic, mentalist, or unqualified, can give us a reliable account of our daily life and experience. Substantialism cannot comprehend or express the central and directive reality of the self, which gives both our mind and our body their characteristic operation. We are betrayed by a misleading abstraction when we confuse the relation of our mind to our body with the relation of mental to material substance. In our life and experience mind and body are both two and one, distinguishable and not separable. The mind is not a mind apart from the brain; nor is the brain a brain apart from the mind. The substantialist should not put asunder that which nature has joined and made concretely one in the living process of experience.

*I* have a brain, and *I* think, but my *brain* does *not* think.[8] The doctrine of material and mental substances proceeds mistakenly on an initial abstract definition of substantial character which is supposedly preserved throughout. The facts point otherwise. A living body is not reducible to so much chemical composition. And an "intelligent organism" cannot be explained adequately either in terms of the adjective or in terms of the noun. Each one of these is integral with the other. So Goethe cultivated in his Weimar garden the oriental gingo tree with its two-lobed leaf, to remind him of the truth of his own nature:

> Do you not feel it in my poems? -
> I am twofold, and yet one! [9]

Aristotle held to a similar interpretation in his phrase describing man as an animate body. The mind is the form of man's body, even as vision is the form of the eye. Of course, we can distinguish the two, but we should never forget their living unity. There is no vision apart from the eye; but unseeing and apart from its function in our life, an eye is not an eye. The basic truth that is expressed throughout is the principle of vital integrity which is manifest in various degrees, from rudimentary forms of life clear to the heights of intelligent activity.

Against this truth is the error or the basic confusion of the abstractions which tear nature apart and then vainly try to piece it together. Nature is not to be understood as a patchwork, nor as a mosaic, however complicated, and this insight into nature becomes clearer and more convincing as we consider the higher levels of existence. In vital integrity the parts of an organism flow into the whole, and the whole saturates each part. Man, a personal minded body or embodied mind, is the pre-eminent instance of this more and more thoroughly organic character of nature.

Our daily experience shows us that we can recognize neither our mind nor our body, nor yet understand their relation, unless we study the concrete processes of our daily life and thought. Be it noted, however, that in considering these concrete processes of our daily life, we still continue to speak of them as bodily or as mental. We still find it natural to use the terms "body" and "mind" as suitable frameworks of reference to various distinguishable types of activity. We may thus recognize the scope and also the limits of the significant use of the perspective of substantialism. Mind and body are traditional ways by which we indicate certain processes and activities of our experience. These ways of abstract reference need to be revised or supplemented by the more direct appeal to the dynamics of bodily and mental life. Now we ask: This standpoint of activism towards which we are turning, is it limited only to our interpretation of ourselves, or is it not rather a fundamental cosmological perspective in which all nature may be viewed and understood significantly? To this question we proceed in our next chapter.

# Part II.

# REALITY AS PROCESS: ACTIVISM

CHAPTER II

# THE WORLD OF CAUSAL MECHANISM

*1. Transitions from Substance to Process in Ancient Thought*

The most characteristic feature of the contemporary outlook on the world has been called "the discovery of Time."[1] The view of reality as ongoing in time has emphasized agencies rather than substances: processes in time rather than substances in space. Before we examine some of the modern developments of thought which have led to these conclusions, it would be well to note briefly a few earlier expressions of this trend of ideas.

The primacy of action in engaging our attention, in stimulating and expressing mental activity, may be noted in the formation of language. Some comparative philologists have held that the earliest words in Indo-European languages were verbs, not nouns. Our distant ancestors spoke first of forms of action and of their own reactions to the ongoing processes of nature all about them. Substantives had a verbal or a participial origin. The Greek *logos*, described in the lexicon as a "verbal noun," meant "word" and also "thought," but it likewise signified reckoning, relating, ordering, or generative principle or force. As was remarked already, the Greek *physis* and the Latin *natura* both had the connotation of productivity, generation, growth-power. When the Ionic explorers of nature asked, "What is the world made of?" their primary stuff or matter was regarded by them also as the root of things. Anaxagoras spoke of his indefinite plurality of elements as "the seeds of existence." He also required a directive agency in the cosmic process and called it *Nous*, Reason; but he wavered in treating it sometimes as a rational power and sometimes as a mechanical disposition.

Aristotle listed Substance as first in his table of categories, but we should not regard him as an unqualified substantialist. Against the Democritean atoms, unalterable bits of solid stuff which can be only joined or torn apart, Aristotle's matter is not any set material substance. It is continually realizing its potentialities, or better, matter is always potentiality involved in the process of realization.

The Stoics of Greece and Rome spoke of the cosmic system or rational scheme of things as the "seed-power" or germinating *logos* of nature. The second leader of the Stoa, Cleanthes, advanced the principle of "tension" in his dynamic cosmology. Unlike the Epicurean theory of atoms, which were unchangeable minimal bits of matter, entirely-filled space, the Stoic doctrine described a world in which everything was in process of transformation due to different degrees of tension. Air flames into fire, liquids become solids or conversely, and things change their qualities and forms of behavior under conditions of increased or relaxed tension. Nature was conceived as a system of stresses or intensities. On the face of it, the doctrine of tension seems to accentuate the Stoic materialism. But tension was used also to explain the course of moral conduct, the wayward indecision or the firm resolution of the will, our petulance or our rational choice in serene conformity to the direction of Divine Providence.

We just noted the dual meaning of *Nous*, Reason, and the Stoic interplay of mechanism and teleology of Divine Providence. We shall recognize a similar problem in the modern theories of activism: how to rise from a view of reality as process, as achieving, to a metaphysical or theological summit of absolute perfection.

The spiritual and definitely religious involvement is fundamental in any thorough activism which recognizes the reality of values. Some cosmological reasoning has started with a spiritual first principle and has contemplated the entire world process in a religious perspective. Throughout the history of philosophy, Neoplatonism has set the pattern for this view of the universe. Nature has been regarded as a theophany, the self-manifestation of Deity. In the cosmic vision of Plotinus, the absolute perfect reality of God was seen as an essentially radiating or "emanating" activity. The hierarchy of existence represented the principal degrees or zones of God's emanation. In gradational order, the Neoplatonist viewed the universe as a system of rationality, as a

26

world of souls, and as a course of material processes. The contending phases of the spiritual and the physical were contemplated in the drama of human life and also in their vast cosmic range. Man's character and career, expressed in each choice and action, were seen as either a step Godward or as a straying towards the abyss. And the vast cosmic range, from divine center to outermost material verge, had already been expressed for the Neoplatonists in that opening utterance of the Fourth Christian Gospel which they lauded as sublime: "The Light shineth in the darkness, and the darkness apprehended or overcame it not."

These few instances from the earlier periods of philosophical thought have been selected as exemplifying the tendency to shift the emphasis in cosmology from substances to processes. These trends towards activism also illustrate the main problem which is bound to confront this sort of cosmology: What sort of activity manifests the essential character of nature? Is the world a mechanical system of tensions, stresses, and drives, or is the mechanical order only the external framework of a rational plan, the staging of the cosmic drama of God's self-utterance in the range of finitude? Modern activism has reaffirmed this fundamental problem. It has assumed several specific forms: the issues between mechanism and teleology, between the finite and the infinite, and the more directly religious problem of theodicy, the explanation of evil in a world under Divine Providence. These problems could be discussed in their Neoplatonic setting, but it will be better to consider some of them in the philosophy of Leibniz, who may be regarded as the preëminent modern pioneer in the cosmology of activism.

## 2. The Activism of Leibniz's Monadology

Leibniz both agreed and disagreed with the Cartesian analysis of the two finite substances, body and mind. He accepted Descartes' definition of mind as thinking substance, for surely thinking activity expressed the essential character of mind. To be a mind is to think. But he found the analysis of material substance by both Descartes and Spinoza unsatisfactory. The definition of body as extended being, in space, was inadequate according to Leibniz. This extensional or dimensional account of bodily existence expressed its common feature but did not grasp its essential character. A chestnut has the size and shape of a brown pebble, but the radical difference between them transcends their similarity in space. So Leibniz reasoned that we do not understand the nature of bodies until we recognize each of them in its characteristic active role. We need a dynamical conception of matter.

Thus the first principle of Leibniz's account of nature is its activism. The world is a system of processes. But as we noted, we have now to face our question: What kind or kinds of processes, and what sort of system, if any? How are we to relate cosmically the different behavior of stones and plants and animals and reasoning men? The old problem of the relation of minds and bodies may be recognized here in a new dynamical setting, but we should seek also some other issues of metaphysical import. How can we recognize both change and permanence, active self-maintenance through growth and development, cosmic system and also unique individuality? Consider a substance. We come to understand it as we learn its predicates, the characteristic ways in which its activity is manifested and identified. It may be similar to other things, but not altogether; finally we must acknowledge it for what it is itself, a unique center of activities. Leibniz used the term "monad" to express this distinctive-representative character. Each monad expresses the universe uniquely in its own manner.

The theory of monads emphasized the dynamical character of nature throughout, as a system of activities, and it also acknowledged the unique individuality of each active center or monad. But how could there be a cosmic system of monads? Leibniz said that the monads had "no windows." Causal interaction between them was as untenable as between the Cartesian two substances. Note, however, that while each monad is unique, it is a unique expression of the universe. What each monad represents in its own manner must ultimately correspond to what every other monad represents. This mutual correspondence of the monads provided the cosmic bond in Leibniz's view of nature. He called it the principle of pre-established harmony and sought to illustrate it in various ways. The monads were compared to a number of synchronized clocks, or less mechanically, to a number of bands or orchestras playing in universal harmony. The doctrine of pre-established harmony became also the chief argument in Leibniz's theology. God is the Great Monad, harmonizing all the others in a cosmic system.

28

Unlike ancient Anaxagoras, Leibniz did not waver in his interpretation of the Great Monad. The author of the pre-established harmony is God, and we are thus assured, not only that there is a system of cosmic activity, but also what sort of a system it is and what direction of activity it indicates. Leibniz demanded an unqualified acknowledgment of the rational purposive activity of the higher monads. This in turn pointed to his theory of the relation of minds and bodies, as a correspondence of higher to lower centers of activity. At lower levels of description, the human organism is a physical-physiological system of processes. In a higher perspective, the human mind is a personality, like Socrates, rationally active, a character of noble integrity and firm convictions. Leibniz used the term "God" not only as a metaphysician but also as a theologian, and so he was involved in the problems of theodicy. God's pre-established harmony explains the rational order in nature and gives cosmic significance to our spiritual activity. In our commitment to virtue, to truth and justice, we are fellow-citizens of the Republic of Minds, God's masterpiece in the universe. But whoever recognizes good must take account of evil. The theological emphasis in Leibniz's conception of the Great Monad, as God, made theodicy, the explanation of evil, a crucial philosophical problem for him. We can only mention this here, for the critical discussion of the problem of evil belongs in our final chapter, on the reality of values.

## 3. The Turn to Activism in Physical Science

The mind's awareness of itself has always been active. Our mind is our experience, and so it has been natural to think of it in terms of process. As we have noted, even the substantialists have defined mind as thinking substance, that is, as a substance characterized by its essential operation. The demand for a dynamical conception of matter, a theory of bodies as centers of activity has marked the leading development of modern physical science. It is beyond our province or competence to review here the detailed technical findings in this field, but the radical change in fundamental cosmic outlook is of major philosophical importance, and we should consider its main outlines.

"Classical" physics and chemistry, until the latter part of the nineteenth century, conceived of nature as a system of substances affecting each other in various uniform ways and relations. The world of our traditional science, as Whitehead put it, consisted of "bits of matter, moving about in space which otherwise is empty, . . . chairs, tables, bits of rock, oceans, animal bodies, vegetable bodies, planets, and suns."[2] Scientific inquiry sought to formulate the universal laws which regulate the interactions of this boundless variety of substances. Scientific analysis also aimed to reduce this infinite variety to its basic constituents. Both of these goals seemed to be attained in the science of our forefathers: in the Newtonian physics and in the standard chemistry with its periodic table of elements. The settled scientist in the course of the nineteenth century was not unaware of some disturbing radical notes in scientific speculation, but in the main he was confident in his grasp of the basic principles of the structure and mechanism of nature. It seemed that further inquiry would be largely in the direction of greater detailed precision, advancing the scientific calculations so many decimal points.

The trend, both experimental and theoretical, during the past half-century has run counter to the substantialism of the earlier physical science. Contemporary research has discredited the analysis of nature into the elements as traditionally conceived, as irreducible varieties of material substance. And it has required the thoroughgoing revision of the classical mechanics. The interplay of the new ideas in chemistry and physics has led scientific theory and its applications to the threshold and over the threshold of a new world of boundless prospects but also of dire perils. The practical aspects of this modern advance have attracted general notice. In the world crisis of our atomic age they have lately been driven home to the anxious attention of us all.

A broad glance at the historical background of the modern development will enable us to understand it more clearly and appreciate its basic significance. The history of ideas records, in its chemical chapters, men's continual wavering between monism and pluralism in their thought of the constitution of matter. As was noted briefly in the previous chapter, Greek philosophy began in the sixth century before our Christian era with inquiries into the basic stuff of which things are made. Thales believed it to be water; his successors advanced alternative doctrines of the ultimate matter: as air, as fire, or some less obviously definable but more fundamental, boundless matrix of all stuffs and substances. These were the first chapters of chemistry, a chemistry of one element. The problem of change, which required solution if the complex variety of things in nature was to be explained, led the Greek mind to the alternative cosmology of pluralism. The world was conceived as a system of numerous permanent elements in ever-changing combinations.

Pluralism in its turn raised two problems which complicated and also deepened the early scientific and philosophical inquiries. What is the number and the character of the constituent elements in nature, and what produces the changing combination or disintegration of the forms which the primary substances assume in the world about us? A variety of answers to these questions reached a climax of Greek naturalism in the atomic theory of Democritus, a contemporary of Socrates. Democritus saw the world as a boundless vortex of atoms, indivisible bits of matter moving in space. These atoms are qualitatively alike but differ in size and shape. Some have projections; others have crevices, still others are smooth, round or oval. These quantitative differences affect behavior of the atoms as they collide with each other. Various clusters or masses of these atoms comprise all the things in nature, and their operation throughout is strictly mechanical.

This atomism may impress us as somewhat crude in its initial statement, but does it not express in its fundamentals the traditional view of physical science? In the nineteenth century Dalton reduced the composition of nature to elementary unchanging particles or atoms. The combination or the separation of them was believed to determine the nature and the behavior of every body.

Atomism from Democritus to Dalton raised the basic problem of accounting for the great variety of things in nature, and also for the changes which these various things undergo. Democritus, holding firm to the qualitative identity of all atoms, indivisible bits of entirely filled space, ascribed the different behavior of various things to the diverse sizes and shapes of the atoms composing them. This explanation seemed inadequate to account for the great complexity of nature. Later chemical speculation followed the lead of Anaxagoras' qualitative pluralism, in maintaining a doctrine of a large number of basic substances differing in kind. Or, moving in the opposite direction, thinkers reverted to monistic surmises and questioned the doctrine of finally irreducible elements. The different forms of matter, it was thought, may allow of rearrangement. By using the right reagents, we may be able to change one substance into another. This was the fond hope of the alchemists who sought the "philosopher's stone" that could turn baser metals into gold.

The alchemists by and large were avid exploiters of nature rather than inquirers, and even among the better ones the lure of the occult prevailed over sober scientific research, like superstition in the reverse. So one of the Medicis, a bold worldly spirit of the Renaissance, maintained his private chapel, to be sure, in any eventuality; but an inconspicuous side-door in it led down a steep stairway to his private alchemical laboratory - there might be something in it! Yet even in the Middle Ages, minds of keener insight considered a deeper principle beyond the brewing pots and vials of the alchemist. So Albertus Magnus reasoned that the various metals may be compounds of more elementary forms of matter. If we could learn the processes of their respective composition, we could subject them to the appropriate conditions and transform their properties. But the chemical combinations of substances in nature are due to their respective affinities for each other, and this variety of correlations, while permitting some transformations, may exclude others.

The systematic advance of physics during the early modern period, especially in the seventeenth century, was not matched by any corresponding progress in chemistry. After the epoch-making work of Lavoisier, however, chemistry made up for lost time, during the nineteenth century. This systematic advance was along definitely pluralistic lines. It emphasized sharply the difference between compounds and elements. But its growing mastery of pluralism also exposed its limitations or at least some its ambiguities. On the one hand, the precise determination of the atomic weights and distinctive qualities of the various elements professed to give us the fundamental and irreducible components of material existence. On the other hand, the remarkable periodicity in the properties of the elements, which made possible their arrangement in the standard table, suggested that there were some basic relations between them, kinships which indicated some more nearly ultimate view of the structure of matter.

Our century began with the gradual unsettlement of the traditional doctrine of elements in several important respects. Some of these supposedly irreducible substances were seen to undergo transformations. Under certain conditions one element could change into another. Increasing evidence pointed to the idea that the elements are not simple irreducible substances but are themselves active systems of some more ultimate constituents.

The experiments which had given rise to the problems also indicated the lines of solutions. Outstandingly important here have been the investigations of the radioactive elements. During the last decade of the nineteenth century Roentgen discovered X rays, and Becquerel observed that uranium ore emits rays of unique penetrating power. This led to the spreading field of radioactive research which has been in the forefront of twentieth century physics. It may be said broadly that the progress of modern physical science has been marked by its perfected knowledge of the variety and nature of radiations.

A plain word of explanation is appropriate at this point. The following very brief review of contemporary experimental and theoretical conclusions makes no pretensions whatever to any degree of specialized technical knowledge. The present author is the veriest layman in this field; he is not competent to question in the slightest the factual reports of modern atomism. But we are all bound to consider critically the interpretation of these reported facts, their significance and their implications for our view of nature and human nature. The "general reader" of the latest works in physics cannot follow the mathematical analyses, but his questions are not to be dismissed as altogether irrelevant. For the physicist with all his arrays of equations is, after all, proposing a certain interpretation of the structure and basic operation of the world. And we are bound to consider and appraise this interpretation of our world, for we ourselves are in it and of it, physicists and laymen alike.

Our forefathers knew one kind of radiation, light, and in trying to explain it they conceived of it either (following Newton) as the corpuscular emission of particles, or (with Huyghens) as an undulating or wave-like propulsion. The ether was regarded as providing a medium of transmission, and it was considered in two ways, to suit the two views of light. Clerk Maxwell later called the ether an invention, and Jeans cited Lord Salisbury's definition of it as "the nominative of the verb 'to undulate.'"[3] Here both the cosmology and the grammar seemed to express diplomatic ambiguity. The question has been raised whether the term "wave" may not be used in a somewhat metaphorical sense, as when we say that a wave of violence is sweeping through our world today.[4]

Theories of light and the basic physical explanation of nature were complicated by the discovery of other varieties of radiation. The application of X rays in medicine has made the name and the use of them familiar to millions of us who do not understand clearly their nature. Without wading too far beyond our technical depth, we should note that modern physical research has revealed the various elements, which had been believed to be indivisible substances, as active systems of postive and negative electrical charges. This is the electronic view of matter. An atom has been represented as a sort of planetary system, with the nucleus of protons and neutrons as the sun and the electrons in their orbits as the planets. The various elements would then differ according to the number of protons, neutrons, and electrons in their atoms. This "planetary" theory of the atoms was a theoretical construction, and it has been subjected to progressive revision to agree with the experimental evidence.

The explanation of light in electromagnetic terms has been involved in a choice between fundamental concepts. As Jeans puts it, "light and indeed radiation of all kinds, is both particles and waves at the same time." But he seems to reconsider his view in another context: "The tendency of modern physics is to resolve the whole material universe into waves, and nothing but waves."[5] Eddington writes to the same effect: "The concept of substance has disappeared from fundamental physics; what we ultimately come down to is *form*. Waves! Waves!! Waves!!!"[6] Bergson had anticipated it in a sharp statement: "There are no things, there are only actions."[7] The complex constitution of matter, the varieties of elements and their properties, have been explained as complex electrical systems undergoing transformation. By bombarding atoms with certain particles, or waves, the modern physicist in his laboratory has effected transformations of one element into another, exceeding the dreams of the old alchemists.

As has already been indicated, the theories of modern physics are in a continual state of revision, not only in details but in some fundamental respects. The science of cosmic processes is itself a science in process. We are advised: "Be prepared to change any conceptions."[8] The lay reader is well instructed not to take as settled statement what the physicists themselves regard as provisional hypothesis or even as speculative surmise. Our account has doubtless many grave defects of an altogether brief and untechnical statement. The defects become more serious still and perhaps insuperable in some basic fields where the usual forms of generally comprehensible exposition do not seem to be available. This difficulty confronts the layman who inquires into the two ideas which physicists regard as most fundamental in the contemporary reconstitution of their science; relativity and quantum theory. The present discussion can consider only some aspects of these basic theories which are relevant to the cosmic view of process and activism.

Einstein's theory of relativity introduced a radical reconstruction of the traditional ideas of space and time and motion. The advance of modern science, starting with the astronomy of Copernicus in the sixteenth century, had expanded immensely the Ptolemaic earth centered universe of the medieval Aristotelians. But this vast modern universe, from stars to atoms, was still a world of objects definitely located or moving in space and time. It was still a world in which you could know where you were and where everything else was, how far and how big or small, definitely. The new theory reconsidered all these aspects of our reliable universe.

The undergraduate student of philosophy, discussing these problems with his roommate majoring in physics, is reminded of ancient Zeno the Eleatic and his paradoxes denying the reality of motion—especially the one about the three chariots. Imagine two chariots of equal length speeding in opposite directions. They would pass each other in shorter time than it would take them to pass a stationary chariot of the same length. But then how can we ever know the real length of the chariots? In fact we may ask: Can we speak of the length of a body by itself, apart from its reference or relation to another body? So the modern exponent of relativity tells us: Magnitude, location, rate or direction of motion, all depend upon the standpoint, or rather moving point, of the observer. The observed priority, simultaneity, or succession of one object in relation to another, all depend upon the state of motion or rest of the observer. Two events that we see or hear "at the same moment" may not be really simultaneous. The terms "now," "before," "after" must all be reformulated in a framework of relativity.

Quantum theory has equally radical implications. Like Einstein's relativity, it was introduced into physics at the beginning of our century. Its pioneer was Max Planck. According to this theory, the course of events in nature is not marked by ongoing strict continuity. It is not like a steady stream, no matter how minimal. It is rather like a dripping flow, drop by drop. Or with a layman's apology for taking such crude liberties with the subtleties of physical theory, let us borrow our simile from Jeans; "In its earliest form, Planck's theory hardly went beyond suggesting that the course of nature proceeded by tiny jumps and jerks, like the hands of a clock."[9]

Our accuracy of measurement is limited by the minuteness of the quanta or jerks. With my faucet I cannot get half a drop. With my watch I cannot get half a second. Our scientific laws and calculations are accurate statistically, determining large scale events. The astronomer can predict eclipses. But in dealing with minute atomic processes of high velocities, the observable determination loses its uniform flow. No effect whatever results until the quantum point is reached for the minimal jerk or jump. The wide-ranging course of quantum mechanics has led it into what physicists themselves call "deep waters," —into questioning or rendering ambiguous the basic principle of causality on which physical science traditionally rested. We should turn more specially to this problem, since it is not clear to us just what is meant by the modern theory of "indeterminacy."

### 4. Causality and Indeterminacy

Causal determination has been traditionally the basic principle, applicable necessarily to the scientific account of every event. It was a fundamental conviction of the ancient Greek mind which inaugurated science and philosophy, that nothing occurs without a cause. The classical inquiries into the nature of things were all based on the assurance that all things do have a nature, a determining character or principle which makes them what they are, in every detail.

Philosophers ancient and modern have differed in their views of the causal agencies in nature and in human life, but they have generally agreed that this world is a system of uniformity and necessity. Nature is not like "a leaky pot," to use Plato's phrase; [10] it is like a well-ordered state, a texture of law, a cosmos. This certainty of the causal order has been regarded generally not as an empirical inference nor as a mere statistical summary but as itself the basis of all scientific explanation. The fundamental presupposition has been that there is and must be a specific cause for each specific event and scientific explanation has consisted in ascertaining this specific cause in each case under investigation. This view, in rigorous insistence and allowing no evasions or exceptions, has marked the traditional scientific temper.

If we inquire into the origin of this idea of causal determination, we find a number of contending proposed explanations. The standard pair of alternatives prior to Kant were those of rationalism and empiricism. For the rationalist the principle of causality was a rational certainty. Descartes regarded it as axiomatic, an "eternal truth." Leibniz expressed a similar rationalistic inherent certainty regarding the causal principle. "Nothing ever comes to pass without there being a cause or at least a reason determining it, that is, something to give an *a priori* reason why it is existent rather than non-existent, and in this wise rather than in any other." [11]

On the other side is preëminently David Hume, whose examination of the complex idea of causal relation marks the climax and also the sceptical turn of modern empiricism. According to him, when we regard two events in our experience, *A* and *B*, as causally related, we find two simpler relations, and we also express a belief in a third, not at all simple. We find that *A* and *B* are contiguous in space and also in temporal succession; the prior we call the cause. But we also maintain that there is a "necessary connection" between them. Now the term "necessary" is a claim on or for experience, not a report of it. Hume explored its empirical origin. All that he could find in experience was what he called a "constant conjunction" of the two events. The advance from the observed constant conjunction to the belief or claim of necessary connection, according to Hume, is due to our habit of association of ideas. We tend to expect or to believe in the future recurrence of previously experienced conjunctions of events, and to this subjective demand of our mind we give objective expression in the idea of causal necessity. This doctrine had sceptical implications which made it unacceptable in scientific thinking. But it was also a challenge to the axiomatic certainty proclaimed by the rationalists. Kant said that on reading Hume he was "roused from his dogmatic slumbers." [12]

Kant's theory represents a critical revision of both rationalism and empiricism. Causal relations apply only to particular events in the course of experience, outside of which causality has no meaning. But the synthesis of cause and effect expresses more than constant or invariable sequence. The effect does not simply follow after the cause; it follows from it, necessarily. Causality cannot therefore be regarded as an empirical inference from experience. It is *a priori*, a category fundamental to the possibility of organized experience. Kant admits no causal relation beyond the process of experience; but likewise he insists that the organization of experience is inherently and necessarily causal.

Kant's *Critique of Pure Reason* was a proposed vindication of universal and necessary scientific knowledge, intended to meet the challenge of Hume's radical empiricism. Some of Kant's contemporaries and successors have questioned whether this challenge was met successfully by him. But for us the important point is that the traditional position of physical science was regarded as challenged by Hume's account of the idea of causal relation and so required a vindication. Classical physics had fixed in the modern mind the conviction of the strict causal nexus in nature. The position of each grain of sand, moving or at rest, is as it is according to strict causal necessity. And in the judgment of Laplace, if one could know the present position of all bodies and the forces operating on them, he would know not only all the past but all the future to the least detail. This traditional conclusion of classical physics, of the causal law as "the calculability of future state from an initial state," is reported emphatically in our day by Philipp Frank: "If the state of the world or of an isolated system is known exactly at one instant of time, then it is known also for all future time." [13]

A twofold problem is raised in the thorough interpretation of the causal principle. Any empiricist questioning of strict causal necessity in nature was recognized as in radical disaccord with classical physics. But the firm insistence on the all-determining causal

mechanism was seen to raise difficulties in the reasonable interpretation of human experience: of purposive characters, freedom
of choice, creative intelligence. How has this twofold issue been
affected by the modern scientific reconstruction? We should consider the revision of the traditional principle of causality which
the new physical science seems to demand. And we should inquire
what this new idea of the causal mechanism implies for our view
of physical nature, and further for our view of man's status and
role and career.

The lay reader of contemporary physics is startled by the use
of terms like "spontaneity" and "indeterminacy" in nature. He
has been under the impression that only unscientific minds ever
entertain such ideas about the course of physical existence. What
could our physicists mean by using such words in their scientific
reports of nature? Consider the disintegration of radioactive elements which results in the formation of other elements. We are
told that a particular radium atom disintegrates for no cause that
can be ascertained. The physicist has calculated the rate at which
a number of radium atoms disintegrate, but not the causal conditions which operate in individual cases. These seem to occur
spontaneously, as if by mere chance. The layman asks: Does the
physicist regard the atom's disintegration as really spontaneous?
Or does he mean that we are unable to identify the factors causing
the disintegration of a particular radium atom, but that we still
regard the process in question as somehow strictly determined
and necessary? Deterministic philosophers have held that the view
of a certain event as spontaneous or free is due to our ignorance
of the operating cause. But they have had to meet the objection
that our insistence that an event is causally determined, where no
operating cause is ascertainable, manifests the opposite kind of
ignorance.

This whole problem has become accentuated in interpreting
the so-called "uncertainty relations" formulated by Heisenberg.
We know that the use of statistical methods yields reliable and
highly accurate forecasts of trends and results of human behavior,
but the conduct of a specific individual may remain indeterminate. Likewise so-called macroscopic physics, dealing with large-
scale operations of material bodies, proceeds on the principles of
strict causal determinism. But it is otherwise with microscopic
physics. In Heisenberg's view, "natural science is not Nature her-

self but a part of the relation between Man and Nature, and therefore is dependent on Man." [14] If what we are examining is an electron, its behavior is affected by the light and other radiations which we need in order to observe it. As Heisenberg again states it, "it is impossible to determine accurately *both* the position and the direction and speed of a particle at the same instant." [15] In ascertaining either one of these, we miss the other.

Here we are faced by several alternative interpretations. Does the principle of uncertainty relations mean that we cannot ascertain precisely minimal processes, which we nevertheless regard as strictly determined in each case? The alleged indeterminacy, then, would belong to our theory of knowledge. Or is this a principle of cosmology: does it indicate a lapse from causal determination in the basic structure of nature? On this issue there seems to be considerable disagreement among physicists, and also various revisions of individual opinion in successive treatises. A number of scientists have demanded or have contemplated a reinterpretation of the evidence in microscopic physics which does not set aside the fundamental scientific principle of determinism. So Schrödinger suggests the interpretation that "there *is* a fully determined physical object in existence, but I can never know all about it." [16] Louis de Broglie has confessed a certain attitude of indecision. While regarding quantum physics as indeterministic, he has entertained the possibility that "some day or other, physics will return to the paths of determinism and that then the present stage of this science will seem to us to have been a momentary detour during which the insufficiency of our conceptions had forced us to abandon provisionally our following exactly the determinism of phenomena on the atomic scale." [17]

In this connection we should note the very significant idea of complementarity advanced by Niels Bohr. Instead of considering quantum physics as plainly rejecting the determinism of classical physics, Bohr regards the quantal viewpoint as complementary, "the expression of a rational synthesis of the wealth of experience in this field, which exceeds the limits to which the application of the concept of causality is naturally confined." [18] In a more recent statement of his views, he points out that "the fundamental difference with respect to the analysis of phenomena in classical and in quantum physics is that in the former the interaction between the objects and the measuring instrutments may be neglected or compensated for, while in the latter this interaction forms an integral part of the phenomena."[19]

Other physicists have been inclined towards a position of probabilism in the sense of accepting a degree of unaccountable spontaneity in nature. Thus Eddington maintained a "principle of indeterminacy" as fundamental in nature. In his judgment, we cannot identify or predict an atom's position and velocity at the same moment because "there is no strict causal behavior anywhere."[20] He restated this conclusion in a later revised formulation: "The present system of fundamental laws does not furnish a complete set of rules for the calculation of the future."[21] Some contemporary physicists have expressed the general view of indeterminacy more emphatically, but also with considerable systematic qualms. The new quantum mechanics has been used to sustain the belief in free-will, by describing the cerebral processes which provide the conditions for our actions as small-scale phenomena analogous to atomic reactions. In this way the principle of indeterminacy has been applied to volition. By a strange confusion of the most complex mental processes with the most elementary atomic reactions, some physicists have reasoned that the mind can direct an electrical charge between two courses of motion. This speculative élan has sometimes been carried to great lengths. The principle of uncertainty or indeterminacy has been generally limited to single atoms, but bolder speculation has extended it also to masses of particles. The future course of a million atoms, we have been told, is as indeterminate as the course of any one of them. For all we know, extraordinary events contrary to the alleged laws of nature do occur now and then. And so we have been informed, in a scientific treatise: miracles may not be without ground.

Theologians have found comfort in this sort of reassurance, but may have been disturbed by the suggested analogy between a million atoms and the miracles reported in the various religious traditions of mankind. Is the bringing of a dead man back to life by a word of proclaimed divine authority to be regarded as a memorable quantum jump? And if it is to be reinterpreted in that way, then how are we to understand its religious significance? The criticaly minded layman must be perplexed by the bold venture of some physicists into the domain of the supernatural.

Jeans has reminded us of a reported saying of Plato's that God for ever geometrizes. The world of modern physics, he thinks, cannot be conceived adequately in mechanistic terms. "The universe begins to look more like a great thought than like a great machine." It is a system of mathematical design, and "the great Architect of the Universe now begins to appear as a pure mathematician." [22] Eddington's ironical comment may be appended: "My opinion of pure mathematicians, though respectful, is not so exalted as that." [23] The surmises about the supernatural have some very confusing implications which have proved disquieting to the scientific conscience, even while entertaining these speculative conjectures. Thus H. A. Wilson concludes his treatise on *The Mysteries of the Atom* with a word of quandary and caution: "A theory which merely gives the relative probabilities of various possible events and leaves what actually happens either to pure chance, whatever that may mean, or to supernatural guidance can hardly be the physicist's final solution of his problem." [24]

There seems to be a sort of impasse here due to a contention between too little and too much, and a difficulty of finding the right rational mean. The indeterminacy or uncertainty principle means more than the generally recognized inability to attain the needed scientific precision of statement in some fields of investigation. But there is natural scientific reluctance to proceed from this admission to the unqualified surrender of causality in the sense of conceding an element of chance and spontaneity in nature itself. The balancing intermediate position seems to be still a desired rather than a realized attainment. We may refer here to the comments of the author of the quantum theory, Max Planck, who proposes a reinterpretation of the concept of causality in physics. According to Planck, "an occurrence is causally determined if it can be predicted with certainty." [25] He is careful to point out that predictability is an infallible criterion of the presence of a causal relationship, but is not synonymous with it. There are causally related processes, such as weather changes, which are not accurately predictable. This last qualification is more far-reaching than is generally realized. In fact, "it is never possible to predict a physical occurrence with unlimited precision." [26]

Planck indicates a twofold process of translation that is involved in scientific thought and introduces a twofold uncertainty. The scientist must ever be translating the occurrences of direct sense-experience into the world picture of physics, and then retranslating it from that world picture into sense data. He interprets the experiment he is actually performing as an instance of the general law, and he applies the general law to the specific instance under observation. In classical physics this twofold translation was available with increasing precision through the continual perfection of technical measurement. But in quantum mechanics the situation is different. Here the theoretical construction of the scientific world picture has shifted so far from the world of ordinary sense perception that, though we may continue to use traditional terms and concepts, they are no longer applicable in their ordinary meaning.

Planck returns to his initial criterion of causal determination of an occurence. The degree of accurate prediction depends upon the theoretical framework of the event, and, Planck adds, it depends upon the predictor. "The law of causality is neither true nor false. It is rather a heuristic principle, a signpost."[27] It serves to guide investigation and to further it. It shows us the direction we must follow if we are to achieve fruitful knowledge and greater precision in our formulation of it.

## 5. *Mechanism and Teleology*

It is interesting to note that even in his radical reconstruction of the traditional cosmological framework, the modern scientist still thinks of nature, if no longer as a machine, yet as some sort of a mechanism. Lord Kelvin said that he could understand that of which he could construct a mechanical model. The physicists in our day are reassured when they can formulate the constitution of nature in their mathematical equations. But the physicist's basic adherence to the physical pattern has not altered radically; his slant and outlook are still mechanistic. Old Democritus had sought to reduce all reality to atoms moving in empty space. The modern physicist deals with electrical charges in a four-dimensional world of space-time. But if either of them were to consider men's purposes or meanings at all, it would be only in order somehow to fit them into some mechanistic pattern. Thus, as we have noted, when the advocate of indeterminism entertains a belief in free will, he considers it on the analogy of indeterminate and unpredictable quantum jumps, of the microscopic cerebral "small-scale phenomena involving relatively few particles."[28]

The meaning of purpose and choice and valuation, which is crucial to our own self-understanding, cannot be explained by the modern atomist any more than by the ancient. And so the problem which confronted Plato confronts us also: How are we to recognize our character in its fullness, not only the complex mechanism of our operations in space-time but our meaning and value to ourselves and to others, the aims and ideals to which we commit our careers? This is the agelong philosophical problem of mechanism and teleology. The discussion of it in terms of activism or a cosmology of processes serves especially well to manifest some significant features of our philosophy of cosmic perspectives.

The emphasis on teleology and value was fundamental in the philosophy of Plato. A crucial question in his account of anything was this: "Is it for the best?" In his hierarchy of Ideas or essential principles of reality, the highest place was accorded to the Idea of Good, or the principle of value. In Plato's idealism the derogation of matter is both a cosmological and a valuational judgment. Matter is factually existent but it does not express the essential character of reality and is thus called non-being. Likewise matter is the medium of instability and confusion, of corruption and evil.

The systematic introduction of teleology was an outstanding feature of Aristotle's cosmology. It is given explicitly in his analysis of causality, and in considering it we can see the connection of our present discussion with the topic of the previous section. Aristotle distinguished four varieties or four meanings of cause. Necessary to the production of a thing is material cause, namely that from which it is made: the marble or bronze for the statue, the silver for the plate. Secondly, we recognize formal cause, that into which a thing is made, its form or pattern or essential determination: the statue or the vase or whatever is to be produced. In the third place, we require efficient causation: the actual process of carving or moulding or otherwise giving the material its form and realization. Lastly—and this is the most important point for our present discussion—Aristotle acknowledged "final cause," that for the sake of which a thing is made, its end or purpose. In thus including teleological principles of explanation in his account of nature, Aristotle followed the Platonic lead, that is, to a certain extent. While he did not demand the appeal to value in every causal explanation, he did recognize in certain fields the dominance of teleological, value-tending considerations.

Both the knowledge and the movement of many things are rooted in values, in goodness and beauty.

This recognition of teleological determinants was accentuated in the Stoic doctrine of the rational direction of the world by Divine Providence. There is a mechanical order in nature, the mechanism of tension in the material components of things. But the entire cosmic process to the least detail manifests the operation of the universal plan. Human life and conduct cannot be understood without the recognition of purpose. Opposed to all this teleology were the atomists, followers of Democritus and Epicurus. They reduced all existence to the whirl of atomic clusters in space. This unqualified mechanism, with its ambiguous unaccountable swerve of atoms in any direction at any time, appeared absurd to the Stoics. So Cicero asked ironically: Can we suppose that the mere shaking out of a mass of letters in a box could ever produce a great poem?

So we have before us the two alternatives. The issue between them is outstanding in the development of the history of philosophy, affecting ethics, social theory, theology. As we may readily judge, medieval Christian philosophy emphasized teleology, Divine Providence, both in human experience and in the general account of nature. But the revival of naturalism in the Renaissance and the spread of modern physical science in the seventeenth century promoted a mechanistic cosmology. Bacon dispraised teleology and called it ironically a virgin dedicated to God but barren. Hobbes rejected any explanatory use of purpose. Like the Epicureans, he undertook to establish his scientific philosophy on the sole foundation of matter in motion in space. Spinoza likewise ruled out Aristotle's final causes.

The rejection of teleology has characterized systematic modern science. The heavens that had been declaring immemorially the glory of God were charted in the mathematical formulae of celestial mechanics. Harvey ranged physiology alongside the other physical sciences by his mechanical explanation of the pumping heart and the circulation of the blood. The success of the mechanistic procedure in the physical sciences was not sporadic or incidental. The strict explanations were extended to one field after another, with increasing precision, predicting eclipses to the second, verifying inferences experimentally to the least detail. There seemed to be no doubt that the application of mechanistic methods to other fields of research, to any field, would only be a question of time, an eventual certainty.

The firm mechanist has regarded any concession to teleology as weak surrender to unscientific obscurantism. In this verdict not even the greatest have been spared, not even Newton. As is well known, in all his epoch-making studies of the cosmic mechanism, Newton himself never quite renounced his high respect for the teleological argument for God's existence. At the conclusion of his *Principia* he wrote: "This most beautiful system of the sun, planets, and comets, could only proceed from the counsel and dominion of an intelligent and powerful Being." When this passage is mentioned, the comment of the average physical scientist is apt to be a reference to Newton's conventional prejudices, or to his oncoming senility.

The mechanical explanation of nature was impressively convincing by its simple consistency of application. Things are what they are, in their place and position and condition and process, merely as they are determined by the forces operating on them. The full ascertainment of these forces would indicate to us unmistakably and precisely the future course of events in the field under investigation. Nature manifests neither purpose nor choice but only the exertion of forces and the mechanics of motions. As soon as the strict scientific methods have been fully applied to human conduct and social processes, anthropology in all its phases will become a precise science. We shall have then not only a scientific knowledge of man's past but also a forecast of human affairs individual and social.

This mechanistic determinism has invaded certain fields of the social sciences, where it has been deemed good scientific method to explain the historical course of customs and social changes on the pattern of structures and processes in physical nature. The outstanding example of this mechanistic invasion of the social sciences is in dialectical materialism, the materialistic interpretation of history enforced by the Marxist educational systems of the Communist countries.

It is at this point, however,—the application of strict mechanism to human experience—that the advocates of teleology have always taken their firm stand. And from this besieged stronghold teleologists have made repeated sorties, with varying success. While the seventeenth century was marked by the spreading advance of the mechanistic theory, the eighteenth century witnessed an upsurge of teleology which reached uncritical excesses and produced in due time a sharp reaction.

The leading mind in this eighteenth century trend towards teleology was Leibniz. The doctrine of pre-established harmony and the theodicy to which Leibniz proceeded marked the temper of opinion, which expressed itself in philosophical and theological works and also in the less tightly reasoned, more popular versions of essayists and poets.

Teleology stressed the principle of universal harmony and design in nature. Shortly before the publication of Leibniz's *Theodicy,* Shaftesbury had developed the teleology of a harmonious cosmos in his work, *The Moralists,* which bore the sub-title "A Philosophical Rhapsody." Shaftesbury's cosmology was marked by an aesthetic approach to nature. The universe is like a work of art; we should contemplate it in its cosmic range and system of relations. If we do so, we can see the alleged evils in the world in their proper relation and context. Like partial discords in a larger harmony, like shadows that set off the light effects in a picture, so it is with the seemingly meaningless and wrong aspects of existence. They all have their place and role; they subserve the large purpose and swell the universal harmony.

Leibniz and Shaftesbury together represent the lofty ground from which the universal design in nature was contemplated. As may be readily judged, this philosophical bent emphasized the teleological argument for God's existence. But beyond this, in theology and in philosophy alike, it tended to interpret the divine design in nature anthropocentrically, that is, as conducing to man's advantage and perfection. Thus we may elicit the fuller statement of teleological reasoning: the world process evidences its direction by Divine Providence, and it is designed to promote man's happiness and perfection.

It requires no stretch of the imagination to see the lengths to which this sort of teleological speculation could go. In ponderous treatises, unreadable today, the divine design in nature was explored and God's existence was demonstrated from the formation of rocks, from the life of fishes, of birds: petrotheology, ichthyotheology, ornithotheology! In winter, it was sagely cogitated, water as it freezes in the streams, rises to the top, in order that the ice may not immobilize and kill the fish, man's food supply. A chorus of didactic poets, many of them Germans, versified the teleological argument. The Hamburg senator Brockes devoted his leisure to rhyming his inventory of God's wonders in nature designed for man's good. A climax of this edifying poetry is his eulogy of the goose:

> Goose-grease doth relieve consumption; goose-gall lotion, too,
>     is good;
> Goose is good to eat; for dizzy spells we often use its blood;
> Skin and feathers likewise useful: doth not this bird radiate
> God's omnipotence, God's wisdom, and God's love for man's
>     estate?

This solemn nonsense was laid low by the shafts of Voltaire's satire. Note the remarkable design of Divine Providence which directed great rivers to bring them to the sea in convenient proximity to men's important centers of navigation! And this design could be shown to operate in reverse, baffling to theodicy: "Flies are born to be eaten by spiders, which are in turn devoured by swallows, and swallows by shrikes, and shrikes by eagles, and eagles are born to be killed by men, who in turn live to kill each other and to be consumed by worms or by devils at least in a thousand cases to one." [29] We may surmise what ironical use Voltaire could have made of the malaria cycle as traced by modern parasitologists.

Notwithstanding this barrage of satire, teleology even in its extreme versions did not yield ground in certain dogmatical strongholds. During the thirties of the last century, a series of so-called "Bridgewater Treatises" expounded the theological use of design in nature. The titles of two of them indicate their general theme and specific arguments: "The Adaptation of External Nature to the Moral and Intellectual Condition of Man," —"The Hand, Its Mechanism and Vital Endowments as Evincing Design." We should note that this sort of writing was not all on a low dogmatic level and beneath scientific notice.

Mechanism and teleology have both had their extreme apologists. We have exposed some of their excesses so as to seek a more reasonable course in dealing with the issues which they raise. A sound scientific and philosophical view of nature is one which acknowledges all the evidence that nature supplies, all of it.

Where some of the evidence does not fit the settled theoretical moulds, the right procedure is not to dismiss the evidence but to refashion the moulds and the theories. As we have noted, that is just what science has been doing in its own domain, reconstructing the entire framework of classical physics and chemistry and calling for some revision of the traditional ideas of causal determinism.

One important point to respect in our philosophy of perspectives is the different relative extent and significance of the various phases of nature. We should not ignore the characteristic expressions of nature in certain contexts, nor should we dogmatically read into nature, in every context, features which it reveals in some contexts. This is a caution which both the mechanist and the teleologist should heed. Teleology may be essential to our full understanding of some processes, but it is not essential or not applicable at all to the explanation of other very extensive regions of existence. Mechanism is the appropriate scientific category in dealing with the vast world of physical phenomena, but it may not provide an adequate approach to the interpretation of human affairs.

Lotze showed respect for the sound principle of procedure when he concluded the second book of his *Metaphysics* by pointing out "how absolutely universal is the extent, and at the same time how completely subordinate the significance, of . . . mechanism . . . in the structure of the world" Lotze's conclusion may be improved by a restatement. It may be taken to mean that every form of existence and every process of nature has a material aspect and requires or admits of a mechanistic account and explanation, but that mechanism is inadequate for the interpretation of the significance of reality as a whole, which points to a divine plan. This is, in fact, very close to Lotze's meaning; but it needs a revision in dealing with the problem before us. Lotze spoke of the universal extent of mechanism. By this we should understand that every process has a physical aspect, and every living process has a physiological aspect. This aspect is the one with which physical science is concerned in its understanding of the vast range of nature. And even in the field of mental activities and human affairs there is a mechanistic phase which physiological psychology and other related sciences study. But human intelligence manifests other aspects of reality which cannot be adequately expressed in mechanistic terms and which require for their full interpretation teleological principles and the recognition of values. So revising Lotze, we should reaffirm the universal extent of mechanism and recognize its adequacy in dealing with the vast scope of physical nature, but also admit its incapacity to do full justice to the activity and the significance of mind. Human life has a mechanical framework, but it is characteristically purposive.

We need some clarification here. We have just spoken of mind or human life as purposive, and we shall consider further the importance of teleology for full humanistic interpretation. But the question may be raised: Is the acknowledgment of purpose essential only to the understanding of man's *mental* activities, or is it also required for dealing appropriately with man as a *living* being? Is teleology a mental or more broadly a biological category? The consideration of the biological scope of purposive explanation is very obviously connected with our understanding of evolution, and so we shall postpone it to our next chapter. Here in dealing with the problem of teleology we should concentrate on mental human activities.

Our problem is primarily psychological, but a considerable number of psychologists may set it aside. The behaviorists are concerned with the investigable mechanics of so-called mental experiences and with our observable actions. Thus the behaviorist's account of thinking connects it with the physiological processes of speech, especially the laryngeal reactions. Two centuries ago the French materialist LaMettrie expressed a similar view. J. B. Watson, the leader of the behaviorists, writes: "What the psychologists have hitherto called thought is in short nothing but talking to ourselves," and again: "Thinking is merely talking, but talking with concealed musculature." [30] The expressions "nothing but" and "merely" in these quoted passages should not be overlooked. They indicate abstract onesidedness and oversimplification, which is especially unwarranted in dealing with such complex processes as mental activity.

While Watson has tended to qualify his statement that "laryngeal movement as such plays the predominant role in thought," [31] his emphasis on the physiological part of the process has not been altered. But when the behaviorist explains thinking thus in mechanistic terms, his own theory must be regarded as merely a physiological process, and then what could be the meaning of the *truth* which is claimed for the theory? This basic quandary of unqualified materialism is especially embarrassing in psychology. We pointed out earlier that, while physical science deals with physical processes, it is itself not physical. Newton's theory of gravitation cannot itself be considered as a merely gravitational process. In the case of psychology, however, not only the interpretation but also what is being interpreted and investigated have a logical aspect which should not be ignored, if there is to be any science, anything proved or refuted. Whitehead expressed this point with keen irony: "A consistent behaviorist cannot find it important to refute my ideas. He can only behave."[32] Behaviorism illustrates in a striking form the baffling character of a rigidly materialistic theory. A doctrine which explains thinking in a way that rules out truth, in claiming to be true, in effect unsays itself. The behaviorist should have learned his lessons from Emerson's lines, which can be adapted to his need:

> They reckon ill who leave me out;
> When me they fly, I am the wings.[33]

The defect of unqualified mechanism is clear: it does not provide for the genuine recognition of purposive and productive mental activities. But we should be warned that this recognition is not assured by the mere assertion of a design in nature. Some forms of teleology have been as alien to mental achievement as any mechanism. If we regard the world process, and so the course of human affairs, as predestined from all eternity by Divine Providence, then our lives must be considered as merely the detailed exposition of the Almighty's plan. The extreme form of this doctrine has been the fatalism of Islam, according to which all our acts and words and thoughts are inscribed eternally in the book of Allah.

Bergson called our attention sharply to the defectiveness of this sort of teleology. "As in the mechanistic hypothesis, here again it is supposed that *all is given*. Finalism thus understood is only inverted mechanism."[34] The teleology of divine predestination is quite as unavailable for humanistic interpretation as extreme mechanism, and for the same reason. Both of these doctrines fail to recognize the integral and productive character of human personality. The purposive nature of mental activity is marked by involvement in real alternatives, in which decision and action are neither mechanically predetermined nor divinely foreordained, but truly self-expressive, the expressions of a self which is progressively achieving its character. Men's careers evince a self-reconstitutive capacity in nature. In mechanistic explanation the present is always understood as the effect of the past, and any future always in terms of its past. In humanistic interpretation of purposive activities, the present reveals more fully its productive character both in its bond with the past and in the progressive achievement of its future. This is the life of man as we directly know it, in all the fields of preference, choice, decision, devotion to values and ideals of whatever sort.

Thus we may return to the basic problem which confronts the cosmology of processes. It is a problem similar to that which we considered in the earlier doctrine of substantialism. How are we to represent reality so as to give due acknowledgment to all its types and grades of manifestation? If the variety of processes in nature is ultimately reducible to a uniformly mechanical character, not only biology but also psychology and all the humanistic sciences would have to learn their final wisdom from physics. But if nature is a hierarchy of processes, then its various aspects may be regarded as stages or grades in the scale, which require different principles of interpretation.

Activism centers its attention not on things but on doings and goings. It is said of Clerk Maxwell that as a boy he always asked about anything that interested him: "What is the go of it?" and more searchingly, "What is the particular go of it?"[35] That is a very good approach into the particular kind of process which characterizes any thing with which we may be dealing. What sort of activities are evidenced in physical nature and in man's lives and careers? We should not ignore or neglect any one of them; we should acknowledge them all in our view of the world, and we should seek to relate them in our philosophy of cosmic perspectives.

It may be seen clearly that the modern dynamical reconstruction in physical science has not settled the perennial issue in philosophy. It has reopened it in a new setting. It has driven home the realization of a fundamental philosophical truth, that the real character of nature cannot be grasped fully in terms of the traditional mechanistic principles. Philosophy should understand this truth sufficiently to add its corollary: that reality cannot be fully understood in terms of any one abstract perspective. Some modern physicists have expressed a spirit of reserved judgment which many philosophers would do well to emulate. So Jeans writes: "Many would hold that, from the broad philosophical standpoint, the outstanding achievement of twentieth century physics is not the theory of relativity with its welding of space and time, or the theory of quanta with its present apparent negation of the laws of causation, or the dissection of the atom with the resultant discovery that things are not what they seem; it is the general recognition that we are not yet in contact with ultimate reality." [36] This view need not be sceptical; it can be an outlook of expanding prospects and of readiness for a revised survey. It may express a growing conviction that nature has neither bottom nor top. This conviction is sound, for it leads to a reasonable and critical use of our abstractions. If no one of them can be regarded as the single absolute top or bottom, we may be more fully emancipated from dogmatism of any sort. And then we can recognize in balanced relative emphasis the principal aspects of reality which are manifested in our experience. We may adapt to this purpose Professor Margenau's wise counsel of "humility to grant that knowledge in one domain does not render us wise enough to foretell another." [37]

If we adopt this general outlook in philosophical procedure, we may recognize better both the proper place and also the limitations of traditional mechanism as a cosmological category. Mechanism has both the merits and the defects of a wholesale "by and large" framework. It serves physical science well in its description and explanation of large-scale processes. And it is applicable also in humanistic research, especially in some of the social sciences, where the determination of human affairs can be indicated statistically with a considerable degree of uniformity. But the traditional causal mechanism shows its limitations in physical science when it deals with the most elementary atomic processes. And mechanical explanations prove inadequate and indeed irrelevant in our interpretation of the full range of mental activities, the integrity and the productive character of personality.

In a significant way the traditional causal mechanism shows its limitations at the two ends of the cosmic order: at its simplest and most elementary atomic processes and also at the highest and most complex experiences of our mental personal life. The latter of these defects of mechanism has long been recognized by reflective men. The former has been discovered by recent physical research.

Scientists and philosophers should be on their guard to avoid reverting to the old confusion in a new form. The human limitations of mechanism cannot be overcome by restating it in atomistic terms. Free will and purposive activity are not to be explained in terms of quantum mechanics. The principle of indeterminacy or "uncertainty relations" does not imply freedom of choice or spiritual guidance or anything of the sort. That kind of speculation indicates lamentable confusion of basic ideas, which the more philosophical physicists have been able to avoid. Truly philosophical insight points in a radically different direction. Freedom of choice in the sense of self-expression, guidance of thought and conduct by the pursuit and organization of values, purposive activity and achieved integrity of personal character: these are not to be sought in the quantum jumps of the physics laboratory, but in the ideas and ideals that characterize the higher life of men.

It is not by further knowledge of the atom but by deeper self-understanding that both the physicists and the rest of us plain laymen can reach the truth that makes us free persons in truly humane societies. Physical science has split the atoms; we now need the wisdom that shall bind men to live together in justice and in peace. The pursuit of this wisdom is a perennial task of philosophy. It moves us to our further quest of cosmic perspectives.

# CHAPTER III.

# THE WORLD OF EVOLUTION

## 1. *Evolutionary Ideas before Darwin*

Our examination of the principal world-views has led us already to consider their anticipation in classical antiquity. This procedure has its merits but also needs some caution lest it mislead us. The true understanding of the development of ideas should seek a balanced view between two extremes. The first warning is familiar. We should beware of misconstruing old doctrines by reading into them our own newer meanings. But on the other hand, we should not, with complacent modernity, proceed as it were in a historical vacuum and ignore the ramified ancestry of our own speculations. The good counsel is not single but twofold: Do not try to pour your new wine into old bottles, but also do not forget that there have been vineyards and vintners long before you.

This twofold caution is especially important in dealing with the theory of evolution. Its scientific formulation by Charles Darwin and his successors has been made possible by definitely modern methods and instruments of scientific research, partly or wholly unavailable to earlier minds. But the basic idea, the evolutionary approach to the study of nature, has its roots deep in earlier speculations. Ancient true surmises and persistent errors were both effective in the directing of modern inquiries. And in studying the growth of evolutionary ideas it is interesting to find that error is not always more ancient than truth. The learning of this lesson may be salutary all around.

It should be clear that we are tracing here in broad outline the early approaches to the general idea of evolution, the developmental outlook on nature. Darwin's theory was a definite application of this outlook to the specific problems of biology. But Darwin was well aware of the larger bearings of his doctrine, and these bearings have been explored in the varieties of modern evolutionism. Our survey of the earlier surmises will enable us to note better the important revisions to which the evolutionary ways of thought have been subjected as a result of Darwin's epoch-making work.

The beginnings of evolutionary thinking have been traced to the very first period of ancient Greek philosophy. As we have already noted, the idea of *physis* or nature as a process of generation was germinal in Greek science and philosophy from the outset. That this generative process was one of development from simple to complex forms of life was a natural trend of thought, and it found very early expressions.

The Milesian philosopher Anaximander may be called the pioneer evolutionist of classical antiquity. This Ionian groped after the idea of transformation of species by adaptation to environment. Of course, he thought, the highly developed mammals must have been generated from lower organisms, and this process of development could not have originated on dry land. So he surmised that the first forms of life were seaborn. We may observe here the likely influence of the doctrine of his elder fellow-countryman Thales, that water is the primary stuff of all existence. While Anaximander did not accept such a simplified cosmology and described the primary matter as a boundless matrix of no specific qualities, still he must have preferred to consider the elemental slime of the watery deeps rather than the solid definite earth as the cosmic womb in which life was first begotten. "Animals came into being from the water as it evaporated from the Sun. Man was originally very similar to a different animal, namely the fish." [1] The aquatic animals, he thought, were encased by a bark-like skin which cracked off as they rose to dry land. But unlike other animals which can quickly find their food, human offspring need a long period of suckling during which they are helpless. The first coastal ventures of the fish-men must have been short-lived. Man must have developed very slowly from his fishy state to survival and procreation on dry land.

Empedocles, of Agrigentum in Sicily, pursued this line of

thought farther and in greater detail. Like Anaximander he believed in the first origins of life by spontaneous generation, but he had more extensive surmises about the production of the higher forms of animals. In the boundless stir of existence, all sorts of mixtures were apt to be produced; neckless heads, arms without shoulders, eyes lacking foreheads, ox-headed men and hybrid creatures. Obviously these misfits could not survive, but by good fortune of nature other forms of life had the structure and the organs to nourish and sustain themselves and reproduce their kind.

We seem to have here an approach to the idea of the survival of the fittest, and along with it, the issue between a mechanistic interpretation of biological processes and some recognition of teleology. Empedocles regarded the entire course of nature as mechanical. His contemporary Anaxagoras relied on the organizing direction of *Nous,* Reason, though, as Socrates told us, he did not follow his rational principle consistently. But Aristotle, definitely recognizing final or purposive causation of living forms, criticized the mechanistic doctrine: "Empedocles . . . was in error when he said that many of the characters presented by animals were merely the results of incidental occurrences during their development."[2] In Aristotle's judgment, the course of nature manifests purposive and necessary causation. The hierarchy of living beings rises from rudimentary mass to higher and more complex plant and animal forms. But this rise is not to be interpreted as a temporal succession from a higher to a lower species, and definitely not as a fortuitous process. Aristotle saw the biological world not as an evolutionary series in time but as a gradation of essential types. It should be added, however, that his exposition has sometimes inclined his readers to an evolutionary misinterpretation.

Modern evolutionists have learned from Aristotle despite their disagreement with his basic conceptions. Darwin himself wrote: "Linnaeus and Cuvier have been my two gods, though in very different ways, but they were mere schoolboys to old Aristotle."[3] The phrase "in very different ways" is significant here, for both Linnaeus and Cuvier, like Aristotle, held to the permanence of species. Darwin could learn from those whose theories he was supplanting.

The evolutionary ideas in the verses of Empedocles were

echoed but not repeated in the great poem of the Roman Epic-urean, Lucretius, *On the Nature of Things*. Lucretius rejected any doctrine of design in nature or Divine Providence and re-garded the course of nature as nothing but a whirling process of atomic clusters in empty space. He did point out that some atomic compounds were creatures unfit for survival but he did not por-tray any evolutionary succession from lower to higher forms of life by gradual variation of structures adapted to the environment. The ancient atomists shared with modern advocates of evolution a mechanistic outlook and resistance to design in nature, but they were not themselves evolutionists.

Between Lucretius and the Renaissance, Patristic and Scholas-tic thinkers resisted the mechanism of the atomists and insisted on recognizing the Divine design in nature.

The spread of broadly evolutionary or developmental thinking after the Renaissance was varied and extensive. We should cite the important contributions to evolutionism made by a number of modern philosophers. The zoölogist Osborn has emphasized this point: "A hard preliminary battle had to be fought by the philoso-phers for natural causation as against supernatural interference in the governing of the living world. Here lies the main debt of natu-ral science to philosophy; and to omit mention of the great names of the seventeenth and eighteenth centuries would leave a serious gap in these outlines. The natural philosophers were more scien-tific than the professed scientists." [4]

Among the philosophers who had some share in evolutionary speculation, we may mention especially Kant, whose philosophy in so many ways was the principal turning point or crossroad in the development of modern thought. Kant's evolutionary thinking proceeded from an early readiness for mechanistic explanation towards a later prevailing teleological emphasis.

The idea of a series or scale of living beings as "a system follow-ing a genetic principle" would seem to have been in harmony with Kant's early cosmogony. He was prepared to follow the broad lines of descent as far as the evidence allowed. The fundamental principle of mechanism was acknowledged by him as essential to physical science, and he could see why scientists proceeded to use it also in dealing with living organisms. But in this latter applica-tion, he came to regard mechanism as deficient and to require the recognition of teleology. Kant accentuated this conclusion in his

58

*Critique of Judgment:* "It is . . . quite certain that we cannot adequately cognize, much less explain, organized beings in their internal possibility according to mere mechanical principles of nature, and we can say boldly it is alike certain that it is absurd for men to make any such attempt or to hope that another *Newton* will arise in the future, who shall make comprehensible by us the production of a blade of grass according to natural laws which no design has ordered." [5]

This passage was written seventy years before Darwin's *Origin of Species.* And was it really so bold and unscientific as it sounds on first reading? As a report of the evidence available in Kant's day, the conclusion was not altogether unwarranted. Biological science had been slow in developing its modern methods. It included noteworthy researches in its special branches, starting early with Vesalius's work on anatomy and Harvey's explanation of the circulation of the blood, but it had no comprehensive view of the science of life to compare with Newton's achievement in physical science. It was 1802 when the general term "biology" was first introduced by Lamarck. In the particular biological fields the established scientists in the main adhered to the doctrine of fixity of species, and evolutionary ideas were resisted as radical speculations. The French naturalist Bonnet introduced the term "evolution," but used it to describe a theory deriving the higher animals from germs preformed in the lower species. This idea of preformation had a long history and was related to the theological doctrine of traducianism, to which St. Augustine had leaned, that since Adam all souls have been transmitted through one generation after another.

The contest of biological ideas in the eighteenth century was led by Linnaeus and Buffon, both of them, like Bonnet, contemporaries of Kant. Linnaeus began with the firm conviction that each species must be regarded as God's definite and fixed creation from the beginning. He reaffirmed his conviction: "No new species." He conceived of his work in botany and zoölogy as consisting mainly in full and adequate classification of plant and animal forms. Only later in life did he make some concessions, by suggesting that the seeming new species might be explained as hybrids produced by intercrossing. Unlike the conservatism of Linnaeus, Buffon's outlook in biology was marked by imaginative boldness and range. He proceeded on the principle that animal species vary with the change of environment. It has been difficult to appraise reliably Buffon's contribution to evolution, for he had not quite abandoned the idea of an original creation, and so regarded the changed species as degenerations of the original forms. But he had made definite advances in evolutionary theory. The struggle for existence and the survival of the fittest were both ideas familiar to him. Before Malthus he wrote of the boundless fertility of all species and the countless obstacles which they must face on all sides and which permit only a certain number to survive.

The eighteenth century was an age in which the struggle of ideas invaded literature and found poetic expression. So theodicy and the problem of evil were argued in rhyme by Voltaire and Alexander Pope and Edward Young. Albrecht von Haller combined biology with optimistic verse. On an incomparably higher plane as a poet and as a thinker stood Goethe, and his contribution to evolutionary ideas was very significant. He set out from a fundamental conviction of the integral life and unity of all nature. Goethe emphasized the belief in the modification or metamorphosis of plant and animal forms from simpler types, and originally from a single one. He inclined towards the theory that acquired modifications are transmitted to offspring.

Erasmus Darwin, grandfather of the great scientist, combined scientific work with poems on nature. Like Anaximander, he traced the early course of living beings from the watery mass and slime of the seas to dry land, first to amphibious and then to land-inhabiting animals. Species have been modified by suitable reactions to the environment, "and many of these acquired forms or propensities are transmitted to their posterity."[6] Thus mankind may have descended from a race of monkeys that had acquired a perfected hand through muscular ability to put the thumb against the other fingers. This suggestion inspired a parodist:

> There was an ape in days that were earlier;
> Centuries passed and his hair became curlier;
> Centuries more, and his thumb gave a twist,
> And he was a man and a Positivist.[7]

This lampoon did not quite fit Erasmus Darwin, for he recognized the limits of any theory of fortuitous evolution that ruled out altogether some basic teleology.

The entrenched traditional opposition to evolution was not only theological, as witness the debate in 1830 at the Paris Academy of Sciences between the evolutionist Geoffroy St. Hilaire and the paleontologist Cuvier, authoritative defender of Linnaeus at the Collège de France.

## 2. *Lamarck and the Inheritance of Acquired Characters*

Within the evolutionary ranks a radical difference in theory concerned the question whether acquired characteristics are transmitted to posterity. One side of this issue, called Lamarckism after its chief advocate, has maintained that the needs and emergencies of living processes cause animals to improve or change certain organs. The use or disuse or alteration of structure or function, as they serve the vital ends of a species, are preserved and transmitted to offspring. Lamarck presented this doctrine of evolution in his chief work, *Philosophie Zoologique,* published in 1809, the year of Charles Darwin's birth.

Lamarck's long years of experience as botanist and later as zoologist at the Royal Garden in Paris, as well as his extended studies of the European flora and of the natural history of invertebrates led him to general theoretical reflections in biological science. The title of his principal work was intended to express his growing conviction as a scientist, that mere "natural history," in his judgment, is not enough. After describing in small detail all the peculiarities and variations of animal species, we must undertake a zoölogical philosophy, an organization of our basic ideas of the structures and processes of animal life; we must "understand nature itself in each of its productions." [8]

Lamarck was engrossed by the inquiry into the causes of the increasing diversity and growing complexity of animal forms. From the standpoint of a limited geographical and historical range, nature does manifest a certain fixity of species, for a general similarity of living conditions may preserve a general type of structures and functions. But even at close range some adaptive modifications can be noted, and if we take the larger view which biological science requires, transformism of some kind cannot be ignored. From the rudimentary animal forms with scarcely any special organs, to the highest mammals and to man, processes and

61

determining conditions of progressive transformation of species must be operating, which science should explain.

We may say that Lamarck's theory applied to all living beings our common proverb about ourselves, that we are creatures of habit. As he put it, "habits form a second nature." He explained the formation of new species as due to the alteration of structure and function by the exceptional needed use or disuse of organs in various environments. He formulated his conclusions in two general laws:

> "I. In every animal which has not quite passed the limit of its development, the more frequent and sustained use of any organ fortifies that organ little by little, develops and enlarges it, and gives it a strength proportional to the duration of its use; while the constant lapse in the use of an organ insensibly weakens it, causes it to deteriorate, gradually lessens its capacities, and ends by making it disappear.
>
> II. All that nature enables individuals to acquire or to lose by the influence of circumstances in which their race finds itself exposed for a long time, and consequently by the influence of the prevailing dominance of some organ or by the constant lapse in the use of some part, is naturally conserved by transmission to the new individuals which are born, provided that the acquired changes are common to both sexes, or to those which have produced the new individuals." [9]

Lamarck supported these two general conclusions with a great number of examples, illustrating the strengthening, the alteration, the deterioration, or the disappearance of various organs, through prolonged use or disuse respectively. Water birds owe their web feet to their old ancestors' long-repeated stretching of the membranes connecting their claws as they ventured on the water in search of their food. The giraffes lengthened their necks and front feet by reaching for their forage in the higher and higher leafy branches. And Lamarck gave a striking evolutionary biography of the kangaroo with its odd anatomy.

The evidence submitted by Lamarck of the structural and functional changes caused by the use or disuse of various organs has only strengthened commonly held opinions and would scarcely be questioned by anyone. What his critics contested was his confident assertion that these so-called acquired characters are inheritable. Extensive researches have yielded much disproof of his theory, but they have not quite discouraged the Lamarckians.[10] This issue for or against Lamarckism concerned Charles Darwin. It has raised extensive controversy in the later developments of evolutionary theory. In Soviet Russia it has been swept into the shifting currents of ideological propaganda. Even those who do not side conclusively with Lamarck have cited evidence which may be disturbing to his opponents. Thus, for instance, C. Lloyd Morgan mentioned some experiments with white mice reported from Pavlov's laboratory. The first set of mice required 300 trials before they established a conditioned response between the ringing of a bell and their seeming expectancy of food. But their offspring seemed to learn faster: the first lot needed one hundred lessons; the second generation, only thirty, and the third, just five. These experiments were judged as defective in procedure, and the readily suggested Lamarckian inference was subsequently revoked by Pavlov. But despite this revocation, William McDougall continued his own researches with white rats through some twenty-three generations, and rather guardedly concluded: "It begins to look . . . as though Lamarckian transmission were a real process in nature." [11] McDougall's procedure has been criticized, and Lloyd Morgan himself, commenting on Pavlov's experiments and also reporting on thousands of his own, with small birds and their avoidance of nauseous soldier-beetles, remarked that he had never observed an immediate suitable response at the first instance, without any learning.[12]

## 3.  Charles Darwin's Method and Conclusions

Enough has been noted to indicate that Darwin did his work in a period of varied discussions of general evolutionary ideas. The epoch-making significance of his contribution was not in its wholly unprecedented character of originality but in the immense body of carefully organized evidence on which he based his conclusions and in the systematic genius which he manifested in the theoretical interpretation of his data. Especially characteristic was his thoroughness, marked by candor and patience, not to force the evidence but to be guided by it. He was cautious both in his agreement with his predecessors and in his criticism of them.

Darwin's development of his own method may be seen in his reactions to Lamarckism. Could the evolutionary advance from simpler to more complex species be explained by the modification and the inheritance due to the use or disuse of various organs? Darwin's initial attitude towards this doctrine was somewhat receptive, and even in his later reflections he was not altogeher averse to some quasi-Lamarckian concessions; but basically and increasingly he tended to disagree with Lamarck. In a letter to Lyell, 1859, he judged Lamarck's science as "extremely poor: I got not a fact or idea from it." [13] Almost sixteen years earlier he had written to the botanist Hooker: "Heaven forfend me from Lamarck nonsense of a 'tendency to progression,' 'adaptations from the slow willing of animals,' &c.!" But he added: "the conclusions I am led to are not widely different from his; though the means of change are wholly so." [14] The qualification here is important.

In the actual exposition of Darwin's theory there are some Lamarckian trends. While not accepting his predecessor's explanation as adequate, he is not unwilling to admit it on occasion as probably auxiliary. In the first chapter of *The Origin of Species* he reviews the effects of habit and of the use and disuse of parts: "changed habits produce an inherited effect." In the fifth chapter he concludes that "there can be no doubt that use in our domestic animals has strengthened and enlarged certain parts, and disuse diminished them; and that such modifications are inherited." He cites Lamarck's example of the giraffe's long neck, explaining its perpetuation in terms of his own theory but also adding that "the prolonged use of all the parts together with inheritance will have aided in an important manner in their co-ordination." [15] In *The Descent of Man* (1871), comparing the mental powers of men and women, Darwin wrote: "In order that woman should reach the same standard as man, she ought, when nearly adult, to be trained in energy and perseverance, and to have her reason and imagination exercised to the highest point; and then she would probably transmit these qualities chiefly to her adult daughters." But the tenor of this statement is ambiguous, and it is qualified in others; it is tentative, and Darwin added: " I here exceed my proper bounds." [16] Elsewhere in the same work he remarked: "It is familiar to every one that watchmakers and engravers are liable to be short-sighted, whilst men living much out of doors, and especially savages, are generally long-sighted. Short-sight and long-sight certainly tend to be inherited." [17]

Darwin's position thus seems to have included an occasional readiness to avail himself of Lamarckian support, but not as a main reliance. Conversely, while his evolutionary theory emphasized natural selection as the chief factor in the modification and formation of new species, he was careful to state in the last sentence of his Introduction to *The Origin of Species* that "Natural selection has been the most important, but not the exclusive, means of modification." This conclusion was reaffirmed by Darwin at the close of that work.[18] In the Preface to the second edition of *The Descent of Man* Darwin corrected the mistaken impression of some of his critics that he had emphasized exclusively natural selection of so-called spontaneous variations: "Great weight must be attributed to the inherited effects of use and disuse."

With these brief references to Darwin's relation to Lamarckism, and prior to a more direct examination of his theory, we may cite here Darwin's own concise statement of his general thesis: "As many more indivduals of each species are born than can possibly survive; and as, consequently, there is a frequently recurring struggle for existence, it follows that any being, if it vary however slightly in any manner profitable to itself, under the complex and sometimes varying conditions of life, will have a better chance of surviving, and thus be *naturally selected*. From this strong principle of inheritance, any selected variety will tend to propagate its new and modified form." [19]

Darwin himself called this "the doctrine of Malthus, applied to the whole animal and vegetable kingdoms." [20] This acknowledgment recalls the familiar story, recounted in Darwin's autobiography, of his long approach to his general formulation of his theory. His observations during the voyage on the *Beagle*, recorded in his *Journal of Researches,* and his subsequent inquiries led him to the conclusion that species were gradually modified. But he sought a scientific explanation of these evolutionary facts: "How are species modified?" He was aware of the various speculative theories in the field. Neither accepting nor rejecting them wholly, he proceeded first, as he wrote, "on true Baconian principles," collecting data and postponing formulated theory. The evidence which he was amassing pointed to selection as the means of modifying species: that is, in the successful practice of animal breeders and skillful gardeners. His problem, then, was to explain how selection operated in a state of nature. It was at this point that his good fortune in reading Malthus's *Essay on the Principle of Population* suggested to him, by analogy, his own explanatory theory. Malthus had reasoned that in any society the growth of population is bound to be controlled by the limited means of livelihood. Darwin's far-reaching inference from this thesis has been recorded in his autobiography in terms very similar to the concise statement cited above from *The Origin of Species*.[22]

So here he had the natural law of evolution, "leading to the advancement of all organic beings—namely, multiply, vary, let the strongest live and the weakest die." [23] Darwin was not given to rhetorical flights, but in summarizing his long chapter on "Natural Selection; or the Survival of the Fittest," he concluded with a striking figure of speech: "As buds give rise by growth to fresh buds, and these, if vigorous, branch out and overtop on all sides many a feebler branch, so by generation I believe it has been with the great Tree of Life, which fills with dead and broken branches the crust of the earth, and covers the surface with its ever-branching and beautiful ramifications." [24]

We should keep in mind here Darwin's main point of emphasis, and also his areas of theoretical reluctance. He was sure of certain negations and of certain affirmations; but he readily granted some fields of ignorance, and on some basic issues he suspended judgment. He denied supernatural intervention and providential design as explanatory principles in biology. But he also rejected absolute chance in nature. The variations which occur in nature are fortuitous in the sense that no supernatural purpose has produced them. But their preservation and perpetuation through offspring cannot be regarded as unaccountable chance. It has been due to their superior adaptation to the conditions of the environment, contributing to their survival.

His firm maintenance of his theory rested on three principal grounds of reliance, all of them in his judgment duly warranted by extensive evidence. He stated them in the concluding chapter of *The Origin of Species*: "Nothing at first can appear more difficult to believe than that the more complex organs and instincts have been perfected, not by means superior to, though analogous with, human reason, but by the accumulation of innumerable slight variations, each good for the individual possessor. Nevertheless, this difficulty, though appearing to our imagination insuperably great, cannot be considered real if we admit the following propositions, namely, that all parts of the organisation and intincts offer, at least, individual differences—that there is a struggle for existence leading to the preservation of profitable deviations of structure and instinct—and lastly, that gradations in the state of perfection of each organ may have existed, each good of its kind. The truth of these propositions cannot, I think, be disputed." [25]

Convinced of the basic soundness of his guiding ideas, Darwin was yet keenly aware of certain serious difficulties—some of them matters of factual detail, but others involving fundamental issues. Nothing is more striking evidence alike of his thoroughness and of his candor than his delay of more than twice the classic Horatian span of nine years before publishing his systematic work to the world. In fact, though he was slowly perfecting his theory ever since his first clear formulation of it, in 1838, he would not have published it even in 1859, had it not been for the fact that Alfred Russell Wallace had informed him of the conclusions of his own researches, similar to Darwin's. Even then Darwin was inclined to wait yet awhile, but his friends Lyell and Hooker persuaded him to publish first some brief statements of his theory and then the entire *Origin of Species*. Here, as biologists have indicated, the two evolutionists differed on a main point. Wallace explained the evolutionary advance by the survival of "full-formed varieties," adapted to their environment. Darwin emphasized favorable "variations in single characters," which are perpetuated by natural selection.[26]

In citing the difficulties confronting his theory, Darwin was neither overconfident nor unsteady. He considered them at length, classifying them under several heads. "First, Why, if species have descended from other species by fine gradations, do we not everywhere see innumerable transitional forms?" [27] This was the issue between him and Wallace. Further, could we believe in the production by natural selection of modifications altogether alien to a species? How would such a radically altered animal have survived in its intermediate stage, before its modification could effectuate its advantages in survival? Third, how can we explain the almost perfect technique of some of these variations, such as the cell-geometry of the beehive? Fourth, why are crossed varieties fertile, unlike the sterility of crossed species? Darwin examined also other difficulties. One of them, which he regarded as among the gravest charges, was the objection that terrestrial time did not allow sufficient span for the assumed amount of evolutionary changes required by the theory.[28]

More fundamental was the question of absolute origin, the first beginnings of life. Darwin candidly renounced the solution of this problem. With such ultimate questions he had "nothing to do." [29] He proposed to start with life in some elementary simplest forms, and was concerned to trace its evolution into more complex species. The origin of mental powers and the moral sense was clearly recognized as raising problems of a different sort from that of the origin of life. For here we are concerned, not with the first beginnings of biological conditions and reactions in some alleged primitive protoplasm, but with the first manifestations of mental processes and responses in highly developed animals which are here before us for examination.

In his *Descent of Man* Darwin devoted several chapters to the Mental Powers and the Moral Sense. He acknowledged that of all the differences between man and the other animals "the moral sense or conscience is by far the most important." [30] He was not prepared to indicate the precise point in animal evolution where intelligence may be said to have had its first origin and fountain source, or the conditions that then and there first initiated it. But he did regard these mental and moral powers, just as the other biological conditions and faculties, as differing between man and the higher animals in degree rather than in kind. He declared explicitly: "There is no fundamental difference between man and the higher mammals in their mental faculties:" [31] We should proceed evolutionally; we should recognize intelligence and moral judgment where they are clearly manifested and operative, in man, and then we should endeavor to trace their likely anticipations or gropings, in lower forms of life. The animals have the same five senses as man and so must share a common stock of perceptions. Instincts are also shared: the striving for self-preservation, sexual and parental attachment. Likewise, Darwin maintained in a somewhat Lamarckian vein, "some intelligent actions, after being performed during several generations, become converted into instincts and are inherited, as when birds on oceanic islands learn to avoid men." [32]

Darwin's survey of this whole field abounds in anecdotal material of widespread sources. In regard to the gradual development of the moral sense, he relied mainly on certain parental and gregarious instincts, accentuated by group influences and reactions. We can trace the growing efficacy of urging and reproof, and look across the doubtless long span of social evolution to the more definitely human emotions and convictions of obligation and duty and conscience. So he ventured to contemplate a likely natural history of the Golden Rule.[33] The rise from even the highest mammals to man has been very great, but Darwin pointed out some exceptionally impressive instances of animal quasi-moral behavior, and on the other hand, he also indicated that savage man has sometimes perverted his intelligence and has sunk below the beasts. On the last page of *The Descent of Man* he departed from his usually calm and objective exposition to give a sharp reply to some of his critics: "For my own part I would as soon be descended from that heroic little monkey, who braved his dreaded enemy in order to save the life of his keeper, or from that old baboon, who descending from the mountains, carried away in triumph his young comrade from a crowd of astonished dogs—as from a savage who delights to torture his enemies, offers up bloody sacrifices, practices infanticide without remorse, treats his wives like slaves, knows no decency, and is haunted by the grossest superstitions." [34]

The whole discussion of the evolutionary growth of the mental and moral faculties raises again the problem of teleology. Darwin had rejected the traditional doctrine of supernatural design in nature, but he was not unaware that his use of the terms selection, growth, progress carried some teleological connotations. In *The Origin of Species* he had protested that his phrase natural *selection* was strictly speaking a "metaphorical" expression: "in the literal sense of the word, no doubt, natural selection is a false term." [35] But despite this warning, he still proceeded to write: "Man selects only for his own good: Nature only for that of the being which it tends." [36] One of the most striking passages illustrating this ambiguity regarding teleology is towards the end of *The Origin of Species*: "We may look with some confidence to a secure future of great length. And as natural selection works solely by and for the good of each being, all corporeal and mental endowments will tend to progress towards perfection." [37] Surely it is needless to point out that Darwin's use here of the phrase "works solely by and for the good of each being," and of the terms "progress" and "perfection" are nowise warranted by his theory. As his colleague T. H. Huxley insisted, this morally commendatory interpretation of evolution is spurious. Darwinian evolution teaches the factual survival—*or extinction*—of certain species with certain variations in certain environments. The "fittest" are simply those that do survive. But it is interesting to note that the basic idea of development as implying growing perfection and realization of values has tended occasionally to influence the interpretation of biological evolution in its most eminent statement.

## 4.  *Alternatives in Evolutionary Theory*

Our discussion of evolution has brought out a clear distinction between established fact and disputed theoretical alternatives. Darwin's works contained both the extensive statement of biological facts and the outline of his theory, marked by his characteristic fairness and critical reserve. His conclusive report of the main facts, that there has been an origin of species in the immemorial stream of life, that more and more complex species have evolved from simpler forms by suitable adaptation to environmental conditions in the struggle for existence, were based on an immense body of evidence gathered through his long years of patient investigation. Biological research since Darwin's day has greatly multiplied his data and sustained his factual conclusions. Paleontology, comparative anatomy, and embryology have contributed extensive and varied confirmations of his reports of evolutionary descent, both at the lower ranges of animal existence and at the higher levels. The world-wide collection of fossil remains from the successive strata of the earth's crust have exhibited in broad outline the succession of simpler by more complex species. They indicate also the great number of specific processes of evolution as, for instance, the many steps in the evolution of the horse's hoof, corresponding to the third toe of its ancient predecessor, the "eohippus." The embryologists note what has been called the recapitulation of the long series of evolutionary forms by the individual during the several stages of gestation. A human embryo during its course of development recalls in turn its evolutionary kinship with fishes and lizards and of course with other mammals. All along the line, scientific research during the past hundred years has expanded immensely the evidence for the facts of evolution.

But the firm establishment of the data of evolutionary biology has emphasized the recognized need of some basic and ultimate explanation of the process of evolution. And as might be expected, theoretical construction in the many domains of biology has not been lacking. The advocates of the several systematic alternatives have shown speculative vigor and also scientific caution, in varying degrees. The present exposition is intended to outline briefly some of the more important theoretical positions which have been maintained.

## Materialistic Evolutionism

We may note first the materialistic and mechanistic direction followed by a number of evolutionists. Darwin's account of the origin of species replaced the traditional doctrine of creationism and Providential design in nature by a naturalistic report of the factual struggle for existence in nature and of the survival and propagation of species with variations suitable to certain environments. Darwinism thus ranged evolutionary biology alongside the other physical sciences by dismissing any appeal to teleological direction in the origin and development of living forms. This physical naturalistic tenor of Darwinism has been accentuated by materialistic workers in the field, who have advocated a mechanistic theory to account for the evolutionary process all the way through, from the simplest protoplasm to the most complex organization of human life.

Among the advocates of this materialistic-mechanistic theory of evolution, the Jena biologist, Ernst Haeckel (1834-1919) was outstanding both in technical competence and in partisan zeal. But his ventures in final evolutionary theory were various. It should be observed that Haeckel preferred to call his biological philosophy monism rather than materialism. He claimed kinship with Spinoza and Goethe rather than with Holbach. There was a certain strain of ambiguity or indecision in Haeckel's thinking. While his usually prevailing emphasis was on the reduction of "spirit (or energy of thought)" to "energy (moving force)," he also ventured in the opposite direction and sometimes regarded all cells as animated and all force as somehow conscious: " Even the atom is not without a rudimentary form of sensation and will . . . a universal 'soul' of the simplest character." [38] Despite this occasional venture towards hylozoism or panpsychism, Haeckel's dominant tone was mechanistic. One of his contributions to evolutionary theory, to what Lamarck had called zoölogical philosophy, concerns the relation of the individual's development to the general course of evolution. Haeckel elaborated this relation in detail and presented a precise formula for it in his theory of biological transformism. The embryological development of the individual organism recapitulates the previous evolutionary stages, or as he put it, "ontogenesis is a brief and rapid recapitulation of phylogenesis." [39]

## Mendelism, Genetics, and Theory of Mutations

During the years when Darwin was advancing his evolutionary theory of the origin of species, an Austrian naturalist, Gregor Mendel, carefully cultivated peas in his Moravian garden so as to discover the details of their processes of heredity. The publication of his findings attracted little notice until the end of the century, when their importance was at last recognized. His work led to extensive further studies of inheritance and to the development of an entire biological science called genetics. Far-reaching investigations of the order and procedure of heredity, and microscopic study of cell mechanism in its most delicate details have given geneticists deep insight into the inner workings of the evolutionary process.

Mendel in his garden experimented with repeated crossing of plants and recorded the characteristics of the resulting hybrids. Cross a red pea flower with a white, and you get pink blooms. But if you now cross-fertilize these hybrids, you get pinks, reds, and whites in certain definite ratios. If these second lots of reds are pollinated by reds, they will breed true; and likewise the whites; but the pinks will always yield reds and whites as their own hybrid pink color. Furthermore, crossing pinks with whites does not yield reds, and crossing pinks with reds does not yield whites. So it was inferred that there must be some specific factors in the flower cells which determined colors, and similarly other factors controlling other characteristics. Geneticists have called these factors *genes;* they are believed to be arranged in the wriggling filaments in the cell's nucleus which are called chromosomes. Very extensive experiments along these lines have been carried out, notably by T. H. Morgan and his followers. They have worked especially with the fruit fly drosophila, which breeds at a rapid rate and goes through many generations in a very short time. They have not only ascertained the operation of the various genes in determining specific genetic results , but have also mapped out the positions of the genes in the chromosomes of the cells under microscopic observation.

We have given only the barest outline of these researches. The systematic inferences from them have been far-reaching. Darwin's general report of the evolutionary process has been sustained in the main. But modern genetics has enabled biologists to trace in most minute detail what specific factors affect inheritance and in what particular ways. As Weissmann maintained firmly, inherited variation of an organism cannot be the result of habitual use or disuse of certain organs, or of any so-called acquired characters. Changes or variations in the body or soma of an organism do not have hereditary consequences. The geneticists have taught us that the only hereditary factors are those transmitted through the genes in the chromosomes, in those minute parts of the body, the germ plasm in the ova or spermatozoa of the two sexes. Some of these heritable factors are advantageous to the survival and perpetuation of organism, others are disadvantageous or lethal.

Clearly, we are told, a heritable modification of a species, or the production of a new species, can result only from certain specific changes in the germ cells, in the genes and chromosomes. Cross fertilization of certain organisms, of peas or fruit flies, yields changes in specific factors. But what germ cell changes can account for the evolutionary advance from microorganisms to mammals? What are the causes which effect the heritable variations in the germ plasm? The incredible progress in cytology, in the microscopic study of the most minute details of cell structure and operation, has only accentuated the importance of these basic theoretical explanations of the evolutionary processes.

In this perspective of genetics, the study of so-called mutations, especially by the Dutch botanist Hugo de Vries, has raised some interesting problems. As was noted in the previous section, Darwin, in his causal explanation of the evolution of species, did not rule out absolutely the inheritance of acquired characters. In a variation involving change in some organ, he thought, minute granules or so-called "gemmules" flowed through the blood stream into the germ plasm and became hereditary factors in the succeeding generation. This hypothesis of "pangenesis" was advanced "provisionally" by Darwin. It was criticized severely,[40] but it served as a starting point for De Vries. His researches led him to the conclusion that the evolution of one species from another cannot be explained adequately as a gradual transitional process of minute changes. The process involves discontinuities, radical alterations which appear suddenly and which are heritable. These unaccountable variations De Vries called "mutations," and he proposed his theory as a supplement to that of Darwin. In addition to the ordinary forms of gradual variation, De Vries added the evolutionary factor of mutation, by means of which "new types are seen to arise suddenly, sharply, although often not widely distinct from the parental type." [41] In exploring and expanding the factual basis of his theory, he observed some startling changes in cultivated evening primroses which had spread wild in a potato patch. These researches led him to further studies both in Holland and in the United States.

De Vries defended himself against the objection that his cultivated evening primroses, grown wild, were really hybrids, and that his supposed mutations were really the reappearances of some earlier types. He held that his conclusions did not rest on any single batch of data and were too widespread to be so easily dismissed. But even if his general findings were accepted as factually warranted, the problem of their causal explanation still remained unsettled. What is it that effects these sudden mutations, heritable changes in the germ plasm? Are mutations, as Schrödinger recently expressed it, "due to quantum jumps in the gene molecule?" [42]

In one of his earlier works, *Evolution and Adaptation* (1903), T. H. Morgan criticized several alternative causal theories and in his conclusion held to a tentative position. Morgan's researches in *Regeneration* had led him to question the adequacy of Darwin's general theory to explain "the building up of the complete regeneration by slowly acquired steps, that cannot be decisive in the battle for existence." [43] He concluded further that "the *origin* of the power to regenerate" is likewise not explicable on Darwinian grounds.[44] He questioned the explanation that variations have arisen because of their usefulness. (What is the usefulness of the beautiful colors inside the shells of some snails or mollusks?) "The scientific problem of evolution is not to be found in the principle of selection, but in the origin of the variations themselves." [45]

One of Morgan's distinguished students, H. J. Muller, observed some startling mutations as a result of subjecting fruit flies to X-rays. Other kinds of radiation have been used, and these also have produced greatly increased rates and varieties of mutations. The inference would seem to be that heritable changes in the germ plasm, in the genes and chromosomes, are due in a measure to physical or chemical reactions to radiation. This view has clearly far-reaching implications regarding the relation of biological processes to physical and chemical determinants. Some biologists have believed that we may find here an answer to the baffling problem of the origin of life.

### *Vitalism*

The difficulties of mechanistic theories in biology, of the proposals to explain physiological and psychological processes in terms of physical or chemical reactions, have given rise to so-called vitalistic theories. This trend of thought has a long record in the history of ideas, which connects the names of Erigena, Paracelsus, Stahl, Schopenhauer. Vitalism proceeds from the insistence that living beings manifest something basically different from anything in the fields of physics and chemistry. We cannot understand living behavior unless we recognize some special directive power in every organism. This unique biological factor has been called by various names: vital principle, vital force, or as Hans Driesch, a chief recent advocate of the theory, has it, borrowing his term from Aristotle, "entelechy."

Without reporting Driesch's reasoning in detail, we may use some of his arguments as fairly characteristic statements of modern vitalism. This strain of evolutionary theory rejects explicitly any mechanistic reductionism in biology. If we are to explain organic processes adequately, we must include in our theory the operation of a distinctively biological principle, unlike anything manifested in inorganic conditions. The activity of an organism manifests a distinctively non-mechanical "correspondence beween individualized stimuli and individualized effects." [46] These considerations become increasingly decisive when we observe our bodily awareness of ourselves, our use of ourselves both in reacting to external pressure or other stimuli and in the execution of our plans and purposes.

This theory has of course met strong refuffs from the mechanists, but it has also been criticized severely by thinkers who question or who reject materialism. Some of the latter have objected to the vitalists' proposed cleavage between organic and inorganic nature. Why do we need to say that biological processes represent such a complete discontinuity in the world? Why may it not be that the physico-chemical substances and processes, under certain so-called organic conditions, become the matrix for the manifestation of the new properties and new forms of behavior? This is the view of emergent evolution which we shall examine later in this chapter.

Vitalism has been criticized as itself marred by a rigidity similar to that of the mechanistic theory. Instead of postulating a special "vital force" to explain biological processes, we should study the behavior of living beings, recognizing both the features which are shared with physical and chemical reactions, and also the peculiar and distinctive biological characteristics. Among the latter, special attention has been called to organic regeneration or self-repair and restoration, the related biological principle of maintenance of normality, and the factors of integration and coördinated behavior. The emphasis on these aspects is significant and it will be considered in our next section.


## 5. Emphasis on Integration and Maintained Coördination

The exposure of the unsolved problems and the inherent difficulties of maintaining evolutionary biology on a strictly mechanistic basis have led some biologists to radical reconstruction. Darwinism has been acclaimed as putting biology on a scientific level, alongside physics and chemistry. But it has also been maintained that the perplexities of modern biology have been due to its failure to recognize from the outset the unique character of biological processes, which cannot be expressed adequately in terms of physical mechanism.

This principle has been emphasized firmly by a number of biologists, as for instance by Karl von Baer: "Life cannot be explained from something else, but must be conceived and understood in itself." The physiologist, J. S. Haldane, who quotes this statement, insists that biologists must begin with biology, with the actual conditions and activities of life. Haldane may be said to advocate biological activism, with emphasis on the adjective. If we ask, what distinguishes biological, living activity, Haldane points to its coördinated self-maintenance. We may call this the principle of integration or wholeness. Plants, animals, men are all marked by this integral active correlation, in which the parts are truly organs. "There is and there can be no origin of life out of mechanical conditions." [47] The primary fact of life is the concrete reality; only in relation to it or correlation within it do our scientific abstractions of anatomical structure, physiological functions, hereditary and environmental conditions have any meaning.

Instead of the reductionism which would explain living processes as complicated physical and chemical reactions, this theory emphasizes living wholeness as a root principle germinal in nature throughout. Planck, the author of the quantum theory in physics, has been quoted to this effect: "The conception of wholeness must . . . be introduced into physics, as in biology, to make the orderliness of Nature intelligible and capable of formulation." [48] Haldane not only surmises that there has always been life in some rudimentary form; he also holds that "the idea of life is nearer to reality than the ideas of matter and energy." [49] This type of biological theory regards the physical-chemical mechanism as the abstract framework of a reality which to a deeper insight manifests its living and evolving nature.

We seem at this point to be in quest of a cosmic principle which can comprehend both inorganic and biological coördination but is not basically reducible to either of these two. The principle of integration itself or wholeness has been proposed to serve this purpose. Perhaps the most emphatic statement of this view is in the theory of "Holism" (from the Greek *holos*, whole) advocated by the South African statesman, General Smuts. Another term for this cosmology is "integrationism." Smuts viewed the entire world-span, from star dust to rational personality, as "holistic," a hierarchical process from lower to higher levels of integrational activity. Holism is "the ultimate, synthetic, ordering, organizing, regulating activity in the universe which accounts for all the structural grouping and syntheses in it, from the atom and the physico-chemical structures, through the cells and organisms, through Mind in animals, to Personality in man." [50] The holistic activity, or cosmic integration trend, is a boundlessly composite and creative orderliness in nature. It is a dynamic hierarchy, to the full explanation of which mechanistic principles are altogether inadequate and even biological ideas are not fully appropriate. It reaches down to the least evolved existence and points towards the highest and the most complex development. It is material in its rudiments and Divine in its consumation.

On a far less speculative level than Haldane or Smuts, a number of biologists have emphasized the principle of wholeness as fundamental in explaining the behavior and the preservation of living organism. Thus Professor Judson Herrick writes: "Integration is the primordial requirement for survival. The individuation of parts takes place within the integrated whole and must be kept in subordination to it." [51] Likewise Jennings concludes his work, *Behavior of the Lower Organisms*, with a recognition that the maintenance of the normal course of life is the determining factor in modification even at the lowest levels of biological existence: "The behavior becomes modified . . . only as it is to the advantage of the organism that it should be so modified; that is, only as the modification favors the normal current of life activities." [52]

More extensively this general idea has been developed in a very interesting book entitled *The Wisdom of the Body*, by the physiologist W. B. Cannon. His studies of the various complex life processes have emphasized the importance of their interrelation. Cannon has recognized in physiology a principle of manifold balance of conditions which mark the normal life of the body. When this balance is upset in any way, self-repair and regeneration of tissues start without delay, to restore the balanced constitution if possible. These conditions and factors of constancy might be called equilibria, but that word has a physico-chemical connotation which is not quite appropriate in physiology. Cannon has proposed the term *homeostasis*, to signify the coördination of bodily processes, "involving, as they may, the brain and nerves, the heart, lungs, kidneys and spleen, all working coöperatively. . . ." [53]

We cannot summarize here Cannon's various and detailed examination of the "homeostasis" in the many complicated bodily activities: hunger and thirst as means of bodily self-care; the preservation of constancy of the water content and salt content of the blood, the formation and the maintenance of blood sugar, blood protein, blood fat and calcium, the preservation of normal bodily temperature, and the many other general features of bodily stabilization. Cannon cites Claude Bernard's sentence, which J. S. Haldane has called the most pregnant ever framed by a physiologist: "All the vital mechanisms, however varied they may be, have only one object, that of preserving constant the conditions of life in the internal environment." [54]

The problem of the origin of life seems to present a dilemma to biologists: difficulties confront us on each alternative position. The theory of spontaneous generation, which was current in classical antiquity and engaged also considerable modern speculation, has been definitely discounted by modern research, in which the work of Pasteur was outstanding. Pasteur proved that under thoroughly sterile conditions not the least microorganism could arise spontaneously.

But this firm experimental demonstration of the principle *omne vivum ex vivo* — life arises only from living tissue — emphasized the problem of the origin of life on earth. Those who hold that the earliest state on earth was one of non-living matter and who reject any doctrine of special creation, have been led sometimes to conjectural explanations which do not explain. We have been told that cells or spores of living tissues may have been blown through interstellar space to earth and thus started the biological evolutionary process. This is clearly a scientific case of "passing the buck." The problem which we renounce would still be demanding solution up yonder somewhere, on Saturn or on Sirius. How did life originate there?

The more thoroughly it is proved by laboratory experiments that life does not originate spontaneously from non-living material, the more insistent becomes the problem of explaining the very first origination of living organisms. While rejecting the doctrine of spontaneous generation in its usual traditional sense, can it be held that in the laboratory of nature special conditions in the immemorial past may have produced the first living cells? This is a speculative conjecture, and it involves perplexing inferences for the strict materialist. Thus Haeckel rejected quite as firmly as Pasteur the old traditional doctrine of spontaneous generation but maintained that the very first life on earth must have somehow produced itself out of non-living matter, and that species have come from simpler and more rudimentary types and ultimately from the elemental protoplasm. But now consider the original and simplest conceivable blob of living matter: what must have been its first beginning? Haeckel reasoned that this must have taken place by chemical processes unknown to us, in the primordial terrestrial conditions which we cannot reproduce today. At best, he thought, we might suggest the likely transition from simpler inorganic substances and processes to the more complex carbon compounds as proteins or albumins and finally to the simplest recognizable organisms or *monera*. "Organic life itself is a chemico-physical process, based on the metabolism (or interchange of material) of these albuminates." [55] This theory, in Haeckel's judgment, has the merit of deriving life originally from the eternal matter and deriving it by mechanical, chemico-physical processes. In a twofold way it reaffirms his predominantly materialistic position.

On a deeper level of cosmological reflection, the actuality of living and also of mental activities in the world process has been judged to imply a certain self-transcending capacity of nature, which cannot be expressed in merely mechanical-causal terms. We should recognize the emerging of the higher out of the lower, real creative achieving in nature. These two theories, Emergent Evolution and Creative Evolution, will be considered in the two following sections.

## 6. Emergent Evolution

Among the contemporary protagonists of emergent evolution, Samuel Alexander and C. Lloyd Morgan have been outstanding. Morgan, the Bristol biologist, even while venturing boldly to the outermost verge of cosmological speculation, professes a layman's modesty in philosophical commitments. In his many expository works on emergent evolution he repeatedly distinguishes his own position from Alexander's but readily acknowledges him as his master. Alexander for his part, in *Space, Time, and Deity*, which set him outright in the front rank of contemporary philosophers, uses the idea of emergence as a leading principle in his all-comprehensive cosmic theory and pays tribute to Lloyd Morgan's scientific mastery — "Would that my faith were founded on knowledge comparable to his." [56] In general we may say that their main contributions to the doctrine of emergence are complementary. Lloyd Morgan is concerned with elaborating the details of emergent evolution and candidly avows and tries to justify his ultimate philosophical and religious inferences from the theory. Alexander's work is on a far-flung systematic plan. Actually the term "emergence" is not often on his pen-point, and the attentive reader has to be patient to jot on the margin the relatively few times that the word itself is employed. But the principle of emergence is germinal in Alexander's cosmic activism, perhaps the more significant because not always so specifically phrased. In our brief account of emergent evolution, we shall not be concerned so much with the exposition of details and minute distinctions of these two principal versions, but shall make use of them both in examining the main ideas in this interpretation of evolutionism.

The principle of emergence issues from the endeavor to press the theory of evolution to its ultimate cosmological ground. Darwin, as we have noted, did not undertake to explain the origin of life. He investigated the origin of species, always from other species. We should repeat that modern biology, notably since Pasteur, has rejected the traditional notions of spontaneous generation. But biologists also accept the evidence supplied by paleontology and geology that for long cosmic aeons there was no life on earth. Life must have originated somehow. So we are urged to face our issue squarely. In a primordial world of lifeless existence, life and living processes somehow appeared. Does this mean that the primordial world has never been really lifeless, that life in its most elementary forms has always been somehow present? Or shall we infer that there is a certain ultimate power in nature which operates at lifeless levels of existence so as to rise to the attainment of biological organisms and reactions? The emergentist answers the second question in the affirmative. He may also interpret the principle of emergence in such a way as not to negate the first question altogether.

The relation of lifeless to living and to mental existence need not be regarded merely as one of temporal succession. These three may be viewed as fundamental levels of being which characterize the structure and the process of reality essentially and integrally. From biological evolution we may then proceed to cosmic evolution and on to a cosmology of emergence, a theory of activism of self-expanding achievement.

Alexander's statement may be cited here: "New orders of finites come into existence in Time. . . . New complexity of motions come into existence, a new quality emerges. . . ."[57] Two lines from George Meredith's *Modern Love* come to mind:

> What are we first? First, animals; and next,
> Intelligences at a leap. . . .

In considering the relation of the lower or matrix to the higher or emergent character, we are warned to avoid a twofold error. We should not, like the materialists, reduce the higher to the lower and interpret life and mind as simply more complex mechanisms. Nor should we, like so many idealists, overemphasize the higher character and regard the physical quality as essentially a latent form of spirit. At every level of existence we should do justice to the facts: recognize that level for what it is, but also see it as the emergent from lower levels and likewise as the matrix of a higher realization.

In recognizing that the higher qualities or levels are unpredictable from the standpoint of the lower, we do not in any way question their reality. Rather, we acknowledge the ongoing and genuinely self-enhancing character of the world-process throughout. We may see here the error of all crude reductionism. When the behaviorist in psychology declares that he "finds no evidence for 'mental existences' or 'mental processes' of any kind,"[58] he only confesses that he has bound himself to the life-level of physiology and, although a professed psychologist, has not considered mind or characteristically psychological processes at all.

The main stages or levels of existence from the viewpoint of emergent evolution are physical mechanism, life, and mind with its upward reach of spiritual character. Two book titles indicate the boundless range of this cosmology. We may interpose Lloyd Morgan's *Life, Mind, and Spirit* within the infinite span of Alexander's *Space, Time, and Deity.*

Alexander insists on hyphenating "Space-Time," for he regards the two as integral in actuality. "Space-Time" signifies to him mainly the physical cosmos, but he also considers it as "the orders of relations which mathematics investigates," and likewise as the mental space and time of our experience.[59] It is the fundamental matrix, structure and pattern of all higher emergence. The higher forms of cosmic achievement can be understood truly only if we maintain a firm conviction of the basic reality of Space-Time. This conviction is reflected in Alexander's realistic commitment in theory of knowledge and in metaphysics, and also in Lloyd Morgan's reaffirmed naturalism. In tracing the emergence of life and of mind, and in reaching towards the divine summits of reality, this doctrine should never lose its initial and persistent conviction of physical structure.

With this general cosmological pattern, the specific problem and method of procedure of the theory can be indicated more clearly. Alexander states them at the outset of his work. Philosophy must learn from the sciences what matter and life and mental activity are, and then it must ask "how these orders of fact are related to one another and to the fundamental nature of things." [60]

If we try to characterize in some detail the new emergent quality of life, we find that no mere listing of specific features quite suffices: organization and self-regulation and plasticity of responses and self-reproduction.[61] We are bound to acknowledge the radical rise in complexity and in order of behavior when we proceed from non-living matter to living tissue, and we must also recognize the continuity from physical-chemical to biological existence. Living activity cannot be understood as a mere rearrangement of physical processes, but on the other hand it cannot be explained by the interposition of some occult agency, like the "entelechy" of Hans Driesch and other vitalists. What takes place in the emergence of life is a radical and new ascent in complexity, in organization or relatedness of the material factors, making possible a new type of reaction and operation altogether.

The interpretation of mind in the doctrine of emergent evolution requires a careful statement, for "mind" is used in a twofold sense. In the more usual understanding of the term, mind is the higher order of activity that emerges from the matrix of life processes. But in a less common version, mind may be regarded as a characteristic of the entire structure and process of reality, and in that sense it may be considered as the basic operation of emergence throughout nature rather than as itself a specific emergent. Considering the latter use of the term first, we may note Alexander's statement that "Time is the mind of Space and Space the body of Time." [62] This statement emphasizes the essentially active and emergent character of reality, and recognizes mental activity as the highest known finite level of attained emergence, so it uses the term "mind" to characterize the process of emergence throughout. This way of interpreting mind suggests some idealistic kinships and some wavering in the initial realistic firmness to which we referred.

Mind regarded in the stricter sense of mental activity also seems to point two ways. It is conscious organization and responsiveness, and it is also, more fully, pursuit and achievement of values. The emergence of consciousness covers a widespread gradation of processes, from the most rudimentary behavior of low organisms to the clearest and most complex intelligence in man. Lloyd Morgan's book, *Life at the Crossways*, indicates by its title his keen sense of the gradual rise from merely physiological to more and more definitely conscious and mental processes. So we may ask: why does, not only the chick but perhaps even the amoeba, accept some particles as food and reject others? [63] Can we note here a hint of that "fore-plan" which marks more and more definitely mental activities? Mind as the higher level emerging from the matrix of life seems to be characterized by a conative order, by the consciousness of ends to be pursued and attained.

The interpretation of values in the philosophy of emergent evolution shows some important aspects but also raises difficulties in the doctrine. The nature and the structure of reality at any level has characteristics appropriate to that level. Now "mind is the highest finite empirical reality we know." [64] We should expect expressions or aspects of reality which are natural to a mental response but cannot be regarded as objective in a non-mental perspective. Such seems to be the status of values in Alexander's cosmology. He calls values "tertiary qualities." In his theory of knowledge both the primary and the secondary qualities of

Lockean discussion are regarded as objective. So we may say: the primrose is really yellow just as it is really round. But it is beautiful only in the mind's response to it: the mind, that is, of Wordsworth, not of Peter Bell. The present discussion is not concerned mainly with theory of knowledge, and we shall not press the main issues raised at this point. We may ask in passing whether the color of a flower is presented to a prism as it is presented even to Peter Bell.

To be sure, as we have learned already from T. H. Green, values are "relative to values for, of, or in a person." [65] And we read in a recent treatise by a distinguished biologist: "True values are always personal perquisites. . . . There are no impersonal values." [66] But not only values are thus uniquely manifested to emergent mind. In a real sense every quality of nature comes to have a somewhat new character in the emergent mental perspective. Precisely the advocate of emergent evolution should not, in calling values "tertiary qualities," question their objectivity. Qualities are objectively real — at their respective levels. Values are as real or as objective as the mental or personal activities in which they are characteristically manifested. Lloyd Morgan expresses his recognition of this point: "Under relational treatment no value is what it is and as it is apart from someone for whom it 'has value.' In relatedness value comes to its own as constitutive of reality." [67]

We may consider this important point further, for it concerns the basic meaning of value. Values are correlative with personality. Not only are they characteristically expressed in the activities of persons, but anything may manifest a value-character when considered in a personal perspective. If we ask more particularly what aspects of personal experience reveal value, the answer should be sought in purposive demands and satisfactions, or better in fulfilment of personality. John Stuart Mill defined matter as "a permanent possibility of sensation." [68] May we venture a definition of value as "the impending prospect of fulfilment"? And the prospect is also a demand, both challenge and commitment. Relative appraisal of values, preference and choice, should follow along the same line of thought. In any situation the highest value should be that which best expresses the fulfilment or the fullest realization of personality, in individual experience and in social interrelation.

We may turn briefly to Alexander's constructive account of the emergence of values. Towards the close of his work he considers evolution as the natural history of values. "Darwinism is sometimes thought to be indifferent to value. It is in fact the history of how values come into existence in the world of life.... The doctrine of natural selection explains not how types are generated but how they come to have value. It is so far from being indifferent to value that it is wholly concerned with value; its very meaning is that values emerge through the trial of various types under certain external conditions, which trial determines whether in virtue of its gifts or constitution a type is worthy." [69]

In its intention, as a contribution to a value-naturalism, the passage just quoted is significant. And as an intended expansion of evolutionism to truly cosmic range through the principle of emergence, it is also important. But as an account of Darwinism, it is open to serious objections. We have already recognized and need not repeat here that Darwinian evolution is not concerned with the "worth" of any type, be it its goodness and nobility or the reverse. Darwinism is concerned with the conditions under which certain species survive or perish. But there is a sense in which emergent evolution may be interpreted as a cosmic optimistic vision, of the ascent through life and mind to spiritual activity, to pursuit and realization of values. In this definitely non-Darwinian sense we may read the words of Alexander and only wish that we had his further interpretation of them, of both parts of his statement: "The universe works in experience so as to secure the survival of good, or rather that which survives in the long run in the contest establishes its value thereby and is good. ... "Morality is the nature of things." [70]

Activism is characteristically the philosophy of an expanding universe, and the theory of emergent evolution, as it rules out the reduction of the higher to the lower levels, also precludes any idea of a closed and definitive system of reality. Mental activity is the highest finite level of nature that we know; but mind also in its turn must point to a still higher summit. We cannot assign any limits to creative intelligence, in genius or saint, and even at less sublime levels, mental and spiritual activity manifest a reach or aspiration towards a still higher reality. Alexander calls this ever emergent quality "Deity." We cannot define it, and we cannot say that it exists, for by its very nature it is ever potential, the infinite divine Beyond. While we are convinced that "all values are conserved in God's deity," we should not regard Deity as a value or regard it in terms of truth or goodness or justice. Deity is ultrahuman, and belongs not to the order of mind and value but to the order of perfection. Therein it alone is worthy of worship.[71] In his interpretation of religion Alexander uses the term "God" to mean the ongoing reality as infinitely perfectible, or as he expresses it, "the whole universe with a nisus to deity. . . . God is . . . the power that makes for deity." [72] Lloyd Morgan is frankly closer to the more personal view of God. He uses more readily the language of traditional religion and is not unresponsive to mystical insight which in his judgment alone "touches the eternal verities of a spiritual religion." [73]

## 7. Creative Evolution

In his insistence on the unique reality of living processes Henri Bergson agrees with the advocates of emergent evolution. But his own theory has unique features which call for distinctive exposition. Bergson's thought is original, and his style reveals literary excellence characterized especially by a mastery of metaphor in which no contemporary philosopher has approached him. His pages are alive with similes that illumine his discussion but also sometimes offer us brilliant comparisons in place of real elucidation.

Bergson's interpretation of nature is marked by his outstanding recognition of flowing change. He criticizes the sciences and philosophies of the past for their failure to give due recognition to the integral ongoing current of existence. In terms of theory of knowledge, he exposes the inadequacy of mere intellectual construction with its schematic procedure. If we may preface our discussion by summarizing some of his main charges, he objects to the misinterpretation of real time as a succession of discrete extents or moments; he exposes the misleading view of the course of existence as a series of events; against both the mechanistic outlook on nature as predetermined in every detail and the eternally planned teleology of providential design, he champions the recognition of really creative conciousness and the living stream of reality.

Systematically, we should begin with Bergson's account of

Time, for it reveals clearly the basic pattern of his philosophy. He criticizes traditional thinking for its "spatialization" of time as a sum or collection of longer or shorter lengths or stretches. This is clock time or calendar time, artificially ticking off its minutes and hours or dating its days and months and years. Quite different is the real time of living activity. Bergson calls this pure time *durée réelle*, real duration. It is not a series nor even a pulsation but a flowing stream. It is "the continuous process of the past which gnaws into the future and swells as it advances."  [74]

Now, to be sure, we may point out that whenever we think of time, we as it were fix our location in the stream: what time is it, or in what year, B.C or A.D., did that event take place? But that only indicates the schematic procedure of the intellect; it divides the living flowing unity into parts, of which it then makes a collection and a system. The scientific intellect sees in nature series and chains of events, and then proceeds to trace their causal linkage. Bergson does not reject this intellectual procedure as wholly misleading. For certain purposes of abstract physical science it serves quite well. But it can never do full justice to living processes or to consciousness, and it can never give us a true understanding of evolution.

Instead of foisting upon our interpretation of life our inept mechanistic explanations, we should begin by a straightforward study of the living experience itself. This living activity is an ever changing and ever unique flux. We can observe this directly in ourselves. "For a conscious being, to exist is to change, to change is to mature, to mature is to go on creating oneself endlessly. Should the same be said of existence in general?" [75] Bergson's answer is affirmative, and he undertakes to justify it on a vast scale. He maintains the principle of activism in cosmology without reservations. "There are no things, there are only actions." [76] The cosmic agency, all-pervading in every living process, is the creative flood itself, manifested throughout nature. Bergson calls it the *élan vital*, the vital urge. He warns us never to forget its two fundamental characteristics, both of which rule out the routine application to biology of the abstract mechanism of physics or chemistry. We may call these two characteristics fluidity and creative novelty or unpredictable direction of growth. The course of life is a real current, and its future streaming cannot be formulated as a bare result of any antecedent factors.

Bergson takes his stand here in opposing not only any form of mechanistic determinism in biology but also the traditional teleologies of providential design. Despite their apparent opposition, these two doctrines share a common error; they both regard the stream of life as determined or as wholly planned in advance. But a living process is neither the mere effect of an antecedent cause nor the inevitable execution of a plan. The teleology that it reveals is its own creative designing, inexhaustible, unpredictable, a genuine evolution. We can observe this creative activity in process throughout nature, and we can recognize it directly in our own experience. "Every human work in which there is invention, every voluntary act in which there is freedom, every movement of an organism that manifests spontaneity, brings something new into the world." [77]

It should be clear that Bergson's insistence on the unpredictable creativity of living processes does not exclude absolutely the use of causal explanation in biology. Our abstract mechanism, which serves us well enough perhaps, though not perfectly, in physics and chemistry, has its part in biology also. But in biology its part is nowise the chief role. The failure to grasp this truth is the basic error of all merely intellectual "scientific" interpretations. Bergson's verdict here is underscored in his text: *The intellect is characterized by a natural inability to comprehend life.* [78] Our mechanistic plotting of the evolutionary course of life in a series of clumsy abstractions; the straight lines that we draw between the points on our graphs, never delineate the flowing curve of real living existence.

Bergson speaks of intellectual knowledge as "cinematographic." It reduces the movement or flow of life to a series of snapshots, and then it undertakes to recompose their serial succession into a sort of continuity. "Things are constituted by the instantaneous cut which the understanding practises, at a given moment, on a flux . . . and what is mysterious when we compare the cuts together becomes clear when we relate them to the flux." [79] Intellect here needs its completion or better, its revision or replacement by intuition and instinct. We should "replace the rigidity of a diagram by the suppleness of life." [80]

The relation of these two, intellect and instinct, should be clearly recognized. Instinct is not to be regarded as a low form of undeveloped intelligence, nor is the intellect to be mistaken for the mature advance upon instinct. Instinct and intelligence are two distinct currents in the stream of evolution. The former proceeds to its perfection among the insects; the latter, among the vertebrates and preëminently in man. The two are both "opposite and complementary." [81] We should grasp their distinctive functions in the living process. Intelligence is regarded by Bergson as a manufacturing or fabricating faculty. The intellect constructs artificial objects, tools, schemes, forms, concepts, frameworks, patterns and systems of relations. Instinct is marked by a certain direct unreasoned sympathy which goes unthinking to the heart of its object, intuitive and unerring.

The achievements of the intellect are evident to us in all the fields of our mental activity, but the instinctive processes have not been so well understood, yet without the clear recognition of them we cannot grasp the characteristic nature of life or evolution. Bergson has cited a number of striking examples of the instinctive expertness of certain wasps which sting their victims (caterpillars, beetles, spiders) in specific nerve centers in such a way as to paralyze but not kill them, and then lay their eggs on them, thus providing their future larva with fresh food. Here is a cricket stung in three definite nerve centers, or a caterpillar which has not only been paralyzed at nine different vital points but has also had its head squeezed in the wasp's mandibles enough to immmobilize but not to kill it. When entomology has explained to us the detailed operation of all this surgical mastery of insects, we shall have a better insight into the nature of instinct. But even now we can recognize in instinctive activity the direct way in which life has proceeded to meet and to surmount its problems.

We may thus note the different roles of intelligence and instinct in the life process and in its evolution. Bergson underscores and distinguishes them in a striking statement of characteristic style: *"There are things that intelligence alone is able to seek, but which, by itself, it will never find. These things instinct alone could find, but it will never seek them."*[82]

In one of his last works, *The Two Sources of Morality and Religion*, Bergson traces the divergent paths and also the intercrossing of instinct and intelligence on the higher levels of human experience. Corresponding to the direct unreasoned effectiveness of instinct in animal behavior, he points to the role of intuition and mystical insight in the spiritual life of humanity. The mystic's direct communion with God may be regarded as the consumation of the *élan vital*: "the establishment of a contact, consequently a partial coincidence, with the creative effort of which life is the manifestation." [83]

At its summit, in the mystic's consciousness, Bergson's creative evolution ascends the range of spiritual experience. But in its very inception and fountain source also Bergson recognizes an agency analogous to consciousness. The *élan vital*, "the vital urge," consists in "a need of creation." [84] We may say that nature is stirred by a creative outpouring. In the language of our experience we at once think of consciousness, and Bergson uses that term but with reservations: "Life is connected either with consciousness or with something that resembles it. . . . For want of a better word we have called it consciousness. . . ." [85] He adds that he does not mean the narrowed consciousness that functions in us. Consciousness or supraconsciousness, it is some sort of creative activity. It is ever stirring amidst whatever is inert in existence. Indeed we can view life as the continual interplay of these two: "consciousness launched into matter." [86]

This creative activity, here called "consciousness," is the *élan vital*, "the motive principle of evolution." [87] Immersed in matter, it spurts out in ever new currents. We can regard plant and animal life as the two main directions of its outpouring, two ways of accumulating energy and then letting it flow into flexible channels, to "accomplish infinitely varied kinds of work." [88] Thus there is the chlorophyllian function of the plant: "what corresponds . . . to the sensibility of the animal is the impressionability . . . of (the plant's) chlorophyl to light." [89] And as has been noted already, in the evolution of animal life also the *élan vital* streams out in two characteristic reactions, instinct and intelligence. All the way through, Bergson emphasizes the vital urge, *élan vital*, as the creative heart and dynamic of reality. We should get into the evolutionary movement itself, instead of "scientifically" reducing it to fragments, which we then artificially try to recompose. Real insight into the nature of consciousness and the stream of evolving life requires intuition as well as intellect, whether we are seeking to probe its most elementary origins or aspire to contemplate its divine summits. "So understood, philosophy is not only the turning of the mind homeward, the coincidence of human consciousness with the living principle whence it emanates, a contact with the creative effort: it is the study of becoming in general, it is true evolutionism and consequently the true continuation of science." [90]

## 8. *Evolution, Teleology, and Values*

Our survey of the varieties of evolutionary theory has indicated two contending tendencies of interpretation which were already noted more broadly in our previous chapter. The larger philosophical view of nature raises the issue between mechanism and teleology, and this issue is accentuated in biology even more than in the other physical sciences, or better, the fundamental account of biological processes emphasizes the issue in a distinctive way which is decisive.

Physics and chemistry in their own fields and perspectives proceed on a mechanistic basis. It would be only confusing to import teleological reasoning into astronomy or geology. Modern physical science has made its great advances precisely because it has recognized and respected its own appropriate postulates. Our problem here arises when we turn from strict physics to a more integral view of nature and human nature. The commitment to mechanistic categories, which is essential to the effective physical account of nature, misses somehow the characteristic interpretation of human lives. Valid in its own fields and on its own postulates, physical science seems to indicate the need of other cosmic perspectives, if we are to understand ourselves and our own scientific activities as well as the physical system of the world with which we are dealing. So we may say that while the principle of teleology is not required, is indeed excluded, in physical science itself, it is raised as a problem by physical science in its relation to an ultimate philosophical interpretation of reality.

The role of teleological reasoning in biology seems to be a different one, but about this alleged difference there has been a radical controversy in evolutionary theory. We should appraise this disputed evolutionary teleology by considering the contending views about it.

One side of this argument, as we have already noted, is the mechanistic interpretation of evolution. The materialistic evolutionist judges that Darwin's principal systematic achievement was his integration of biology with the other physical sciences, his exclusion of providential or any other kind of design as a biological explanatory principle. According to this view, the fuller development of evolutionary biology must be only along these mechanistic lines. Against any appeal to design in biological theory or against any interpretation of adaptation or fitness as in any sense purposive, is the demand for a mechanistic explanation analogous to that in physics and chemistry.

This mechanistic rejection of purposive adaptation in any form has been criticized as failing to do justice to many facts in biological evolution. Without reverting to the traditional doctrine of providential design in nature, some biologists have found it necessary to include in their evolutionary theories the recognition of teleology in some form. Even those who would not go the whole length with Bergson or with Lloyd Morgan and Alexander or with Driesch have felt bound to admit the inadequacy of a rigidly mechanistic theory in biology. Surely the evolutionist cannot use the principle of adaptation without acknowledging its ultimate teleological or quasi-teleological implications. Against the mechanist's claim to Darwinian leadership, it has been maintained, for instance by J. S. Haldane, that "the theory of natural selection does not constitute the smallest step in the direction of a mechanistic conception of life." Variation and hereditary transmission cannot be understood rightly if we regard them as mere physico-chemical effects of the environment on the plant or animal. The living organism manifests some sort of purposive agency and initiative. "Heritable variation must be regarded as a fresh striking out of life." [91]

The critics of a rigidly mechanistic theory in biology have cited a mass of evidence indicating something analogous to purposive behavior, not only among mammals and birds but also at lower levels, especially among insects. The elaborate organization of some insect life, in ant-hills or beehives, has seemed to point beyond a strictly mechanistic explanation. Not only the functional explanations of behavior but also the structural variation of organs adapted to definite conditions of the environment appears perplexing to a strictly physico-chemical theory of evolution. Critics have pointed out that the organism seems to proceed on some sort of a self-preserving, self-promoting plan, with an initiative in variation and integration. Especially in the attainment of certain complex structures, as for instance in the evolution of the eye, a great number of different and very delicate adjustments have to be realized before the organ can function advantageously at all. The explanation of the survival and propagation of the many initial details of such a structure on a factual mechanistic basis seems to strain belief.

On the higher levels of animal life the evidence of dimly manifested and then more definite approaches to some form of mental activity raise further difficulties for the mechanist. As has already been noted, Darwin realized that the evolutionary explanation of mental powers and the moral sense was a requisite part of his theory, and he treated these problems with his characteristic candor and caution, in *The Descent of Man*. His work in this field stimulated his followers to important extensive studies of the evolution of mind. Distinguished writings in this field are Edward Westermarck's *Origin and Development of the Moral Ideas*, L. T. Hobhouse's *Morals in Evolution*, and Alexander Sutherland's *Origin and Growth of the Moral Instinct*. Westermarck and Hobhouse center their attention on the historical evolution of morals in human life from the earliest primitive societies. Sutherland endeavors to follow Darwin further in tracing the first beginnings or antecedents of moral activity in the instincts and reactions in animal behavior. The specific theoretical explanations advanced by these and other investigators may vary in details or in some major principles, but they all share the evolutionary outlook. We are told that in the far-flowing stream of life, organisms develop increasingly complex cerebro-neural systems capable of conscious reactions, and then mental response, moral behavior, understanding, and judgment of values. Animal gregariousness and the herd instinct develop into human social-mindedness; the urge for fighting back and retaliation grows into a sense of retribution, with the recognition of justice and punitive law in prospect; the parental instinct and group solidarity mature into conscious sympathy and benevolence; the effective restraint of offending members and the corresponding individual sense of group compulsion ripen into a consciousness of moral obligation, duty and conscience. The regard for the preservation of the herd or flock grows and may gain precedence over the concern for individual survival. In these and other ways, Darwin's followers undertook to trace the preface and the first chapters of evolutionary morals.

In a broader survey, not limited to moral behavior and not always used in evolutionistic perspectives, the beginnings of mental reactions in the life of the higher animals have likewise been made the subject of many detailed investigations. It may suffice here to mention one outstanding example of this type of inquiry, Wolfgang Köhler's work, *The Mentality of Apes*. Köhler noted that the brain structure and the bodily chemistry of the higher apes show greater similarity to those of human organisms than to those of the lower apes. He studied with especial care the behavior of some chimpanzees which seemed in many ways like human responses, and he raised the question whether the apes may not show intelligence analogous to ours. If this question is answered affirmatively, we may be in a position to recognize in the first or primitive instances of animal intelligence some of the characteristic factors in the evolution of mind.

Köhler does not proceed to dogmatic conclusions, but his researches indicate several lines of evidence for what may fairly be called a definite trend towards mentality in the behavior of the higher apes. The chimpanzees which he observed were capable of using roundabout methods of catching their objects; they showed some grasp of what the total situation required. They used strings or sticks or other implements to pull or push the food in the desired box or bag hanging or swinging out of their unaided reach. They would scratch a stone from the ground and throw it after an animal which they might be chasing; or, unable to move a heavy box on which they had to climb in order to grab the food suspended above their heads, they would first take out the stones that had been packed in it. They would join two sticks to lengthen their pole to the needed length, or pile up one box on top of another — four of them on one occasion — to gain the required height. This work was done sometimes in collaboration. They showed capacity for planning with foresight and with some control of their very strong appetites. On their being driven from their stockade to their sleeping pens in the evening, they had to cross a spot covered with lush green plants of which they are very fond. At first they all stormed upon the juicy fodder, but when the keeper drove them more insistently towards their pens, one of the chimpanzees would suddenly stop eating and begin hastily to tear up the weeds and so would carry a tremendous bundle of them to his den.[92]

An account of some analogous reactions of wild wolves, some of them as it were animal gropings after moral responses, has been given to us in a truly amazing story of life in the polar regions beyond the reach of any settled human habitation, in Lois Crisler's recent book, *Arctic Wild*. While some of these researches have been pursued without any explicitly evolutionistic purpose, they all have bearing on evolutionary theory. One interpretation of them is to regard so-called mental behavior as the factual effect of biological reactions. But even on a basically mechanistic view of biological processes, this account must still recognize clearly the eventual attainment of mind. How is this recognition to be understood? Either we should adhere rigidly to the exclusively mechanistic perspective, in which case we miss the fundamental characteristics of mind. Or we may acknowledge the distinctive character of mental activity, of thought and understanding and purposive conduct and moral judgment. In that case we should discern in the evolutionary course the attainment of non-mechanical activities, teleological and rational. We should then require a reinterpretation of the evolutionary process, to account for this attainment; we should have to supplement or expand the evolutionary perspective by some other views of nature and of human character.

The former, mechanistic explanation of the origin and development of mind, as gradually evolved from organic reactions and manifesting only physical and physiological properties, would claim the merit of undeviating naturalism in its explicit rejection of teleology in any form, admitting only purposeless behavior, determined mechanically. But then consistently it could not recognize genuinely purposive activity or pursuit of values anywhere, even at our human level. This view suffers from the essential defect of a rigid materialism, for it cannot account for itself as a theory or for its claims to truth and validity. Reason surely cannot thus reason itself out of existence.

If we appraise the second view, which recognizes unambiguously mind and its various forms of intelligent activity, the farther inferences from it are very significant. The first one — a revision of evolutionary doctrine to include the clear explanation of mind — is illustrated in the theories of creative evolution and emergent evolution. Secondly, these two theories in their respective ways may proceed to a more expansive cosmic outlook, on nature and on human character, from a number of significant approaches. Reality is complex, and nature is not to be exhausted in any one abstract formula. The physical sciences express in their postulates a view of the cosmic mechanism, and their formulations of the structure and laws of nature have fully justified their mechanistic perspective. Evolutionary biology has shown its merit in appropriating to its use, as much as suitable, the physico-chemical outlook on nature. This principle in biological method was defended with balanced judgment even before Darwin's work by the great physiologist Johannes Müller: "Though there appears to be something in the phenomena of living beings which cannot be explained by ordinary mechanical, physical, or chemical laws, much may be so explained, and we may without fear push these explanations as far as we can, so long as we keep to the solid ground of observation and experiment."[93] The last clause here is important in guiding sound fundamental theory in biology. Its distinctive problem, the understanding of living processes in their evolution, especially at its higher stages, has confronted the systematic evolutionist with the need of understanding the origin or the emergence of mind and of accounting for the boundless development of intelligence and of the values with which human beings have been characteristically identified. Evolutionary biology, allied as it is on the one hand with the physical sciences and indeed having its basis in them, seems to open new vistas on reality, human and social perspectives to which no rigidly mechanistic formulas can do full justice.

These new vistas and the problems which they raise are shown in the expansion of evolutionary ideas in the various fields of the humanities. The basic idea of evolution, the principle of development as a cosmic category, has proved fruitful in many humanistic inquiries. All of us know the productive work which has been done in the evolution of social and economic institutions, the evolution of language, of art, of religion. We have just been considering briefly the investigation of the evolution of morals. The title of a notable treatise by Edward Caird comes to mind: *The Evolution of Theology in the Greek Philosophers.*

The examination of this varied material or even a cursory glance over the bibliographies in these respective fields would show the fruitful expansion of the humanistic outlook by the application of the evolutionary principle. Our insight into any human activity is clarified and deepened as we come to understand its gradual development. The genesis of ideas, practices, and institutions has some roots in physiological reactions to conditions in the environment. Searching inquiries in these fields indicate man's groping and then more definite advance from organic drives to intelligent purposes. We may trace the growth of the human animal to full rational stature. And we may thus perceive that even at his full maturity man never quite surmounts his animal rootage. He is ever illustrating the truth of Aristotle's definition of him as a rational animal. In his most primitive state he is not altogether a beast, and at the highest levels of his civilized existence he is never purely rational. He needs the two perspectives, related, to manifest his full nature.

All these inquiries may be described as studies in the evolution of values. And values are characteristically expressed in contending interplay. This dramatic perspective of our experience will be the special topic of our last chapter and can only be mentioned here by way of anticipation. What we specially note at this point is the twofold, Janus-like outlook of the basic principle of evolution as it is applied in the various humanities. The development of social and economic processes and institutions is obviously bound up with climate, food-supply, and other environmental conditions, as well as with human demands and ideals. Language has its organic medium as well as its almost boundless range of intellectual and poetic expression. The arts have yielded the high achievements of creative genius, but they have their physical and physiological aspects. All along the line, evolution in the humanities has been a dual manifestation of the complexity of human nature, emphasizing the need for a philosophy of perspectives, to do justice to the many basic aspects of reality.

We may indicate here in a brief statement our general conclusion in this study of the World of Evolution. Evolutionary biology, in one direction, is marked by a thoroughly justified factual-mechanistic account of living processes. But the further evolutionary insight has opened up another perspective of the genetic principle of development. Animal behavior that at its rudimentary beginnings seems to be only very complicated chemistry, manifests increasingly at its higher levels a teleological tendency, and then unambiguously purposive and intelligent activity. The evolutionary biologist was bound to include man in his zoological museum, but the course of evolution in human life could not be understood or explained fully in the earlier terms, as survival or extinction by fortuitously fit or unfit adaptations to certain environments, as a mere mechanics of behavior.

The genetic process at human levels is a process increasingly directed by intelligence, a process of purposive activity, of choice between contending values, of achieving not only organic but also spiritual integration and fulfillment. This sort of genetic process is not a mere series of events but a significant career, which we call history. The principle of evolution as used in the various humanities manifests characteristically this historical aspect. We are thus naturally led towards our next philosophical perspective: the World as History.

PART III.

THE REALITY OF VALUES

# CHAPTER IV.

# THE WORLD AS HISTORY

## 1. Nature and History: A Preliminary View

The historical pattern of ideas is a characteristic expression of activism. The view of the cosmos as process would seem to imply a cosmic history. The evolutionary outlook, the emphasis on genetic methods of research, scientific explanation in terms of development, all these suggest a historical slant of thought. This inference is not altogether misleading, and some thinkers have followed its lead, but it has also been resisted.

Thus John Dewey entertained the idea of natural history as a proper scientific designation: "Aside from mathematics, all knowledge is historical: chemistry, geology, physiology, as well as anthropology and those human events to which, arrogantly, we usually restrict the title of history."[1] Hegel, on the other hand, rejected the appropriateness of the term "natural history." He declared roundly: "Nature has no history."[2]

Francis Bacon included as an important part in his projected reconstruction of science and philosophy a series of encyclopedic historical surveys of nature. He drew up a list of about one hundred thirty "histories" of various fields of research and himself explored some of them and outlined others. Only a few need be mentioned here: history of the sympathy and antipathy of things; of sulphur, mercury, and salt; of winds; of life and death. His catalogue of particular histories indicated his projected encyclopedia of nature: from comets and meteors to floods and drouths, earthquakes and eruptions, serpents and flies—all the way to man, his frame and limbs and humors, gestation and nourishment, faculties, arts and crafts, culture and technology. The Baconian procedure may be lauded as expressing a sound naturalistic treatment of man, or it may be criticized as lumping things together without due distinction.

Our initial difficulty at this point is in part owing to an ambiguity in our use or interpretation of history as a cosmic category. We have noted already that the various cosmic perspectives are both related and also have their distinct range and relevance. So history strictly or characteristically considered, will be seen to concern distinctively human affairs. But this historical character, which is preëminently manifested in the careers of men and peoples, may also be regarded as a cosmic aspect which we can recognize in a measure, though far less relevantly or less significantly, in other, but not in all, fields of nature. We shall take up this problem further in a later section of this chapter.

## 2. *Knowledge and Truth in Historical Inquiry*

We may consider first the subject matter, the scope and characteristic outlook of historical inquiry. How do they differ from those of the other sciences? The unquestionably scientific investigations in physics and chemistry explore their respective fields of nature with a view to reaching universal systematic conclusions, usually in formulated uniformities and laws. This procedure is necessarily abstract. It describes general classes or types of objects, conditions, processes, and reactions. Its experiments allow for many particular deviations, and they discount many inessential deviations. To be sure, the seemingly unique or the incidental may themselves become the objects of special inquiry, but again only for the sake of finding in them that which is sought throughout all investigation, namely some type of uniform behavior. The formulated law, we are told, is valid of the ideal experiment, though not in strict detail of each particular instance. Physical science studies these particular instances for the sake of reaching some general conclusions about the sort or class to which they belong: phosphorus or fruit flies or whatever else.

This abstract procedure of physical science is a condition of its attaining formal precision. As we all know, the mind buys precision at the price of abstraction. The most precise and formally the most perfect sciences are the most abstract. We may see this principle most strikingly illustrated in mathematics. So plain geometry begins by abstracting from the boundless complex reality all phases except those that characterize two-dimensional space. It defines precisely the sort of plane figure which it proposes to analyze, say, a right triangle. It is not concerned with the adequacy of the alleged triangle drawn on the blackboard. Indeed the reflective geometer knows full well that no one has ever drawn or could draw, has seen or could ever see a right triangle, not really. He knows that a triangle of straight lines is only an abstract concept of his reason; yet of this abstract triangle alone are his theorems truly valid. That is why our geometry does not state that the figure *ABC is* a right triangle; it invites us to consider it thus abstractly: *"Let ABC* be a right triangle."

What is so patently clear in geometry can be recognized also in the sciences which deal with the various factually existent fields of nature, from astronomy to biology. There is, however, a discrepancy here which should be understood, for it is only apparent. Unlike the mathematician's concern with the abstractions of reason, the physical scientist investigates the world of factual existence. The chemist surely does not say abstractly: *"Let* this be sulphuric acid." Nevertheless the natural scientist like the mathematician aims at formulating the general properties of this or that *class* of factual things or processes. Now these two characteristics of scientific knowledge—its abstract analysis and its description or explanation in general formulae—these are unavailable in historical inquiry. This point should be clarified and we may thus be led to see more definitely the character and the scope and content of historical knowledge.

The great prestige of modern physical science has influenced our minds to insist on abstract scientific formulation as an essential requirement of all real knowledge. Modern rationalists have tended to follow Descartes and Spinoza in exalting the "geometrical method" and demanding mathematical demonstration as an essential requirement of true conclusions. Furthermore the investigation of facts and causal uniformities has been selected as the reliable method of ascertaining the laws of nature. In this twofold way physical science and real knowledge have tended to become synonymous for the modern mind.

This kind of so-called scientism has infected many historians and other workers in the humanistic fields, and not a few philosophers. So we have zealous workers who have tried in their own ways to be scientific historians or scientific biographers. Against this tendency, others have cited the radical difference between a scientific and a truly historical approach to the study of human affairs. This difference is dual: first, it is in the concrete subject matter which history shares with the other humanities and social studies; and secondly, it is a quality peculiar to historical inquiries. The first characteristic, concrete subject matter, is preëminent in all history. It may be noted that even the so-called social scientist, while he investigates concrete human conditions and institutions, is seeking to grasp in some description or analysis a universal interpretation of certain social patterns. This aim has often been judged to be misguided and to account for some of the misdirections of social inquiries. Now the historian, it would seem, should be definitely safeguarded from straying into abstractions. By the very demands of his inquiry he must be concerned directly with concrete events: the decline and fall of the Roman Empire, the rise of the Dutch Republic. If he proceeds beyond this, to the study of the decline and fall of empires, or the rise of republics, he may be said to be crossing the border line from history to social theory or social philosophy.

A second characteristic of history is its concern with the temporal course of events. Despite the physical scientist's experimental investigation of conditions and processes in time, there is a certain connotation of timelessness in the formulated laws and truths of science. But the historian is thoroughly immersed in the stream of time, and for this further and specifically historical reason his knowledge cannot have the abstract precision of scientific laws. The physicist and the chemist seek to ascertain what takes place universally under certain types of conditions. The historian tries to learn what took place specifically then and there. The truth of historical conclusions requires a perspective of temporal relativity. But this view disturbs our basic conception of real truth as universal and in a sense eternal. What is ever true, we say, is true forever. At this point we should do well to distinguish truth in a certain specific time-context from abstract universal validity. Which way our logical emphasis inclines would depend upon what qualities of truth we choose to accentuate: its abstract, formal universality or its concrete vitality.

The historical series of events are not only irreversible; they are also induplicable. Scientific universal equations are ruled out in history because historical events are not repeatable. We shall consider later in this chapter the old doctrine of eternal recurrence and its radical difficulties when considered in a historical perspective. Here it may suffice to reflect that the very recurrence, so-called, of a historical situation would make it also different from its preceding occurrence, for its background and historical context would not be the same. The historian is committed to his unique event: the Battle of Tours or the Battle of Waterloo or the Battle of Gettysburg. Each one of these is itself, or better, it was what it was, in its particular time and place.

This point is not to be taken too rigidly. Unless it is duly qualified it will turn out to be again a half-truth and an exposure to error. The general abstract formulations of the physical scientist rely for their validity on the direct investigation of actual and concrete facts. And on the other hand, as we shall have to point out and even to accentuate, the historian's exploration of concrete sources and special documentation must aim at reaching some eventual interpretation in the universal terms of significance or importance of values. The difference here is mainly one of emphasis; but let us not dismiss it as merely a difference of emphasis, for after all, emphasis here is decisively important.

Turning now to consider the contents and the scope of history, we are confronted by a traditional restriction which, we should note, has been challenged. This restriction may be readily seen in our university programs. Although we find many workers in the history of science, the history of literature or of art, of religion or philosophy, these courses are not listed by our departments of history. The titular historian deals primarily with the political or military or naval course of events. We should not overstress these restrictions, and besides, they have been contested. The great historians have realized that thorough historical inquiry is bound to consider all aspects and expressions of human life. But there is a reason for the historian's main concentration on the course of external events. Inquiries into the historical development of art or literature, religion or philosophy inevitably involve critical interpretation and evaluation. They demand considerable competence in their respective fields of human advancement. So the professional historian who is aiming at factual objectivity usually limits himself to the study of those events which can be

107

plainly narrated. Wilhelm von Humboldt and Leopold von Ranke agreed that the historian's task is to report the actual course of events; in Ranke's words, "how it really took place, *wie es eigentlich gewesen ist.*" [3]

Actually even the most resolutely objective or factual historical report cannot dispense wholly with interpretation or evaluation. Evaluation, judgment of relative importance, is involved in the very selection of the specific factual events which are investigated and recorded. As Burckhardt told us, history is "the record of that which one age finds worthy of note in another." [4] The indiscriminate reporting of actual facts or events is neither good science nor good history. But we should not prejudge offhand what is indiscriminate and of no consequence in either of these two types of inquiry. When Tolstoy lampoons the misguided zeal which compiles "a catalogue of a million beetles," and when Frederick Harrison satirizes the "intellectual fussiness" that "learns by heart the Post Office directory," [5] both of them are exposing obvious misdirections of research; but they may also be failing to do justice to the importance of thoroughness in matters of detail. The need of investigation is to combine factual documentation with critical insight. The great historians, from Thucydides to Gibbon and to Macaulay, combined reliable accounts of actual events with evaluative judgments of their importance and significance. The sound historian's insistence on a resolutely objective initial exploration is due to his demand for a balanced, fair, and solidly founded interpretation. He would refrain from premature judging because he is aiming at a sound verdict. He starts with factual objectivity, so that he may be enabled to reach objective critical conclusions. As J. B. Bury stated, in this sort of inquiry "we are brought face to face with a philosophical problem." [6]

## 3. Problems in the History of Ideas

The need of critical objectivity in ascertaining the facts is especially important in the history of ideas. From the very outset these ideas involve interpretation and evaluation. We should consider, therefore, what methods characterize the reliable and significant history of ideas: what kind of documentation, what kind of fidelity to sources, what textual and other accuracy? Our consideration here will not be limited to the history of philosophy, even though we shall deal largely with it. In my work on a history of philosophy I was repeatedly impressed by many characteristic problems of procedure and interpretation which had been brought to my attention in dealing with other fields of historical and broadly humanistic inquiry.

We should recognize the distinctive method of the historian of ideas, for it is determined by the character of his subject matter. While all historical writing involves selection, in political or military history the materials that are examined are themselves objective, external events. The Battle of Trafalgar, the American presidential campaign of 1860, proceeded in this or in that particular way which should be reported accurately, with adequate documentation. But in the history of ideas, of art or literature or religion or philosophy, the material itself is ideal. The various external occurrences are together as in fact they are, there to be ascertained and recorded. But the events and the contents of literature or of religion belong together, so that the parts reveal the whole and the whole affects the parts. The historian of ideas and ideal values cannot be satisfied with the mere rehearsal of details, no matter how accurate or how fully documented. The historian of ideas has to be correct, yes, but he must also be true in his interpretation.

At this point we should be well advised to watch our step. As we have already observed, just because the historian of ideas is bound to be involved in interpretation, and because he aims at a true interpretation, he also like all good historians should beware of premature and uncritical commitment. He seeks the truth, and so he should have the real facts. He should not begin with his conclusions. In his attitude and in his detailed procedure he should avoid doctrinaire pre-judgment of his material. Before he speaks for or against his ideas, they should be allowed to testify for themselves in a fair court. This initial self-admonition to objective exposition is the more important, the greater and the more influential or controversial historically the ideas or the thinkers are which the historian is examining. But in another way the warning is sound also in dealing with what may not be so well known or what has not aroused so much contention.

There are many difficulties here which the historian of ideas

**109**

must resolutely strive to overcome. There are, first of all, the barriers of cultural remoteness, both of time and of language. The first barrier, of time, can be met in considerable degree by the cultivation of a historical sense, a critical judgment that demands imagination as well as insight. The second obstacle or gap, of language, must be scaled or else it may betray us into confusions. Was it Mommsen who refused to rely on any documents which he could not examine in their original texts? As we all know, the Greek term *logos* signified "word" as well as "thought." The historian of ideas is engaged in a sort of double translation, which should be doubly reliable. Here are the words of Descartes or of Kant which must be translated into ideas, meanings, and these in turn must be retranslated into the language of the historian's exposition.

These difficulties of reliable translation are magnified when we are dealing with ancient writings. The problems of Biblical criticism provide striking examples of this. The medieval Geiler of Kaisersberg said that Holy Scripture is like a wax nose: everyone moulds it to suit himself. Histories of philosophy likewise illustrate this same hazard of hanging an interpretation of a doctrine on a debatable rendering of an important word. The cautious student feels bound in some cases to avoid mistranslation by simply citing the original term. He thus surrenders his problem to his reader. Two or three instances from Plato and Aristotle may serve to illustrate this point. Plato in his doctrine of the tripartite nature of man distinguished our reason, our desires or appetites, and what he calls *thymós*. This term has been rendered variously by English translators and commentators, as spirit, spiritedness, or spirited vigor, vital drive, or will-energy. There is a native English word, mettle, which perhaps conveys Plato's meaning. Or consider the term *eudaimonía* in Aristotle's ethics. How commonly it is translated by "happiness," with the result that many English readers get a confused idea of Aristotle as a sort of utilitarian! While Aristotle did not mean to exclude happiness from his ideal of the good and perfect life, he surely was not thinking of happiness in the sense of mere pleasure. So the more careful student of Aristotle endeavors to interpret *eudaimonía* as well-being or welfare, but he wishes for some English term that will do full justice to the Aristotelian principle. Even more striking is the difficulty of explaining the term *cátharsis* in Aristotle's *Poetics*. Here a long controversy has been waged through the ages by translators and commentators in all European languages. When Aristotle declared that tragedy arouses the emotions of pity and terror in a way that affects their *cátharsis*, did he intend to signify by his term the purgation of the passions, or their purification or refinement or expiation? It is small wonder that many students of the *Poetics* have been obliged to reach the conclusion that by *cátharsis* Aristotle must have meant simply cathársis. We have changed the accent of the word, but have not mastered its meaning.

A second barrier to adequate historical knowledge or true interpretation is the fragmentary character or the insufficiency of our source material. This is, of course, generally the case in dealing with ancient thinkers and ideas. In so many cases time has robbed us of our data and evidence. It is commonly known that our accounts of the Pre-Socratic philosophers are to a considerable degree conjectural. And even an outstanding thinker like Aristotle has to be interpreted with reserve, not only regarding some special terms, as we have just noted, but more generally in the exposition of his doctrines. Consider, for instance, his treatment of the problem of human destiny, debated by Mohammedan and Christian commentators for centuries during the Middle Ages and the Renaissance.

This difficulty confronts us in studying some modern thinkers. Several of Hegel's works, as we know, are really compilations prepared by his editors from his lecture notes and from various students' notebooks. A different compilation of this sort of material would yield a different volume, as we can see by comparing Hegel's *Philosophy of Fine Art* in the standard edition of the last century, from which Osmaston's English translation was made, with the revised version of the Hegelian Aesthetics in Lasson's more recent edition. To claim textual final accuracy in dealing with such sources is to encroach on the prerogatives of Omniscience. Our difficulties with Leibniz are both similar and different. When he died in 1716, considerable parts of his writings were still unpublished and were scattered among his official, diplomatic and other papers in his desk and filing cabinets. As some of his correspondence was very likely concerned with confidential and controversial matters, or even with court intrigues, the Hanover authorities put all Leibniz's papers under lock and key. From time to time for two centuries extracts from these materials were released for publication. Only in our time is the full edition of Leibniz's works in process of publication, to be completed in some forty stout volumes. The chapters on Leibniz in the future histories of philosophy should be much more informing and more reliable in many respects.

Some of these uncertainties in the history of philosophy concern only details, but some of them affect our whole understanding of a great system of thought. The so-called Socratic-Platonic problem is an outstanding instance of this perplexity of the historian of ideas. In his *Dialogues* Plato uses Socrates as his chief spokesman. How much of the teaching thus voiced by Socrates is actual Socratic doctrine which Plato is fairly reporting, and how much of it is really Platonic development or revision of Socratic ideas, or quite definitely the view of Plato himself? This is the same kind of problem as that which confronts students of the New Testament. The difference of style between the first three so-called Synoptic Gospels and the Fourth Gospel is unmistakable. Are the words ascribed to Jesus in the Fourth Gospel a literally accurate record, or are they a deeply significant interpretation from the point of view of the author?

The thorough historian of ideas knows that he cannot overcome all of these difficulties, but he does his best to surmount his barriers. He tries to get as close as he can to his original sources and to achieve detailed textual mastery, but he can never remain satisfied with that sort of precision. While he studies his original texts, he cannot ignore his secondary sources, the commentaries or critical interpretations by other students in his field. Thus Platonism is to a large extent what it has meant to Platonists through the ages. Yet the historian cannot be content with approach at second hand. Many confusions in the histories of philosophy have been due to the fact that commentators have been satisfied with quoting other commentators instead of going directly to their fountain sources.

Both of these counsels of warning are important, and a historian of ideas cannot afford to neglect either of them. The penetrating insight which yields truth in historical inquiry is of two sorts, or better, it has a dual aspect. On the one hand, it requires a thorough mastery of all available evidence achieved by a direct study of the original sources. On the other hand, it involves a fair critical reaction to all the responses that the ideas which are investigated have evoked from other minds. The historian of an idea must study that idea in its historical development, and so he must study its alternative interpretations. He must begin with a record or a report of the idea in its initial statement, and he must eventually proceed to the interpretation of its historical career and its developing significance in the course of thought.

As these two requirements in historical inquiry are gradually realized, the critical historian may come to possess not only full detailed knowledge of the materials but, at least to a certain degree, a fulfillment of knowledge, an integral understanding of his subject that grasps its essential spirit. This insight may enable him to recognize the importance of formerly neglected sources, to perceive the unreliability of certain details, that they are alien to the structure and meaning of the whole and are very likely spurious. It is in this way that many traditional doctrines have been revised and corrected factually by the guidance of more adequate interpretation.

Critical inquiry thus enables us to seek and to find the better truth, by teaching us where to look for it. The history of science abounds in striking instances of these advances in understanding the constitution and course of nature. Even more informing to our purpose is the evidence supplied in the various fields of humanistic studies. May we turn a moment to cite two instances of art criticism, which indicate these factually productive results of historical insight in the various humanities? All of us know the famous profile portrait of a lady, of Beatrice d'Este or perhaps of another Beatrice, the original of which is in the Ambrosian Gallery in Milan. Tradition had regarded it as the work of Leonardo Da Vinci. But contemporary experts on Italian Renaissance art have rejected this traditional belief and have ascribed the portrait to Ambrogio Da Predis. This revised view of the celebrated portrait is generally accepted now. Consider the possible bases on which such a critical reappraisal might rest. It might be due to the discovery of new evidence, in biographical or other art archives, which warrants or compels the ascription of the picture to Da Predis. Or it might be due to such a thorough reinterpretation of the art procedures of both Ambrogio and Leonardo as would require the revision of the traditional belief.

Our other example is really astonishing. It concerns Goethe when he was a student at Strassburg. The young poet was carried away by the beauty of the Strassburg cathedral which he studied zealously from every point of view. The dean of the cathedral took notice of the young man and engaged him one day in conversation. Goethe expressed his admiration for the great church, but ventured to say that it would have been even more beautiful if it had included a small spire in the middle. Amazed by this comment, original on the young man's part, the priest invited him to examine the old plans of the cathedral, showing that the initial architect had included such a spire, which the later builders had omitted. Young Goethe had absorbed so thoroughly the artistic character of the structure that he saw what it required for its living integrity. By understanding its materials fully, the mind is enabled to reconstruct the past truly and more completely.

At this point we should recognize clearly the vital power of the creative imagination in productive historical inquiry. Great historical interpretation manifests some poetical, that is creative and organizing insight. This historical imagination should not be confused with fanciful or sentimental imagining. In the powerful statement of Trevelyan, it is "imagination pursuing the fact and fastening upon it. . . . Let the science and the research of the historian find the fact, and let his imagination and art make clear its significance." [7] Corresponding to the distinction between merely fanciful imagining and the truly creative imagination in poetry, we may note the difference between the pedestrian documented correctness of some historical records and the living revelation of historical reality by the imaginative insight of genius. Coleridge's words about Shakespeare may be applied also to the great historian: in both of them we may observe thought and imagination vying for mastery. Distinction of literary style enhances the power of thorough historical exposition, or surely at least it need not conflict with it. As Mandell Creighton expressed it, "you don't have to be dull, to prove that you can write history." [8] Among modern historians Macaulay is a test case in this discussion. He has been sometimes dismissed as a "literary historian." But modern masters of historical inquiry have esteemed him very highly. Stubbs and Creighton and Lord Acton in Britain agreed with Mommsen and Harnack in Germany in ranking Macaulay as the greatest of historians. [9]

Returning to the history of ideas, we should note that there also thorough critical study illumined by creative imaginative insight can reveal the living integrity of the past. It likewise yields firmer factual grasp. It may lead to needed textual emendation, to the deletion of unwarranted readings. It may justify the use of interpretative terms which may not appear verbatim in the texts. As an example of the first sort of textual revision, consider the passage from the Sermon on the Mount where Jesus is reported as saying: "Whosoever is angry with his brother without a cause shall be in danger of the judgment." So the verse reads in the various traditional translations. But Tolstoy, studying the Gospels with intense concern, expressed his conviction that the words "without a cause" must be an interpolation. Surely, he thought, Jesus meant to condemn anger unreservedly. And Tolstoy's judgment of critical insight was sustained by the textual research of New Testament scholars, showing that the oldest manuscripts of the Gospel of Matthew do not have those words. They are excluded from the text in the revised versions.

The second kind of critical historical exposition may also be readily illustrated. Students of Leibniz's philosophy have used the phrase "Monad of monads" to describe his idea of God. But Bertrand Russell told us that this particular phrase has not been found in the text of Leibniz's published writings. Of course, the complete edition of the philosopher' works, which is now in progress, may supply this textual lack. Even if it does not, however, many critical historians will still maintain that the phrase "Monad of monads" has been suitably used by Leibniz's successors to characterize his doctrine of God. Or take the term "Scotism" in ethical theory. Duns Scotus, as we know, taught that not rational necessity but the fiat of God's will is the source and the ground of law. The laws of nature are divine edicts, and they would have been different had the Creator decreed otherwise. Duns Scotus himself did not apply this doctrine to the field of moral laws. But his voluntarism did point towards the view that truthfulness and justice are virtues, not because of their inherent worth but basically because God's will has so decided. This radical inference from Duns Scotus's ideas was actually drawn by William of Occam. The careful historian of philosophy who cites this sort of ethics from Occam may also properly call it Scotism because it is what the philosophy of Duns Scotus signified and

**115**

implied. A similar comment is applicable to the words commonly attributed to Tertullian, *"Credo quia absurdum—*I believe it just because it is absurd."

Another instance which comes naturally to our minds is the interpretation of the Hegelian dialectic as a triad of thesis-antithesis-synthesis. This exposition has been followed generally by the historians of modern philosophy, but it has been contested by some recent students. Whichever way this divergence of views may be settled eventually, it will provide an example of the historian's procedure of seeking some suitable framework of interpretation within which to comprehend a complex body of doctrine.

We have considered briefly some of the characteristics of historical inquiry, especially in the field of ideas, both its limitations and difficulties and also the penetrating insight which it can yield when pursued competently. As we noted, critical selection is essential to significant interpretation. The historian of philosophy may be called the biographer of the important ideas in the thought of the past. His problems are akin to the problems of the biographer, and besides, his work includes some biography in the more usual sense.

A biographer's purpose is to achieve integrity and essential significance and fairness in his portrayal. But he knows that his interpretation will represent to a considerable extent his own slant of evaluation. The difficulty of a thoroughly balanced and critical appraisal confronts the historian of philosophy alike in dealing with the doctrines which he himself supports and with those which he opposes. Here again we may note that while mastery of the sources is necessary, it does not suffice for a fair evaluation. The distorted exposition in alleged historical accounts that are partisan in spirit is evidenced in the violent controversial literature which has confused philosophical, theological, and political discussions.

The partisanship of devoted disciples is liable to compromise historical fairness and critical interpretation. The problem becomes still more complicated when a biographer's or a historian's intellectual sympathy or personal devotion contend with a genuine resolution to be objective in exposition. Take, for instance, the well-known biography of Lord Tennyson by his son Hallam. There was certainly no lack of mastery of the biographer's sources here. Hallam Tennyson knew his father's life and character as he knew his alphabet. His difficulty was that he was writing the life of his father and yet was resolved not to write simply as his father's son.

These personal tendencies which so often compromise the critical adequacy of historical or biographical accounts may be seen as projected on a magnified scale in the shifts of social-cultural appraisal. As Hegel told us, ideas have hands and feet; they move through the minds of men and societies, rise or decline in the various turns of culture. What they signify, and indeed what they are, is never set conclusively. Their historical development is their living reality.

The vital ideas in philosophy are not only the heirs of their epochs but also the judges of epochs and of the time process altogether. But the time which they judge may also pass its judgment on them. Both kinds of verdicts have been repeatedly illustrated in the history of philosophy just as in the history of art or of literature. Consider the evaluative curve of the art of Raphael or of El Greco in the history of art criticism; or note that there were two and a half centuries during which scarcely a single important edition of Dante was published. In philosophy also there have been thinkers whose ideas met some major demands of their epoch but who aroused little or no response from later ages. Shaftesbury is an apt example of this sort of great temporary renown followed by comparative oblivion. Again there have been thinkers who in their day were voices crying in the wilderness, whose fame had to wait for its late historical season. Two outstanding contemporary examples of this sort of historical verdict are the philosopher Kierkegaard and the historiographer Giambattista Vico.

A significant point is brought out by this historical reappraisal of philosophical ideas. A philosopher's thinking has an influence in some degree on the minds to which it is addressed. But the changing social climate of opinion itself affects the vitality and the significance of his ideas. To be sure, there are preëminent minds of perennial vitality. As Coleridge once said, every intelligent man is either a Platonist or an Aristotelian. Yet the general fact remains that the social course of responsiveness and emphasis

117

brings the ideas of the past into the center or else out of the center of vital discussion. The histories of philosophy record a continual *ave atque vale*—hail and farewell!

This note of reflection has hopeful but also dismal overtones. The judgment of history may have to wait until it has grown to mature appreciation of certain great ideas; it may also condemn to oblivion ideas of which it is no longer worthy. In the ancient Chinese social system of commemorating ancestors, the forebears of a peasant who had risen to high office were accorded public honor and elevated in rank on the family record, while the condemnation of a criminal also degraded his ancestors and erased the record of their old dignities. In less striking ways, this rewriting of history and biography is a continual process. Extreme examples of it are provided in the flagrant revisions of historical records by the communists, to accord with the radical turns of party politics. After Lavrenty Beria was ejected from his high post as one of the triumvirate following Stalin's death, his enemies in the Kremlin were not content with condemning him to death. They decreed his historical liquidation. They ordered the deletion of the passages in the Soviet Encyclopedia celebrating his work. More instances of this sort may be cited. So the reader who wishes to learn about the philosophy of Karl Marx would look vainly in some standard histories of philosophy of an earlier day, where even the name of Marx is scarcely mentioned. The course of world affairs has compelled today an extended discussion of Marx's ideas.

There is a significant statement by Giovanni Gentile: "Philosophy and its history are together one as process of mind." [10] The knowledge and the truth yielded in historical inquiry are not merely factual data, externally objective. They are living realities. They grow and they also age. In their perennial renaissance or in their eventual eclipse they reveal or else expose their more or less significant manifestations of man's life and thought.

The ascendency and the decline of ideas often appear fortuitous and unpredictable, but they may also reveal certain patterns. This formal design of the historical course of events is scarcely comparable to the causal uniformity formulated in scientific laws. It is more aptly allied to the varied yet recognizable rhythm of poetry. [11] The scanning of this historical rhythm; the epical sweep of movements or epochs in the life of mankind, has been the

118

hope and also the challenge of the more philosophical historians. This sort of integral interpretation demands complete mastery of the materials. It requires caution to avoid premature synthesis and should be undertaken only on the basis of long and thorough investigation. Actually the theoretical designs of philosophical historians have often reflected their own basic valuations and philosophies of life. To St. Augustine, at the beginning of our Christian span, history was the solemn utterance of God's verdict on the career and destiny of mankind. To Auguste Comte, fourteen centuries later, man's historical life revealed his growth from the childhood of theological beliefs, through the adolescent ventures of metaphysical speculation, to the advancing maturity of scientific explanation of the facts of nature and the practical mastery of the principles of social order and progress. Lord Acton viewed history as the agelong conflict of good and evil.[12] Croce in our day conceived of its development in terms of ideal values.[13]

The problem of historical necessity has also evoked various reflections. While Ranke spoke of "the logic of the works of God," [14] Bury called attention to the "contingencies in history." In his essay entitled "Cleopatra's Nose" he developed critically the common view that important historical consequences have often depended on the fortuitous coincidence of apparently unrelated factors: the effects seemingly quite disproportionate to the causes. Bergson also was impressed by the perennial variation of the rhythm, by the factors of hazard and the incursion of novelty in every historical situation. The old words of Herodotus have been cited in our unsteady age: "Anything may happen in the immensity of time." [15] Our age has provided various readings of the history in all the histories, or the ideal eternal history, as Vico called it. They have yielded contrasting versions of our widespread pessimistic temper, whether expressed in theological providential terms or in the irreligious outlook of Spengler. Toynbee's monumental volumes endeavor to scan the rhythm of history in a more reasonable spirit.

All of us who have tried to understand thoroughly some idea, some doctrine or belief or problem, have realized the absolute need of exploring its historical development. The presuming philosopher who operates in a historical vacuum, vain in his supposed originality, or content to follow his own immediate

119

master, is liable sooner or later to realize his frustration. The really great ideas are not all of the past, antiquarian treasures, but neither are they merely of today or of yesterday afternoon. The intelligent mind should prize neither the old for its age nor the new for its novelty. He should observe the fresh foliage but he should also explore the old and spreading roots. Historical inquiry aims to attain reliable knowledge of the actual course of past events. It also reveals to us the foundations of our present station. Through the fuller understanding of the past we are enabled to face more intelligently the problems of today. There is contending interplay of opposite extremes of motivation here, between which the careful historian should seek his reasonable middle course. He cannot be satisfied with mere neutral exploration of the past, for while history includes antiquarian research, it must go beyond digging for its own sake. On the other hand, history cannot be treated as a handmaid of political or social strategy.

The historian's thorough and critical insight into the past gives him a mature balanced view of human life and character, not in abstract formulae but in concrete portrayal. He is thus enabled to view any period, and so his own, the present, in a fair historical perspective. He has learned to study classical antiquity or medieval life with due allowance for his own standpoint; so he can approach his own present likewise with critical objectivity. He must avoid both antiquarian engrossment and tractarian or pamphleteering zeal, and should portray both past and present in fair report. He must grasp and express the perennially modern: understand and depict the Rome of the Romans, even though it be ancient to us, and also in a broad historical view consider our age, modern for us, which will be past history to our distant successors. Thus history, "instead of being a mere sequence of events, becomes the gradual revelation of the spiritual world." [16] May we recall here some wise words by Max Müller: "If we do not understand a thing, if we hardly know what it is, what it means, and how to call it, it is always open to us to try and find out how it has come to be what it is. It is wonderful how this method clears our thoughts, and how it helps us to disentangle the most hopeless tangles which those who came before us have left to us as our inheritance." [17]

## 4. History in Nature

We should now consider the larger cosmic outlook of natural history. Some thinkers have drawn a sharp contrast between the causal uniformity of nature and the dynamic-creative self-achievement of mankind. Kant interpreted the scope of modern physical science, as yielding universally valid knowledge of a causally connected system of events in space and time. From this standpoint every type of process is to be viewed or explained as the necessary result of some variety of antecedent conditions. This system of uniformities is regarded as the general cosmic pattern. The detailed processes, to be sure, are in time, but the necessary connections which they exemplify are basic characteristics of the entire system across the time span of specific occurrences. The book of nature, as read by physical science, has no distinctively historical pages, or we may say that its uniformities are all on one vast cosmic page.

This contrast of the physical scientific and the historical perspective has been accentuated as fundamental. We should recall Hegel's epigram that nature has no history. Thus we may say that physical nature, throughout numberless changes, manifests its basic and invariable uniformities. It does not reveal the progressive development and self-realization of character or else its frustration, decline and fall, which are the marks of a historical perspective. In our day this view has been developed by Collingwood and also by the Spanish philosopher Ortega y Gasset. The so-called science of human nature has been regarded as a misconceived undertaking. It set out from the false presupposition that there is a certain entity called mind which stays put and awaits our analysis. But actually persons are ever in the process of achieving, developing, or misdirecting their character and significance. Their career must be studied in a biographical or historical view. Most emphatically Ortega y Gasset maintains: "Man . . . has no nature; what he has is . . . history." [18] So the proper study of man is history, and we may say explicitly that the various humanities are chapters or branches of history.

This sharp separation of physical nature and human history calls for a cautious reconsideration, especially when we deal with the biological sciences. We have noted that evolutionary ideas

121

have been used extensively and fruitfully in the various humanistic inquiries. Our attention may thus be directed to the essentially genetic and developmental character of evolutionary research, be it biological, anthropological, or explicitly humanistic. This aspect of evolutionism has been related to the basic outlook on reality as process. Is this outlook historical?

We should be on our guard here to avoid a confusion of fundamental ideas. Evolution may be interpreted in the specific Darwinian sense as the causally determined process of the survival of the fittest in the struggle for existence through fortuitous variations adaptable to specific environments. Or evolution may be used in the broader meaning of development of a process or a form of activity differing in kind under a variety of conditions. To be sure, there is a thought common to both of these uses of the term. The historian Bury called it "the *genetic* idea."[19] Darwin's great success in reconstructing biology on this genetic evolutionary basis inspired other workers to apply analogous methods to anthropological and humanistic research. This analogy of method has often been ambiguous. It has been guided by a due recognition of the essential differences between physical process and historical activity. But it has also tended mistakenly to proceed from the acknowledgment of some quasi-historical aspects of the sequence of events in biological evolution, to the inference that human history can also be understood in strictly physical-biological terms.

The distinction here should not be drawn too sharply or rigidly, but neither should it be dismissed. The sound distinction is one of emphasis. Historical studies may retain some elements of "naturalistic" method which is characteristic and dominant in physical science. Science in the form of "natural history" may entertain some aspects of the method which is more clearly and appropriately used in human history. We can understand both the correlation and the distinction between these two as our cosmic outlook proceeds from one of these perspectives to the other.

In making this last distinction we are, of course, clearly aware that we are comparing and also contrasting a necessarily abstract view of reality with one that aims at greater concreteness. From this standpoint it may be said that the abstract universality of the physical sciences cannot grasp fully the concrete reality which is portrayed in the historical perspective. The so-called natural history or history of nature is, as Croce put it, a "pseudo-history."[20] If I am to view anything in nature in a truly historical manner, I should have to cease regarding it as of a certain class of genus and should try to see it concretely in the way in which I would have to consider it if it were human. I might then proceed to study the biography, say, of a grizzly or of a glacier, but as it came to manifest historical portraiture it would tend to lose scientific analysis and definition. The strict scientist might even suspect such accounts as "nature-faking." (In our next section we should consider the opposite procedure, in which the concrete actuality of ongoing human life has been forced, with what may be called "history-faking," into the abstract framework of materialistic determinism.)

Now, as was noted in the previous chapter, it is just some such concrete insight into biological processes which Bergson sought to achieve by his idea of creative evolution. The more directly we observe ourselves the more clearly we see that we never stay put as mere discrete entities, but on the contrary are continually in a process of achieving ourselves. We therefore have no static character that can be described or explained. We require a historical account. What is so evidently characteristic of ourselves is true, in a measure, also of lower forms of life in the stream of evolution. Evolving life manifests the origins and growth of new lives. The study of it is concerned primarily with genesis rather than with the repeated uniformities of abstract science. So Bergson found evolutionary inquiries enlightened by the subordination of the traditional scientific to a creative-historical perspective.[21]

Thus the relations of physical scientific and historical views have been indicated and appraised in terms of contending conceptions of knowledge and insight. The exaltation of abstract formulation of uniformities as essential to scientific knowledge has led to the denial of scientific character to historical inquiry. Did not the historian Renan call history a "poor little conjectural science"?[22] Goethe before him had derided it as a "web of nonsense."[23] From the other standpoint, the emphasis on concrete portrayal as the preëminent achievement of understanding has led to the depreciation of abstract reason and formulated science, as lacking the true insight into reality which history manifests. The cultivation of historical penetration has been advocated as required for the fuller grasp of biological processes, in the views of creative or emergent evolution.

## 5. *The Materialistic Interpretation of History*

In our previous section we indicated the confusion which results from the inept excessive application of a loose quasi-historical method in scientific research, or of rigid quasi-scientific method of historical inquiry. We should beware of "nature faking" in the former case, but also of "history faking" in the latter. The right intelligent procedure demands due distribution of emphasis on the characteristic approach suitable to each of these two types of investigations. The lengths of misdirection to which we may stray if we ignore this warning are shown in the so-called materialistic interpretation of history. Its boasted scientific thoroughness in dealing with historical conditions and activities has yielded only narrowly abstract and artificial accounts. It distorts the concrete human portraiture. It fails to express the distinctive meaning of human characters and events. We have stated here at the outset our conclusion, and we should now proceed to trace the grounds on which it is based.

The materialistic conception of history is derived from the interpretation of human activities in terms of mechanistic determinism. The prestige of modern physical science as the model way of attaining reliable knowledge has motivated the demand to use its principle of causal necessity strictly in humanistic inquiries. The epoch-making success of evolutionism in the biological sciences stimulated the emphasis on physical-physiological methods in anthropology and introduced an expanding and ramified similar procedure in the various humanities.

This general standpoint and method have certain initial systematic merits. The materialistic interpretation of human affairs considers the lives of men and societies as integral with the rest of nature. In his account of history the materialist seeks to trace and formulate causal uniformities analogous to those ascertained in the physical sciences. This mechanistic outlook is due to a basic refusal to recognize any unique and distinctive characteristics of mind. From this point of view "mental activity" should be written in quotation marks, as a traditional misnomer for a certain group of physiological processes. When thinking is classified in the same rubrics with digestion or respiration, the entire treatment of human processes and problems is restated in biological materialistic terms. Men's and women's lives, societies and cultural processes and epochs, are then studied as the botanist or the paleontologist study their respective materials. So Hippolyte Taine, with perhaps an excess of candor, wrote of his historical and literary or ethical studies: "A historian may be permitted the privilege of a naturalist; I have regarded my subject the same as the metamorphosis of an insect. . . . Vice and virtue are products, like vitriol and sugar." [24]

The materialistic account of mind and mental activity is nothing recent. Its first versions are derived from Democritean and Epicurean atomism in classical antiquity. But its specific applications to historical inquiries gained especial emphasis during the nineteenth century. It was reinforced by the spreading influence of evolutionary methods. It was also due to the naturalistic revolt against Hegelian idealism which marked many trends in European and especially German thought about the middle of the last century. Hegel's basic principle—"What is Rational is Real, and what is Real is Rational"—led to a theory of history as the progressive self-revelation of Spirit. This spiritual reading of the historical record might and did incline some of the so-called "Hegelians of the Right" towards modern restatements of the old theological and providential interpretations. But another and an increasing group of Hegel's successors, the "Hegelians of the Left," reacted not only against this type of providential teleology in history, but also against the basic idealism from which it had been derived.

An early leader in this anti-Hegelian insurgence was Ludwig Feuerbach, but the extensive inferences from this reversal of Hegel's philosophy of history were drawn by Karl Marx. They provided the outlines of the dialectical materialism of the "scientific socialists," and they have been fixed today in the official philosophy of the communist governments. Feuerbach began as a Hegelian idealist but turned increasingly towards positivism and materialism. According to him, the idealists had misplaced their emphasis. It is not reason and ideas that move and transform material conditions, but rather these physical and physiological conditions themselves determine the course of ideas in individuals and in societies. Climate and diet shape men's characters. The eighteenth century French materialist La Mettrie had ascribed the "fierce character" of the English as due to their predilection for rare beef.[25] Feuerbach summed up his physiological theory of human personality in a dietetic pun: *"Der Mensch ist was er isst—*Man is what he eats."[26]

The central point in this view is in its initial conception of man. It regards human life as essentially material in nature and mechanical in operation. It therefore undertakes to recount men's ongoing careers as part and parcel of the physical processes, altogether and without qualification. It may yield different versions, but they are different only in the detailed tracing of the various aspects of the physical mechanism of humanity. So history may be traced and explained in its dependence on climatic conditions or on geographical factors determining a pastoral or an agricultural mode of subsistence.

Buckle was a vigorous but not unqualified advocate of historical materialism. In his *History of Civilization in England* he traced the course of historical events to their external causes in the material environment. It should be observed that he did not ignore the operation of "mental laws" and in fact regarded the intellectual and moral factors as increasingly important in the higher development of civilization. He noted the historical role played by religion, literature, and government. But in the earlier stages of historical life Buckle did trace in almost endless detail the "influence of physical laws." He emphasized especially the factors of soil, climate, and food. These three physical conditions determine the population curves of peoples and their manner of subsistence: precarious and ever on the verge of starvation, or else stable in substantial livelihood and rising prosperity. They are the material roots of a stunted and meager society, or of a wide-branching and fruitful national culture. The old saying of Herodotus, that Egypt is the gift of the river Nile, would seem to sum up this general view of history.

Buckle illustrated this general thesis by a wealth of examples drawn from every country. Particularly striking is his reference to the history of the Arabs. Limited to the arid stretches of their original homeland, they lived for centuries nomadic lives of rude indigence. And such is the life of multitudes of them to this day, Bedouins of the desert. But note the radical change of the Arabs

126

THE WORLD AS HISTORY

as their spreading conquests brought them to fertile lands of more temperate climates. The rude nomads became cultivated builders of great cities, patrons of learning and culture, literature, science and philosophy, from Damascus and Cairo eastward to Bagdad and Delhi and westward to Cordova and Granada. Buckle sought to trace causal connections between definite material conditions and specific qualities of human character and behavior. Thus he pointed out that altitude and atmospheric changes affect temperament. People living in volcanic or earthquake areas are marked by high-wrought nerves and agitated imaginings, by dismay and superstitions.

Marx's materialistic interpretation of history was in terms of the economic forces and conditions of production. His choice of the particular version of his thesis is of radical social-revolutionary importance, but speaking systematically, his doctrine is only a variety of the basic materialistic theory. Buckle's account, which we have just mentioned, indicates clearly that the fundamental theory itself, the interpretation of human life in materialistic terms, can be entertained without reference to communism. It has in fact been held by firm capitalists who oppose violently the communistic application of the theory in the economic and political field.

Marx's *Capital* has been described as a materialistic-economic philosophy of history. It was a theory which proceeded from a derogation or dismissal of the traditionally rehearsed historical forces—military or dynastic or religious or racial strains or lusts of personal ambition or rancor—to point out and underscore everywhere the prevailing dynamic of material-economic factors. In *Capital* all history was viewed as mainly a succession of economic conflicts, a class struggle for the means of production under certain material conditions.

The old providential determinism of the theologians was, of course, cast out as dogmatic superstition. The later idealistic philosophy was branded as Hegelian decadence. So Marx wrote in *Capital*: "My dialectical method is not only different from the Hegelian but is fundamentally its direct opposite. For Hegel the thought process . . . is the demiurge (or creator) of the actual, and actual existence is only the outward manifestation of the Idea. But I, on the contrary, regard the ideal as nothing else than the material reality, transposed and translated in the human

127

head." [27] Thus interpreted as a physical dynamic in all human processes, directing and forming them all, the Marxist dialectic was advanced as working with irresistible necessity through the ages towards its inevitable historical climax. Friedrich Engels agreed with Marx in pushing all historical explanations down to their basic roots in the material economic structure of the conditions of production.

An interesting aspect of the communists' dialectical procedure may be noted. On the one hand, their historical method claims the merit of applying the causal determinism of modern science to the explanation of human lives, of integrating the sciences of man with the other sciences of the cosmic mechanism. On the other hand, the communist dialecticians disclaim the crass mechanism of the traditional materialists. They acknowledge the vital factors of intelligence and reason. But these claims and disclaimers are mainly tactical; the basic emphasis on the material factors remains undiminished. History is viewed all along as the ongoing contest of economic groups for the control of the means of production, and the contest itself is regarded as determined throughout by the material conditions characterizing each age. So we read in the *Communist Manifesto*: "In proportion as the bourgeoisie, *i.e.,* capital, is developed, in the same proportion is the proletariat, the modern working class, developed, a class of laborers who live only so long as they find work, and who find work only as their labor increases capital. These laborers, who must sell themselves piecemeal, are a commodity, like every other article of commerce, and are constantly exposed to all the vicissitudes of competition, to all the fluctuations of the market." [28] The important point systematically is that this economic, revolutionary version of historical materialism has its natural kinships with the materialistic account of all human activities—literature, art, religion. Can you imagine Homer in our days of printing presses, or the *Iliad* and Achilles along with gunpowder and modern armaments? Human culture in any of its stages and varieties grows out of certain material conditions, blooms and bears its fruits, ages and withers and rots away in its material soil. It is radically material in constitution all the way through.

Engels estimated this materialistic economic interpretation as "destined to do for history what Darwin's theory has done for biology." [29] Even though this superlative estimate may be questioned, the comparison is very appropriate, alike in indicating the merit of these two theories and also some of their defects. Historical materialism shares with the theory of evolution the positive worth of pointing out the physical factors in biological and human processes. Both doctrines contribute to the scientific integration of the diverse investigations of nature. For surely history does not operate in a physical vacuum, and it is of advantage to bring it down to solid earth. But while the naturalistic approach to historical studies is significant, as correcting the onesidedness of a too exclusively spiritual or else romantic historiography, it is itself onesided and liable to radical distortion of the true total historical picture.

We may recall here Taine's proposed analogies. It is a fact that men and societies are subjected to the action of chemical and physiological conditions similar to those which affect vitriol and sugar or determine the metamorphosis of an insect. But men's reactions to these natural forces differ from those of acids or arthropods, and until we understand these differences we cannot make sense even of the alphabet of history. We need here the balanced insight of Aristotle, whose examination of man's soul was on one hand a part of his general biological inquiries, but on the other hand led him to a recognition of the unique and distinctive character of human nature, rationality. For Aristotle, man was an animal, yes, but a rational and a social-political animal.

The demand which confronts the historian, to portray the ongoing course of human affairs in its material setting, but to portray it as convincingly and genuinely human—this demand illustrates strikingly the basic character of our "philosophy of perspectives." Nature in its boundless variety and complexity can be studied and understood from various standpoints that accentuate its various important phases. We should respect both the interrelation and the distinction of these phases, both the ultimate integrity of nature and the variety of its manifold aspects. A complex and widely ramified inquiry like history must acknowledge, observe, and record the external physical factors operating in men's lives, but it fails to grasp its main theme and problem unless it also recognizes and portrays the distinctively human character of the events which it undertakes to interpret.

The materialistic interpretation of history and the account

of human activities as the operations of mechanical forces has been carried to speculative extremes. The course of historical events has been considered as subject to statistical reckoning, like the formulated calculation of chances in throwing coins or dice. In such mechanistic procedure the available alternatives can be listed and likewise their respective chances of occurring and the eventual playing and playing-out of them all. Across the infinite span of past time, we have been told, all that could ever occur must have already occurred, and many times over. The future "history" can only rehearse the old stories in endless iteration. This is the doctrine of eternal recurrence. It runs counter to any genuine belief in progress, or in a real historical prospect or emergence of values, in growing and ongoing human life. The examination of this unhistorical doctrine, to which we proceed, should enable us to grasp more firmly the essentials of a truly historical outlook.

## 6. The Unhistorical Doctrine of Eternal Recurrence

The doctrine of eternal recurrence has a long record across the whole span of religious and cosmological speculation in the Orient and in our Western civilization. I have traced elsewhere in some detail the development of this view of the world process in many of its varieties,[30] and the present brief discussion of it will be concerned mainly with the contrast which this outlook on human affairs presents to a significantly historical account.

The idea of eternal recurrence has expressed some of the mind's quandaries in trying to grasp the idea of infinity. In the boundless scope of "the two eternities," as Hume called them, "before and after the present state of things," [31] our concepts of variety and ongoing process shrivel into inadequacy. Sooner or later eternity must swallow up the versatility of all existence, and the cosmic table of contents must eventuate in repetition. Infinite time destines all things to ultimate rehearsal. So Lucretius summed it up in four words: *Eadem sunt omnia semper*: All things are always the same." [32] And before him Ecclesiastes: "There is nothing new under the sun."

The baffling character of the idea of eternity may be noted

especially in the Oriental efforts to express it. Nothing in classical antiquity quite approaches the limitless sweep of Brahmanic and even more Buddhist speculation. Only the modern astronomical range of spatial magnitudes, of galaxies and supergalaxies and light years of unthinkable distances, matches the ancient Asiatic straining at eternity. Our Bible tells us that for God a thousand years are as one day and one day as a thousand years. But the ancient Hindu reckoned a day of Brahman as a thousand times four million and twenty thousand years, and likewise Brahman's nights. This combined span of over eight billion years is a world-age; at the close of each such period Brahman re-creates the world. Fifty Brahmanic years of such days and nights have already elapsed, and well-nigh half a trillion years are still to come.

Buddhist cosmology put these staggering Brahmanic calculations in the shade. Its Great World Age or *mahakalpa* consists of four incalculable aeons, and each one of these includes twenty *antara* world-ages. The cosmic calendar proceeds in countless years through the process of the destruction and the renovation of worlds, time without end. And how without end, the Buddhist was never tired of speculating. Man's longevity, beginning with 84,000 years, is each century reduced by one year until it reaches a bare ten years, and then in reverse process is again increased by one year in each century, back to 84,000 years. The span of this double operation, about seventeen million years, is a small *kalpa*. Or suppose it rained over the whole world for three years without any letup: the total number of rain drops would still not reach the length of years in an *asankhyeya kalpa*. Really to grasp its eternal span, we need the magic of numbers. Take a progression of years: $10^2$, $10^4$, $10^8$ . . . —*asankhyeya* would be its 104th term! The great *mahakalpa* is four times longer still. And as if that were not enough, consider that these incalculable aeons of world-creation and world-dissolution are repeated eternally, without end. A Chinese Buddhist folk tale began its "once upon a time" thus: "Ten quadrillion times a hundred quadrillions of *kalpas* ago there lived a righteous king."

Western versions of the doctrine of eternal recurrence do not reach the infinite expanse of Oriental speculation, but they exceed its specification of details and give a more vivid description of the cyclical course of existence:

> Worlds on worlds are rolling ever
> From creation to decay. . . .[33]

Cosmic recurrence was contemplated by Heraclitus and Plato, and especially by the Stoics. While the Roman Stoics did not espouse this doctrine, Marcus Aurelius meditated on the "periodic palingenesis" of all things, the reënactment of the drama of existence in all its scenes and details: "Those that come after us will see nothing new, nor have those before us seen anything more."[34] Should we say that in days to come, again and again, a new Socrates will endure his shrewish wife Xantippe and will drink the hemlock in prison? For it will be the old Socrates, another but yet the same—and so likewise with all the others, and ourselves too: periodic extinctions, periodic rebirths in the countless aeons past and yet to come.

Christian theology rejected the notion of eternal recurrence. In the Christian perspective the course of cosmic and especially human affairs could not be viewed cyclically. Our Western division of historical chronology, B.C. and A.D., is a significant expression of the Christian outlook. The Savior's career in Galilee and Jerusalem was to the Christian view the unique turning point in history, from Creation to the Last Judgment. It was unthinkable to regard the nativity, the crucifixion, the resurrection as periodically reënacted scenes on the stage of eternal recurrence. Professed Christian piety goes hopelessly astray when it reflects that God is bound from all eternity to create all possible forms of existence and to determine eternally the existence of them all, so that nothing new could arise, and the old could only reappear in periodic recurrence. God neither begins nor ends his work in our human sense of these words. "He can act while He reposes, and repose while He acts." So St. Augustine admonished us to "turn away in heart and mind from the unreal and futile cycles of the godless."[35] Religious conviction directed Christian thought towards a historical outlook. "History ceased to be a uniform rhythmic repetition and became a comprehensive whole, a single drama."[36]

The ascendency of a secular outlook in later European reflection was bound to modify the strictly theological interpretation of history, but it should be noted that even the earlier providential determinism of ecclesiastic historians represented an advance over the view of cosmic cyclical rotation of events. History revealed a genuine ongoing course of men and nations, for good or for ill, towards eternal salvation or towards irretrievable ruin. The note of providential unique finality in God's judgment of men anticipated the later grasp of a concrete historical perspective in secular terms.

The modern versions of the idea of eternal recurrence, in literature and in philosophy, show the influence of revived classical speculation. The fascination of the hypothesis has also affected some scientific minds of bold conjecture. The nineteenth century, starting with the romantic poets, entertained the notion of cosmic repetition. Examples can be cited from Shelley and Byron, Hölderlin and Heine and Guyau. Herbert Spencer wrote of the world course as necessarily pendular, a "rhythm in the totality of its changes, . . . alternate eras of Evolution and Dissolution." [37] But the outstanding thinker in this field, who stamped his name upon the doctrine of eternal recurrence, is Friedrich Nietzsche.

Nietzsche was a distinguished specialist in classical scholarship, and it is hardly conceivable that he was unacquainted with the Greek ideas of eternal recurrence. Besides, it would be scarcely reasonable to presume that, as an advocate of this doctrine, he would have held that there could be any really original advocacy of this or of any other idea. Actually he did declare that "in every one of these cycles of human life there will be one hour when for the first time one man, and then many, will perceive the mighty thought of the eternal recurrence of all things:—and for mankind this is always the hour of Noon." [38] We need not pursue further Nietzsche's mistaken conviction of historical priority here. Might not a thorough believer in the doctrine of eternal recurrence point out that in all previous aeons the prophet of that "mighty thought" was, really, the very same Nietzsche? If not the first, he was the foremost protagonist of the cyclical cosmology. What concerns us is his version of it and the interpretation of human life and history to which the doctrine of eternal recurrence led him.

Nietzsche's first expression of this idea has the marks of emotional or even mystical fervor. It was a sort of philosophical inspiration: "This life, as thou livest it at present, and hast lived it, thou must live it once more, and also innumerable times . . .

**133**

all the unspeakably small and great in thy life must come to thee again, and all in the same series and sequence. . . . The eternal sand-glass of existence will ever be turned once more, and thou with it, thou speck of dust!" [39] He wrote to his friend Peter Gast: "My emotional intensities make me shudder and laugh. . . . On my horizon have risen thoughts such as I have not yet seen." [40] But he also intended to undertake extensive scientific training to enable him to come before the world with a thorough demonstration of the doctrine. His poor health and especially his ailing eyes compelled him to abandon these plans. His formal exposition of eternal recurrence is brief, but the influence of the idea on his later thinking was radical.

The cyclic-recurrent course of existence is, according to Nietzsche, a necessary inference from the principle of the conservation of energy. This principle, that the total amount of force in the world is a constant quantity, implies that the world-energy, however vast, is yet calculable, a finite and not an infinite amount. Space is also finite; or better, space, like matter, is an abstract form. Everything real is energy. But time is real and infinite, eternal. The present, like a gate that swings both ways, opens on the endless spans of the past and the future. In the eternity already past every possible event, that is, every conceivable combination of energy factors, must already have occurred, not once only but many times over. And the future can bring forth nothing new but only repetitions of the past. The versatility of existence is vast but yet finite, and it is exhausted in eternity. "An infinite process cannot be conceived otherwise than as periodic." [41]

It is clear that Nietzsche's account lumps together human and historical processes with the rest of existence in the same mechanistic view of the world as a "monster of energy." He makes no provision for the inclusion of context, rational meaning and purpose, or for values as principles in his interpretation of human activities. But while ruling out rationality explicitly, he yet relies on abstract logic to yield him his necessary conclusions. We are bound to ask: In a world-process of sheer mechanism, "the chaos of the universe," as he called it, how can we know that any particular combination has occurred more than once, or that it will recur along with certain other definite combinations in "the same order," again and again? For all we know, the alphabet of events may get itself to twirling around some $u$ or $v$ and never reach any conceivable $z$! Nietzsche recognized this perplexing alternative, "the existence of some sort of irregularity and incomplete circular form in the world." [42] But he set it aside in his confident reliance on eternity. With eternity as an ally, we are bound to have all combinations again and again, without exception.

Nietzsche's failure to understand the interplay of identity and difference in every repetition renders his account of a course of events, and especially of historical activities, ineptly abstract and artificial. Bare identity is a bare and empty notion. We are told that there are no two identical Greek vases in existence. And in physical nature likewise no two leaves are the same, nor any two grains of sand, not really—if for no other reason, simply on account of the different setting and context. The same thing, the same event, as we say, would in its very recurrence be yet another. It is not the same fine bowl of soup that in a chaotic menu might be served to us again as dessert. It was not the same sun that rose and that set on the Battle of Waterloo. Neither the communists nor ourselves were the same after Stalingrad as before. To regard human activities and reactions as bare mechanical combinations in the twirling cosmic roulette is to miss the essential character of historical events. Every historical occurrence is what it is in its concrete actuality. It cannot be understood if considered abstractly as a kind of combination of "energy factors" which is somehow identical in this or that or any other total situation. Historical insight requires recognition both of the concreteness and of the contextual integrity of every historical event.

The defectiveness and the unhistorical character of the idea of eternal recurrence and cyclical cosmology become even more evident when we consider the significance, the value, and generally the normative aspect of human activities which the historian is bound to include in his accounts. Meaning and value are inexhaustible, and at every turn of human living, as the context of experience shifts in any direction, the alternatives are undergoing revision, and the eventual decision and action are proceeding to their unique and unprecedented expression.

The true understanding of human affairs in historical portrayal is thus incompatible with any merely mechanical view of eternal recurrence. The historical perspective is the perspective

**135**

not of cyclical repetitions but of ongoing significant activities, of development or decline, achievement or frustration, with background and prospect ever shifting, in inexhaustible and often baffling complexity. For good or for ill, the interplay of alternatives is never the same, as values in continual revision are always impending or receding.

The principle of emergence, which we found to be fruitful but also perplexing in the evolutionary cosmology, seems to express an essential characteristic of the historical process. It needs careful consideration.

## 7. The Historical Emergence of Values

Hegel developed his ethics by tracing the social realization of personality through the expanding spheres of institutional participation in the lives of others: in the home, the civic community, the state, and the all-comprehending scope of civilization. This expansive realization of personal values, according to him, expresses the fundamental meaning of history. The meaning is dual. History manifests the ever fuller significance of free self-realization. History is also the ongoing verdict of men's activities by the standards of emerging and gradually established values. Hegel formulated the first of these principles in very positive terms: "The history of the world is nothing but the development of the Idea of Freedom." The second principle he cited from a famous line by the poet Schiller: "The history of the world is the world's court of judgment." [43]

Without any further preoccupation with Hegelian exposition, we may keep in mind these two aspects of history which may be related in the idea of the historical emergence of values. In returning here to the basic notion of emergence, which we considered in the previous chapter in evolutionary terms, we may observe from the outset that it seems especially suitable to historical treatment. Historical events cannot be regarded as the bare mechanical results of antecedent conditions, as consequences which can be predicted reliably and in detail. In proceeding from the past to the future, historical processes manifest a certain characteristic overplus. The overplus is characteristic in a two-fold way: the result cannot be anticipated fully by no matter how thorough understanding of the former situation; yet when the event is realized later in actuality, it can be seen and understood as the full fruition of its antecedent character. There is historical determination, and there is also historical genuine growth, and unless we recognize them both, we fail to do adequate justice to the historical course of events. This twofold meaning we intend to express by the idea of the historical emergence of values.

In grasping the dual meaning of the idea of emergence in history, it is important that each of its two aspects be duly recognized. That there is some overplus, something impending and in some sense really new, seems to be implied in the very character of historical process. It is a process of growth, or decay, that is, a process of ongoing activities involving individual and social values, of which only the event can tell us in its due time. Here Auguste Comte found the sharp difference between physical science and historical inquiry: "History is not a thing that can be deduced." [44] Reliable deduction or prediction is unavailable in history because the historical event, unlike the mechanical process in physical science, is not regarded as a certain *kind* of event. It is that particular concrete event. It does not stay put either in conceptual analysis or in actuality. Its full significance is being continually manifested, but it is at no point completely and factually settled.

While we keep in mind the concretely ongoing and developing character of historical activities, we should also recognize, if not a finality, yet a certain genuine determination of events. After all, the past is passed; it is there, to be observed and reported. Neither individuals nor societies and nations can unsay their record. The past awaits its eventual fuller fruition, but surely it is also a factor in determining that fruition. If the latter truth be overlooked, the former by itself may lapse into an error. We may be told that the past is never factually definitive. It always was viewed in a certain perspective, which is continually altering. The past is ever in a process of revision. In the developing course of historical interpretation, periodically, as we have been told, "a different Caesar crosses the Rubicon." [45] This is in a certain sense true—that is, so long as we do not also imply that any Caesar is ever crossing the Delaware. That is to say, the historical evidence never remains fixed in every way, and no history is written once for all. But in this ongoing process, ongoing also in its recording, there are definite elements, there are specific data and facts. They are being progressively realized and understood and interpreted, but their actuality should be respected and reported accurately.

Isn't this the dual insight which we emphasize when we insist on the importance of preserving a historical sense in our appraisal of ancient ideas? We traced in our previous chapter certain early approaches to the doctrine of evolution. We should not fail to note in classical speculation the groping after the evolutionary outlook; but we should not read too much of our own meaning into the fragmentary sayings of Anaximander or Empedocles, almost two and a half millenia before *The Origin of Species,* and regard them as advocates of Darwin's theory. With this twofold qualification, we may include Anaximander and Empedocles in the history of evolutionary ideas—but not Pythagoras! History always discloses a certain factual character of events, to be ascertained and recorded by the historian. This factual character determines in a real measure the historical further unfoldment of the events, which the historian must pursue. The historical past cannot be unsaid, but it is not said fully once for all. History must trace, and it must also await, its fuller fruition, in part already determined, in part yet to be realized.

Samuel Alexander's contemplation of evolution as the natural history of values[46] may be considered here in a more definitely historical outlook. Using the term evolution in the broad sense of development, we may reaffirm that history is the natural evolution of values. The historical process is the occasion for the manifestation of values, and also the testing ground on which they are realized and preserved, or discredited and negated. This process may be studied in its large outlines or in its specific expressions of certain particular values. We shall not overload our exposition with too many examples; one or two may suffice.

The long series of evolving animal life may be traced as providing in ever fuller measure the conditions of stimulus and response, of consciousness, which eventually reach the level of definitely mental activity. Once attained, mind or spirit may be recognized as the characteristic fruition of life; but while we may observe evidences of its potentiality through a considerable range of the biological reactions, we should beware not to read more in the lower stages than they actually yield. Gradual emergence is just what we should note here: the matrix or the predisposing conditions of mind considerably down the scale, and then its full and definite operation on the higher levels. As General Smuts put it sharply, "it is just as wrong for Idealism to deny the world before the appearance of Spirit, as it is for Naturalism to deny Spirit when eventually it did appear in the world." [47]

Mind or spirit may operate at a very low range of reactions, or it may rise to the highest creative activities of genius. And even at the higher stages it is often liable to backslide. Values emerge and are also eclipsed. Fulfillment and degradation mark the unsteady rhythm of the best of us, individuals and societies. History is both an inspiring and a disheartening and dismal record. Both of these aspects of the historical career of values in our Western civilization may be illustrated by considering the ancient classical and the modern meanings of the two words, aristocracy and democracy. Plato used "aristocracy" in the lofty sense justified by its etymology, meaning "dominance of the best." In individual lives or in the ordering of societies and states, the ideal principle of aristocracy meant that the highest and the best capacity of man, his reason, should be given the rule and the direction of human life. In our modern use the term aristocracy has been degraded to mean the rule by special privilege of a social élite or even of prevailing wealth.

Against the discreditable strain in Western history epitomized by the shifting meaning of "aristocracy," consider the inspiring note in the historical elevation of the word "democracy." To Plato and Aristotle democracy was a corrupt form of government and social order, rule by the *demos* or the masses, the many, *hoi polloi*. The derogatory meaning of these terms indicated the basic contempt of the Greek élite for the common people. The democratic ideal as we know it is the social-political expression of the Christian regard for the infinite worth of personality, of any man irrespective of birth or external conditions, each man's unique and infinite worth in God's sight. The words "democracy," "the people," in their historical shift of meaning express the emergence and the development of humane values in our Western social history. To realize the far-reaching contrast between even the best of classical antiquity and our modern liberal spirit, just try to imagine Plato advocating "government of the *demos*, by the *demos*, and for the *demos!*"

We shall broadly recognize in the historical course of events, as we do in our own lives, advance and decline, achievement or frustration of acknowledged values. But the specific judgment is not so readily settled even in personal reflection, and in historical reference it is often highly debatable. Many writers today describe Western culture as on the verge of collapse. But this contemporary spirit of defeatism is scarcely justified. Western history records other periods of mortal threat which our civilization has withstood. What we regard as crises are really the characteristic expressions of the historical situation in a transitional period: a period of decisive issues and contending directions of social action.

It may help to balance our present judgment about world affairs if we consider two earlier crises in Western civilization, in each of which old traditional values were radically disrupted and new values emerged dominant, but in which eventually the old and the new fructified each other. Both of these critical transitions are so outstandingly important that by reference to them we distinguish the principal periods of history, as ancient, medieval, and modern. What characterized each one of them was the historical emergence and reconstitution of values. In order to understand clearly these historical crises we should assume the right point of view. Today we are, of course, judging our tragic problems from the shaky ground on which we ourselves stand. We should similarly regard the earlier crossroads in our civilization from the viewpoint of those who were confronted with them.

Consider in this spirit the radical turn from ancient to medieval civilization. How must this critical situation have appeared to representative classical minds: to educated Roman statesmen, Greek scientists and philosophers, to the cultured society of antiquity? Their great system of life was unsettled and tottering to its ruin. Man's reason and creative genius had achieved in Greece epic and dramatic poetry, incomparable art, systematic science and philosophy. The organizing imperial majesty of Rome had maintained ordered social life from Britain to Syria. Roman law and Roman peace, *Pax Romana,* had become abiding symbols of stability. This entire cultural edifice was being shaken to its foundations. Hordes of fierce savage men clad in animal skins were breaking through the farflung ramparts of the Roman empire, laying waste the noble classical world in flames and carnage, drawing ever closer to the Eternal City. And while the political and economic structures of antiquity were thus cracking under the barbarian shocks, the inner life and spirit of classical culture was being disrupted by the widespread advance of a Jewish religious cult called Christianity. To the devotees of this cult, Greek art and Roman majesty and all the proud achievements of classical genius were worldly vanities. In the sight of their God and Divine Savior, the weary and the heavy laden, the meek and the merciful and the long-suffering martyrs were the blessed souls. The Christians looked beyond this world, to the divine grace of the life to come. They awaited the fall of Rome as God's judgment on the sin and corruption of the classical world, the downfall of its pride and power. As this new religion was winning converts on every side, where was Rome to find the vigor and the resolution to withstand the barbarian invasions?

This struggle of social ideals did have many tragic consequences. The Roman imperial system was laid low, and the Eternal City was devastated. For several centuries civilization seemed extinguished in Europe. But new values emerged in the gradual development of medieval culture. In this work of spreading enlightenment, the leadership was Christian. The followers of the Galilean Savior, whom the proud classical minds had scorned as fanatics, as they established the new religion over the ruins of Greek and Roman antiquity, did not negate altogether the classical values. They transformed them and gave them new spiritual meaning. The wisdom of Plato and Aristotle and the Stoic sages was reinterpreted in the language of Christian reflection and devotion.

The new medieval Christian civilization which developed and held sway in Europe for a thousand years was both a negation and a revision of the values of classical antiquity. The medieval mind was theological in its outlook, submissive to Church authority, largely negligent of the secular interests and achievements of men. It revealed the human capacities for saintliness, but it did not satisfy or express the whole nature or personality of men. The faith of the scholastic Catholic philosopher was a faith seeking to understand, but a faith committed to its doctrines whether understood or not.

141

Yet increasing numbers of these medieval minds caught the ancient Greek interest in the investigation of nature, the classical enthusiasm for critical inquiry and for secular achievement. A new crisis was thus brewing. The old proud spirit of worldliness was once more abroad, threatening the Kingdom of God and Christ. We call this transitional period the Renaissance; out of it has come our Western world system and its culture. The new spirit was a spirit of independent inquiry and a zest for worldliness in every respect, up and down in the scale of human values. Instead of poring over sermons and theological treatises, men turned once more to the literature and philosophy of classical antiquity. Instead of accepting without question the doctrines of the Church, men sought by themselves knowledge of nature. Instead of glorifying the monastic denial of the world, men chose by preference active secular careers, the profits, the power, and the pleasures of living in the world here and now. The new modern spirit was critical, inquiring, but also passionate and violent. It set proofs above prayers, and prosperity above piety.

We may see clearly how perverse and how disastrous this early modern upheaval must have appeared to some of the church leaders and to their loyal followers, four or five centuries ago. They saw the striving of the Renaissance as the rebellion of men's sinful pride and lust, the war of Satan against the Kingdom of God. But the course of modern civilization, which issued from that struggle of contending values, did not follow either of the two opposite directions exclusively. It sought and it is still seeking a satisfactory harmony of medieval-Christian and ancient classical ideals. It rejected or outgrew much of the dogmatism of the medieval system, but it did not lose the influence of Christianity. It emulated the inquiring and creative intelligence of classical antiquity, but it soon realized that a mere classical revival was of no avail unless modern minds attacked their own problems in a critical way.

Our modern age at its best has represented a synthesis of ancient and medieval values. At its best it has sought to reconcile and harmonize the naturalism and the rationalism of classical antiquity with the spirit of Christian devotion. But this harmony is a very exceptional achievement. We find more generally in modern society the unsettled issue beween contending values. And this raises the basic problem of emphasis in historical valu-

142

ation. Can we speak reasonably of a rise and fall, achievement or decline on a broad historical plane? The study of the emergence of values in the course of history thus leads us towards a critical appraisal of the belief in social progress.

## 8. *The Idea of Progress and the Judgment of Civilization*

The view of history as the stage or the medium for the emergence of values is a view of contending activities, impending alternatives and issues awaiting resolution. Each turn in the historical course of events is really some sort of crossroads of eventual choice or at any rate of ongoing determination. Biographers as well as historians are continually engaged in explaining or appraising these turns to the right or to the left, advance or detour or retreat in this or in that field of value realization. But there is a broader and a more searching question of overall evaluation. Does the historical course manifest any significant trend upward and forward? Is the movement of history an epical rhythm of positive achievement, or a tragic downfall which we can scan, or is it fortuitous and unmeaning sequence, random futility? How warranted are we in speaking of historical growth and development? This concern about the ripening and realization of values, about the reality of historical mellowing, is expressed in the problem of Progress.

It should be needless to point out that we are not concerned here with some common uses of the word "progress" as a continued movement forward in space or advance in time or increase in size of certain processes and conditions. The idea of progress which we are now considering may be stated in the simplest terms as a change for the better. The recognition of progress in any activity is a judgment of it in terms of impending values, and a judgment of positive evaluation. "Great is truth, and will prevail." We should note that the connotation of the idea of progress is thoroughly personal and definitely secular. Let us consider these two features of our belief. First, it is counter to any materialistic account of human activities in terms of mechanical determination. We use the word progress loosely when we speak of the progress of a storm or of some plant and animal decay. Progress has no meaning apart from values, values concretely being realized in ongoing activity. Our lives, we say, are not a mere series of predetermined

143

effects, wound up mechanisms. Human choice and eventual action signify the genuine emergence of values, values that were not but now are, and are yet to be more fully.

Despite the incongruity of a thoroughly mechanistic cosmology and the idea of progress, many materialists have of course traced progress and retrogression in their histories, natural or human. In fact, one of the first thinkers to use the term progress was the Roman poet of atomism, Lucretius. Like his masters, Democritus and Epicurus, he described all events in nature, including human lives, as fortuitous contacts and collisions of material particles. But he also traced the stages of men's rise to more and more effective and satisfactory ways and conditions of life. And here the poet of the atomic swirl, despite his mechanical theory, recognized the directive power of reason in man's rise to civilization. "Ships and agriculture, fortifications and laws, arms, roads, clothing and all else of this kind, life's prizes, its luxuries also from first to last, poetry and pictures, the shaping of statues by the artist, all these as man progressed gradually step by step were taught by practice and the experiments of the active mind. So by degrees time brings up before us every single thing, and reason lifts it into the precincts of light. For their intellect saw one thing after another grow famous amongst the arts, until these came to the highest point." [48]

The definitely human-personal non-mechanical connotation of the idea of progress is also thoroughly secular. While it transcends the perspective of strictly causal determination, it is also to be distinguished from the opposite rigid Providential determinism of some types of theology. Consider an extreme variety of the latter, the notion of *kismet* or fate in Mohammedan countries. The Islamic doctrine, that all our thoughts and words and deeds are eternally written in the book of Allah, rules out any belief in progress. On this basis there can be no view of human achievement. History can only be the unrolling of Allah's everlasting scroll.

We noted earlier Bergson's criticism of this sort of divinely predestined finalism. But many Christian theologians who do not expound predestination in its extreme forms, fatalist or Calvinist or even Augustinian, are yet finally insistent on Providential direction of men's lives and of the historical process. In that outlook the idea of progress, meaning men's own active achievement and increasing possession of values, must appear very ambiguous, or else impious.

The ancient classical inclination towards cyclical view of the world process and eternal recurrence was counter to any firm grasp of the idea of progress. The medieval providential determinism and the dispraise of any human initiative or capacity productive of real good pointed to a similar conclusion by a different course of inference. The clear idea of progress is thus a modern expression, notably since "the century of genius," the seventeenth. It was due to the thinking of deliberately secular minds, for, as the historian Bury reflected, "so long as the doctrine of Providence was indisputably in the ascendant, a doctrine of Progress could not arise." [49] The belief in progress has been called the modern man's religion, and so some traditional religionists have suspected it as ungodly presumption.

In our day of world crises and general social-cultural dismay, a devout despair about men's spiritual capacities of initiative or attainment has found expression in theologies of pious self-abasement. "The belief that the development of human capacities radically alters the human situation" [50] has been rejected as erroneous or even as absurd insolence towards God. Less extreme reflection in this field recognizes the seemingly limitless range of human development and yet maintains man's ultimate finitude and utter need of God's grace. Some of the more rigorous judges of man's basic ineptitude have seemed to proceed on the principle that "complete terrestrial pessimism is the key to celestial optimism." Their theology is premised on the contrite declaration in the Liturgy, "There is no health in us." Our helplessness and total depravity must be recognized as incapable of initiating or achieving any real good. By no work of our own can we advance one single step towards God. Our "best intentions and most strenuous efforts are but 'filthy rags' in his sight." [51]

The characteristic perspective of the idea of progress is thus a secular outlook which acknowledges unambiguously personal and spiritual activities and values. This outlook is historical and non-theological but it is not to be regarded as irreligious. It simply faces a human problem in a human way. In this view of human lives and historical processes, the idea of progress has real meaning. Here we can raise the question of progress significantly. We can raise the question, but how is it to be answered?

145

The offhand answer in general discussion is apt to be affirmative. In the growing complexity of modern life, nothing seems more obvious than the progressive mastery of the forces and resources of nature for human use. We are harnessing nature to do our bidding in more and more various and extensive ways. We are discovering and utilizing ever-increasing supplies of food and more secure subsistence. We are solving the secrets of dread diseases, steadily lengthening the average span of human life. We are perfecting transportation and communication to incredible degrees, so that we have almost wiped out the barriers of space and time. We are placing within the reach of growing millions the appliances making possible a more effective and comfortable household economy, as well as educational and artistic advantages. And our systems of universal public education are preparing our young people to outstrip us and move on to still larger horizons.

This broad optimistic evaluation may be noted in the eulogistic tone of the term "modern." The modern is by common consent the better, and better still is the newest model with the latest improvements. The general matter-of-course expectation of all the modern conveniences is typical of our society. The average citizen has at his service appliances which were beyond the dreams of kings and barons not so long ago, historically speaking. A visit to Holyrood or Warwick Castle, or even to Versailles, would clinch this point.

This common sense optimism has found scientific support in the doctrine of evolution. Despite the basic distinction between the evolutionary outlook, and that of historical progress in the realization of values, the biological idea of evolution has been used loosely in the sense of development to express confidence in the ongoing betterment of living beings and especially of the human species. Darwin himself yielded sometimes to this sort of reflection. Surely nature that has advanced from amoeba and worm to mammals and to men, surely humanity that has risen from savagery to civilization makes the conviction of continued progress a reasonable belief. This evolutionary idea of progress has been challenged sternly. T. H. Huxley, himself a leading champion of Darwinian biology, warned us against the optimistic inferences that were often derived from it. The historian Bury cited Huxley's words that he knew "no study which is so saddening as that of the evolution of humanity as it is set forth in the annals of history." [52] And long before Darwin and Huxley, and beyond the range of evolutionary biology, the idea of historical progress has met through the ages detailed and radical negation.

Pessimism is one of the perennial themes of man's thought and feelings. The study of it has shown its deep and ramified roots in all fields of human experience. The tragic view of life will be found to engage our attention in our next chapter, on "The World as Drama." Here we shall be concerned only with the pessimistic denial of historical progress. This is the despair of civilization, the grim conviction that men are unfit for reliable social achievement. Consider any of the great values of a life worth living: health, happiness, knowledge, justice, peace. Does history give us any convincing evidence of men's advance in the attainment or assured possesssion of these cherished blessings? Notwithstanding our greatest medical triumphs, civilized man is still a physical and mental invalid, for his manner of life corrupts his body and mind faster than medicine can cure or alleviate his ills. Our complex social system is stirring more wants and lusts than our means and capacities can satisfy, and we are doomed to ever varying disappointments and unhappiness. Our increased knowledge of details has left us no less baffled than our ancestors by the ultimate secrets of reality. And as to justice and peace, history is a record of dismay, of instability and disaster. In vain presumption, nations build their edifices of justice and peaceful order, build for the centuries systems which do not outlast their own seasons. Chamberlain announced his "peace in our time," and the next year the world was in flames. Schopenhauer spurned the idealist's lofty description of history as man's achievement of freedom or the agelong court of justice. History, he said, is but a succession of cat-fights: one long war chapter after another, with some blank half-pages perchance for the brief war-weary peace.

Both the pessimistic and the optimistic recitals can be expanded to any length without modifying the final refrains. To critical appraisal, the evidence cited by each of them is impressive, but their contrary conclusions are unconvincing. We cannot dismiss either of them as merely temperamental reactions, or as subjective inferences from personal wellbeing or woes, or as the expressions of their respective historical periods, of relative stability and peace or of crisis and chaos. Examples supporting each of these explanations can be cited, but also notable instances to the contrary. We do not need to quote Rousseau's protest to Voltaire, which has been judged as maudlin: "Sated with glory and disillusioned about vain greatness, you live free and in the lap of plenty. . . . Yet you find only evil on earth. And I, unknown, poor, and tortured by an incurable malady, I meditate joyously in my retreat and find that all is good." [53] Better evidence is provided by Condorcet's *Historical Outlines of the Progress of the Human Spirit.* This monumental record of the steady forward march of humanity, in its nine historical stages from the earliest beginnings to modern history, was composed by a man who expressed the noblest principles of the French Revolution, who resisted its corruption and the brutalities of the Terror, and as a result was in flight from the police and had to complete his work in various hiding places, with the specter of the guillotine ever before him.

We should better consider the historical evidence on its merits. And here we are bound to note that the very immensity and complexity of the historical material precludes any final rigid conclusion of approval or condemnation. One can follow Spengler in assembling a mass of historical data that make plausible his thesis of the decline and breakdown of Western civilization. But a different collection of historical evidence could be marshalled to support the opposite thesis. We cannot settle this issue by a mere counsel of moderation and seek a golden mean between Spengler and Condorcet. The right way out of our perplexity is through studying the process of civilization more critically.

The history of civilization cannot be described fairly either by an upward curve of progress or by a downward curve of degradation or by a random line of meaningless fortuity. As distinguished from primitive life or from barbaric epochs, our modern civilization is both better and worse, but we should explain this seemingly evasive appraisal. The historical course towards civilization is a process of increasing complexity and of expanding range of human powers and activities. It is as the transition from childhood to adolescence and to maturity. Men's abilities and the scope of individual careers and social-historical policies and institutions sweep out in both directions, for good or for ill. History shows in ever wider reach how high man can rise and also how low he can sink. Men's resources multiply, their technical and other powers of realizing their purposes, but also their misdirections and perversities. Achievement and frustration, creative advance and corruption contend precariously at each turn of the historical course. The outcome is often complicated by conditions not altogether within man's control, but it depends basically upon his choice between alternative interests, purposes, and values. And that choice is ever more momentous.

This outlook is neither one of bland optimism nor of pessimistic dismay, but of clear-sighted and responsible view of the historical course of events.It conceives of history as growth or expansion in the range of men's activities, the scope and signficance of their projects and problems, the importance of their issues, and the gravity of their decisions, for good or for ill. Can we think of any other period in history when this judgment of civilization and of the basic idea of progress has been evinced more clearly than in our atomic age? The theoretical and technical achievements of modern science have unlocked natural resources and energies available for human use, beyond the wildest dreams of yesterday. We are at the threshhold of an age of unparalleled increase in the means of perfecting human welfare in all directions. But the released atomic energies are also engines of destruction, and we find ourselves on the verge, and almost over the verge, of exploding our whole civilization and ourselves to smithereens. Our belief in progress has both an inspiring and a tragic aspect. It should express a clear awareness of the expanding range and complexity of our modern life. Before us are marvelous opportunities for unprecedented cultural achievement, but also stunning perils of castastrophic disaster. Our destiny hangs upon our choice of conflicting values. If ever there was an all-human drama enacted before us and within us, that sways our entire lives on the balance, bodies and souls, here it is, and we cannot shirk it. We are thus led inevitably from the historical to the dramatic perspective.

# CHAPTER V

# THE WORLD AS DRAMA

## 1. From History to Drama

The idea of history, philosophically interpreted, expresses the value aspect of reality, as we know it characteristically in human activities. But, as has just been noted, there is another and essential phase of value, the dramatic, which is manifested in history but which calls for more direct and special study. We should examine this dramatic character of values as involving an interplay or counteraction of alternatives.

The physical scientist is concerned with the observed uniform connectedness of events and with their manifest patterns of operation. In tracing the causal processes from antecedents to consequents he does not investigate any purposive agencies. He not only ignores teleology but he explicitly rules it out as an irrelevant and scientifically confusing category. The philosophical expression of this non-teleological outlook may be noted early, in Francis Bacon's and Hobbes's rejection of Aristotle's "final causes." But many philosophers and some scientists have pointed out that this scientific neglect of purpose needs revision if we are to have a more adequate and integral view of reality. "Scientifically one abstracts from all agency. Dramatically one is concerned with that agency from which in science one abstracts." [1]

The dramatic view becomes convincingly appropriate as soon as we consider anything in a personal perspective. We then recognize directly the relevance of interests and purposes and values. The object of our attention is no longer merely some matter out there. It now concerns us as somehow a significant condition or agency. And furthermore, the personal outlook which reveals the value aspects of reality is an outlook of appraisal and eventual choice between contending meanings or purposes or ideals. Our views become issues; our judgments are now verdicts and commitments. Each value manifests its significance and its role in our experience; it pleads for our preference and choice; it vies with some related or opposite value. This is the ongoing drama of our lives.

This so-called bipolarity of alternatives may be seen through the entire series and variety of human activities. In each case a certain value, while it may be viewed in its field as distinguished from other values in other fields, is recognized and appraised more characteristically in its contending relation to some counter value or values. The moment we pass from description or explanation to appraisal, our series is no longer single file. The variety of values manifests in each case certain alternatives. Happiness is, of course, distingished from truth or justice, but it is opposed to misery, signifies freedom from misery, is attained through the avoidance of misery or effective resistance to misery. So with the other values. Truth is realized through the clearance of error; in the very recognition and establishment of truth, error is exposed and discredited. Justice always means fairness, but it is never neutral. It is ever struggling against some injustice, a champion for some right, against entrenched or invading wrongs. Beauty and harmony likewise are steadily or precariously shaping the dull scramble and ugly discord of things into some significant form. These examples may emphasize the issue in appraisal as one of opposition, involving positive and negative value, good against evil. But it is often an issue of preference among available goods or impending evils. The choice may concern relative worth in a hierarchy of values, calling for some prevailing espousal rather than for exclusive approval or utter condemnation. So the Christian gospel did not negate secular attachments altogether, but subordinated them to the spiritual: "He that loveth father and mother more than me is not worthy of me."

History itself has been interpreted as the dramatic struggle of social values. In the words of Berdyaev, "history is a drama which has its acts and logical development, its dénouement and catharsis." [2] Philosophers of history have emphasized the idea of polarity, "the assumption that every force meets with a resistance, a contrary force. . . . Through the great tragedies that history reveals

151

rises the recurrent vision of noble ideals frustrated by the course of actual events."[3] The Christian theologian may follow St. Augustine in reading all history as the sublime contest between the cities of this earth and the City of God. The idealistic philosopher may trace a cosmic rhythm of events through the ages, "one increasing purpose," and witness in the entire course of nature "an ethical Drama."[4] On the opposite side of systematic reflection, the Marxist philosophy of history adopted by the communists interprets the historical process as a struggle of economic interests. Historical epochs are thus regarded as the various stages of the contest for economic dominance. The legal system of each epoch signalizes the interests and values of the prevailing faction in the ceaseless struggle. "All history rests upon antitheses, contrasts, struggles and wars. . . . This drama in all its relations is repeated from community to community, from nation to nation, from state to state."[5] Thus the dialectical materialists of the communist reaction have subverted to their purposes the social conclusions of Hegelian dialectic: "The history of the world is the world's court of judgment."[6] But both materialist and idealist recognize a certain dialectic of alternatives, counteracting in the dramatic issues of impending decision and prevailing outcome.

The term "dramatic" is employed here to indicate the counteraction of alternatives which is so characteristic of the world of values. There is nothing peculiarly original in our use of the dramatic principle in philosophy. Drama has served to express analogically men's estimates of their complex human situation. Is the drama of our lives a tragedy or a comedy? The pessimism of Schopenhauer exposed human life as a tragedy in its essentials but in its ignoble details a comedy. Dante's vision of genius contemplated the world-order and man's life and eternal destiny under God's providence as the Divine Comedy. In our time the Spaniard Miguel de Unamuno advocated a dramatic philosophy in his work, *The Tragic Sense of Life*. William James in a well-known passage portrayed our existence dramatically as a struggle of values: "It *feels* like a real fight, — as if there were something really wild in the universe which we, with all our idealities and faithfulnesses, are needed to redeem."[7] Hartley Burr Alexander wrote a brilliant essay on "Drama as a Cosmic Category." C. Lloyd Morgan contemplated his view of emergent evolution "in dramatic regard."[8] Our discussion in this chapter is intended to reaffirm the significance of including Drama, the dramatic perspective, as one of the principal outlooks on reality which philosophy should consider in its accounts of the world: the dramatic element in the recognition of human experience and its values.

## 2. The Dramatic Principle in the Philosophy of Process

Our earlier discussion of mechanism and teleology in the philosophy of process indicated a fundamental lack or onesidedness in traditional materialism, its failure to recognize a really ongoing and productive character in mental activities. If the entire course of human events to the least detail is regarded as determined by mechanical causation, then responsible and creative activity would seem to lose meaning. The critics of this stereotyped view of nature have urged the need of acknowledging a cosmic principle of purpose as preëminently operative in mental life and as manifested in lesser degrees or as latent also at some, not all, levels of existence. This has been the demand for finalism, for the recognition of teleology as a pattern of nature or type of explanation. In classical antiquity this principle was included in Aristotle's cosmology, in his doctrine of final causes or purposive determination.

But finalism in its turn has often tended towards an opposite variety of rigid determinism, leaving moral responsibility and creative significant activity as ambiguous as in the mechanistic cosmology. We noted Bergson's resistance to this error in his *Creative Evolution* and should again call attention to it. The traditional teleologist, especially when pursuing the theological line, has tended to interpret the purposiveness in nature and human nature as God's eternal design, of which all history, human and cosmic, is simply the detailed execution. Though the fatalistic tenor of this way of thought has been resisted, it has also been openly avowed, as in the Mohammedan dictum that all our words are written in the book of Allah. Mechanistic determinism and divine predestination thus suffer from the same defect. They do not conceive of any really productive achievement in the world. For both of them the universe would seem to be a foregone conclusion all the way through. In such a world-outlook neither scientist nor theologian could recognize a truly dramatic issue in human life, a real contest of alternatives, with a genuine choice in prospect, or actively decisive significance and personal responsibility.

This problem of basic interpretation in cosmology has been considered by a number of modern philosophers. It is involved in the interpretation of activism, and so it has seemed appropriate here to examine its treatment by the outstanding philosopher of process, Whitehead. Our brief discussion cannot pretend to comprehend even in outline Whitehead's entire complex system. We shall try to indicate the dramatic aspects of teleology and value as they are expressed in his activism. It will be our aim to report his ideas as plainly as we can. As readers of his works know, Whitehead's exposition is often clarified by brilliant statements, but it is also clouded by abstruse terms which sometimes require a paraphrase into simpler speech.

Whitehead's cosmological theory is a fundamentl activism. In place of the traditional view of the world as a system of substances, bodily or mental, he emphasizes a dynamical world-outlook. "The reality is the process." And he tends to give his activism a dramatic version. He describes nature as "a theatre for the inter-relations of activities." But he is clearly aware that the view of nature as a system of activities does not disclose offhand its dramatic involvement as a choice between alternative values. So Whitehead asks: the world process is "activity for what, producing what, . . . involving what?" [9]

Whitehead's approach to these questions is from the naturalistic end. He calls his theory "organic mechanism." The noun, mechanism, is intended here to reaffirm his loyalty to the truth of the physical scientific conception of nature. But the adjective, organic, as he uses it, expresses a demand for the needed revision of the scientific truth, to clear it of errors due to onesidedness and over-simplification. Whitehead tells us that "science has always suffered from the vice of overstatement," and that overstatement is also "the chief error in philosophy." [10] Overstatement gives rise to unwarranted dichotomies which rend the seamless garment of nature. If we are to do justice to the basic character of reality as ongoing productive process, we must reject the traditional rigid dualism of mechanism and teleology. This dualism is artificial. Causal mechanism and purposiveness are not incompatible categories; they do not indicate an ultimate cosmic cleavage. Our mechanism can be and should be thoroughly organic. In our cosmology, causality and teleology should manifest two aspects of nature characteristic of the entire span of existence, though in different perspectives we sometimes recognize the special relevance of one and sometimes of the other.

Whitehead clarifies his view by pointing out two other central ideas. We must distinguish but also correlate the idea of sheer matter-of-fact and the idea of importance. Things are presented to us in their factual existence. We trace events to their causal antecedents and to their eventual effects. But we also consider things and processes in a perspective which reveals their dramatic character. We recognize in them a certain involvement in an ongoing and significant activity in which they play their respective roles. In this integral involvement an event discloses not merely its cause and its effect but also its living character, its cosmic roots and its unique fruitage. We recognize it as somehow important. "Have a care," it seems to say to us, "here is something that matters!" [11]

In the basic recognition of the characteristic role and importance of an event, teleology and value gain clear expression. The aspect of importance is thoroughly teleological: importance for what, to what end or purpose? The reintroduction of the category of final causation into cosmology is thus essential to thorough understanding, especially of human activities. "The ultimate motive power, alike in science, in morality and in religion, is the sense of value, the sense of importance." [12]

At this point we may note a crossroad of procedure, and here Whitehead refuses to take the traditional turn with the methodologists of physical science. The usual course of interpretation is familiar to us all. Functional activity at the lower levels of existence has been explained throughout in causal-mechanistic terms. This, of course, has been the suitable procedure in dealing with physical events, to emphasize or rather to treat exclusively their matter-of-fact aspect rather than their aspect of importance. But then, with what Whitehead calls "a colossal example of anti-empirical dogmatism arising from a successful methodology" [13] self-proclaimed scientific philosophers have insisted on applying their exclusively causal-mechanistic interpretation to biological and psychological processes. They have explained away or have ignored those data of our experience which do not fit readily within their schemes of matter-of-fact existence.

Thus we note that most physiologists reject any explanation in terms of purposive order, lest their physiology depart in the least degree from the model science, physics. This sort of reductionism, with its insistence on recognizing in the higher levels of existence only those aspects which are shared with the lower processes of nature, has been carried to great lengths. Elaborate experiments have been devised for the definite purpose of proving that the explanation of biological and mental operations rules out any reference to purposes. As Whitehead remarks with ironical reflection, "scientists animated by the purpose of proving that they are purposeless constitute an interesting subject for study." [14]

It should be clear that this sort of procedure cannot qualify as really scientific philosophy. The truly scientific, that is the knowledge-yielding account of nature in any field of experience is one that does not fail to consider the distinctive features of that field which are presented in that experience. We do not get a good scientific physiology by explaining biological processes exclusively according to the laws of mechanics and ruling out whatever does not fit in that mechanistic framework. We do not get a scientific psychology by treating mental activity simply as the behavior of the bodily organism.

Now we may see clearly Whitehead's turn at the crossroads of methodology to which we referred. Instead of trying to force our account of the higher processes of nature into the mechanistic framework of physics, he insists that we should recognize our distinct task of interpreting the purposive and significant elements of our mental life. As we do this, we may be able to explore the further reaches of teleology and value. We may trace their roots into the nature of things, deeper than is commonly supposed. Here Whitehead advocates a reversal of the traditional scientific procedure. In dealing with the various levels of existence, he urges us, "why construe the later forms by analogy to the earlier forms? Why not reverse the process?" [15] This challenging question recalls the idealistic emphasis on respecting the principle of the oak-in-the-acorn. The course of nature, then, is not a mere sequence or a chain of events. It is a system of processes unfolding a significant action throughout. Teleology and value may thus be involved in the very texture and plot of nature.

The term "organic," as Whitehead uses it, is not strictly biological in intension. It has rather the connotation of integrity. So his cosmology of "organic mechanism" would express the expansion of thought from specialized scientific investigations to a more thorough and comprehensive interpretation of nature and human nature. As we advance from the tracing of various causal linkages to a more cosmic outlook and insight, we cannot avoid thinking about the nature and the implications of thought, about significant moral activity, about the purposive, evaluative, creative processes without which science itself would be unthinkable.

The reader of Whitehead's persuasive exposition needs a warning here. In exposing the narrowness of mechanical reductionism, we are scarcely warranted in proposing to replace it by an overall teleology which would exhibit purposiveness in every process of nature. We should agree that there is a mechanical-causal aspect of every event available for scientific study; for surely there is some physiological and physical medium even for the most purely theoretical reflection. But while the physiological aspect cannot be ignored in considering the visual perceptions of a color-blind person, it may be of minimal relevance in the case of mathematical or metaphysical contemplation.

As we thus note a relative or graduated scale of significance in the use of mechanistic explanation, can we likewise maintain a corresponding application of teleology in different degrees, across the entire span of nature? Whitehead ventures an affirmative answer to this question: there is a "creative urge of the universe as it functions in each single individual occasion." [16] Would this signify the appropriateness of recognizing some specific teleology in every process of nature? It certainly implies a somewhat dramatic element of creativity as well as factual determinateness in each process.

The expression "dramatic" suits Whitehead's world-view. In his *Science and the Modern World* he traces the cosmic import of the classical idea of drama or action. For the Greeks, "nature was a drama in which each thing played its part." The term "drama" meant action, and every thing, by its way of acting, expressed to the classical mind its own peculiar strain in the world-wide ongoing course of existence. On the vast amphitheater of nature, all things enacted their respective roles, heroic or inconsiderable. This dramatic world-view has persisted but has also been transformed in the history of ideas. We may note a redistribution of emphasis in the connotation of the principle of necessity. The

157

Greek *Moira* and *Nemesis* had an unmistakably dramatic character. They could be characters in a tragedy, chief *Dramatis Personae* in the cosmos. Our modern causal necessity is impersonal by comparison. In Whitehead's words, "Fate in Greek tragedy becomes the order of nature in modern thought." But this turn from cosmic drama to causal nexus in our scientific view does not imply that the modern mind has become entirely unresponsive to the dramatic outlook. Against the factual neutrality of physical nature, the tragic involvements of human lives engross modern minds as they engrossed classical antiquity: with a difference which Whitehead points out. "The ancient world takes its stand upon the drama of the Universe, the modern mind upon the inward drama of the Soul." [17]

We may review in brief statement the reinterpretation of teleology and value in Whitehead's activism. As he writes in *Process and Reality,* "one task of a sound metaphysics is to exhibit final and efficient causes in their proper relation to each other." [18] Actual existence in each case is "a matter of fact," but it is also "something that matters." Now we ask: is it something that matters in each case, simply, or in each case only in certain contexts? Whitehead's view seems inclined to the first position, but at any rate it warrants the second. In alluding to the importance and value of any activity, we find beyond the mechanistic framework a certain dramatic perspective. Our philosophy should thus recognize purposiveness and value, not as designs divinely imposed on the course of existence, but as phases ingrained and rooted in the very structure and organism of nature, as basic characteristics of reality as process.

## 3. The Development of Personality: the Problem of the Self

In considering the problem of the self, the first question which might be raised is, why should the self be a problem? If there is anything directly obvious and familiar to us, it is ourselves. But this familiarity becomes unsettled when we try to clarify our meaning. We are reminded of a passage in St. Augustine's *Confessions* where he considers the problem of time. "What is time?" he says. "If no one asks of me, I know; if I wish to explain it to him who asks, I know not." [19] We appreciate the need and also the difficulty of philosophical inquiry when we undertake to grasp in definite statement our ideas of numerous commonplaces in our experience: causal relation, identity and change, unity and plurality, perception and voluntary action — all of which are involved directly or indirectly in our problem of the self. We cannot presume to settle and dispose of them all in our brief discussion, but may we not hope at least to clear up some moot points?

The traditional inquiry into the nature of the self raises the question of the relation of the soul to the body. This problem, as it is spread across the history of thought mainly in terms of the philosophy of substances, was examined in our first chapter. The inadequacy, in various ways, of its main proposed solutions was a factor in turning modern critical reflection, as in Leibniz, from substantialism towards a philosophy of process. We may also note that the true interpretation of the self requires the recognition of its complex character which precludes any abstract oversimplified reductionism. The self has rightly been called a microcosm. Like the complex system of processes which we call nature, the self has a bodily and a mental phase. These two aspects should be neither confused nor separated. We should both distinguish and relate them.

Good philosophy requires the recognition of the various basic perspectives; it must also aim at some significant integration of them. But this integration cannot be achieved through the replacement of one major aspect by another. Sound integration of the various phases or perspectives of reality demands respect for the postulates or abstractions appropriate to each distinguishable systematic standpoint. In our cosmology we should avoid abstract reductionism in any direction. Failure to respect this principle accounts for some of the defects, in different ways, of both materialistic behaviorism and mentalism or panpsychism. The capacity of the self to perceive and to act volutarily in a bodily medium is an indisputable fact of direct experience. But this fact does not warrant the inference that our perceptions and voluntary actions, the contemplation and execution of our purposes, can be understood as merely bodily-physiological processes. Just as little, however, are we justified in inferring that our individual bodily cells feel and think, from the fact that feeling and thinking are our mental activities as persons.

We may recall here in very brief review some of the general

conclusions of our earlier examination of the problem of mind and body. The various forms of both materialism and mentalism, for opposite reasons, fail to explain the relation of the self's activities to bodily processes. Materialism cannot comprehend or recognize the meanings and the values of the self or personality. Mentalism does not express convincingly the physical and physiological accounts of the mechanics of nature in which the self is active.

A third major theory of the mind-body relation, causal interactionism, proceeds from a dualistic cosmology of bodily and mental substances and sharply discriminates their basic characteristics. But then it undertakes to apply the category of physical causality to explain their interaction. Thus interactionism alternates between a materialistic and psychical view of mind. On the theory of a strict dualism of substances, any causal interaction of mind and body, any perception or voluntary action, would appear to be a baffling puzzle. When a physiologist observes his bodily processes and concludes that he has caught a certain infection, is that conclusion itself merely a physiological causal effect? If the answer is affirmative, we have a variety of materialism. But if it is negative, then we cannot avoid our problem by being ambiguous about causal interaction. A bodily process cannot produce a conclusion, cannot be the cause of an idea unless the idea itself is regarded as another bodily process. And an idea cannot be the cause of a bodily action because, strictly speaking, an idea cannot be cause or the effect of anything. Surely we do not regard a conclusion as the causal effect of its premises. And if we state that by causal interaction we mean some other sort of basic connection, then we should recognize that we are proceeding towards another sort of theory.

We are in fact being led to some form of parallelism, the doctrine that material and mental processes stand in some relation of mutual correspondence. But the interpretation of this correspondence requires great caution. Our mental activities do have certain physiological correlates. But can we maintain the converse proposition that every physical process, in galaxies and supergalaxies of boundless space, has its parallel in some mental activity? As was pointed out in our first chapter, psychophysical parallelism requires an important revision. While recognizing a correspondence of mental and physiological processes in broad terms, we need not regard this correlation as coextensive in detail and in both directions. The physical and the mental phases of nature should be related but they should also be distinguished, as two cosmic perspectives. In some contexts the former phase, in other contexts the latter, should be recognized as the more relevant for our interpretation. Philosophy should aim at a synthesis which does justice to the complexity of nature.

It should also be clear that this view of the relation of selves and bodies proceeds from a cosmology of activism, not of substantialism. Both body and mind must be regarded, not as substances or as fragments of reality, but as complexes of events, as processes and activities in the boundless dynamic system of nature.

This approach to our problem, through the distinction and correlation of aspects, enables us also to recognize the characteristic activity of selves in their concern with values. Values are manifested in some personal context. Consider anything in a personal reference, in some relation to some self, and it will manifest value of some sort. The characteristic activity of selves is in the recognition, the pursuit, and the achievement or frustration of meanings and values. In general but essential statement, this may serve as our description of the self and of the ways in which it manifests the nature of reality. It would be a mistake, then, to question the reality of values because they are manifested only in personal experience or reference; but it would also be an error to look for values in a wholly impersonal perspective. Values are as real as persons and selves. To call values merely personal and so not ultimately real would be as misleading as to call nutrition merely physiological, or electricity merely physical. These are all aspects of nature which we should acknowledge. For nature is all that we experience, our own experience of it included. Reality is infinitely complex; it has neither top nor bottom, and sound philosophy is that which undertakes its exploration without abstract constriction and which seeks to correlate its various aspects in some intelligible system.

We have recognized that the relation of the self to the body involves a correspondence of significant activities and of personal meanings and values to physical-physiological processes. We have also concluded that adequate understanding of the entire life-career of an individual requires a correlation of the many aspects in which it can be interpreted systematically. But we still have to consider more closely the characteristic features of these distinguishable aspects of human beings.

What concerns us at this point of our discussion is the clearer view of our careers as persons. We should not expect to dispose of our problem by any abstract formula. Like all real structures, personality has more than one façade. Indeed it would be unreasonable to expect that the self, the most concrete of all realities known to us, should be qualified adequately in any one set of terms. Formal precise definition involves a high degree of abstraction, and that is not applicable to the self. Royce enlightened us on this point: "*Man* you can define; but the true essence of any man, say, for instance, of Abraham Lincoln, remains the endlessly elusive and mysterious object of the biographer's interest. . . . There is no adequate definition or description of Abraham Lincoln, just in so far as he was the unique individual." [20]

The better we come to know ourselves and others, the more thoroughly we can understand the unique and inexhaustible character which nature manifests in every person. So, continually seeking to comprehend the self in some formal definition, we are continually realizing the inadequacy of our proposed formulas. Our very acute analyses, when applied to concrete selves, while they reveal to us many significant aspects, show us also the limitations of any abstract analysis. Like the sap in the growing tree which is continually cracking the rigid bark, so the living reality of the self flows through our conceptual meshes.

At this point we should beware lest our concrete self, transcending abstract description, become in our view of it a mystical nondescript. In acknowledging the unique and indescribable core of personality we are not justified in abandoning all abstractions and proceeding to lyrical mysticism. We still must continue to use definite exploration and analysis as far as they can take us, for that is the way to knowledge in detail. So we may come to see more clearly one side or another side of the self, and that is all a gain. But while we are thus accumulating knowledge, we should not be failing in wisdom if we retain our dominant conviction of the living outpouring personal activity, ever expansive and new and yet unambiguously itself throughout all changes, the unique creative identity of a person's career.

You can test this view of the self concretely in your own experience. What do you really mean when you speak of yourself?

Are you a certain kind of being, a classifiable sort of universal, or are you an irreducible individual, not to be comprehended at all in any terms? Is it not the truth that you are continually and in some respect the former, and always finally the latter? Unique individuality is bound to manifest itself in this or in that manner, and in fact our study of the self is likely to be an inspection of some phase or other of its activity and character. So in dealing with any person we must approach him in some context or relation. In that context or relation he is understandably describable in some terms relevant to the aspect which is considered, be it political, economic, domestic, intellectual, aesthetic, and so forth. But our respective description is always partial and tentative; we are bound to see that it does not do full justice; the formula does not quite fit. We have gained some knowledge of our neighbor or of our customer; but still we lack the complete insight. We cannot set our statement as final and say: he is that and nothing but that. This rigid phrase, "nothing but that," shows its futility unmistakably when we try to apply it to a self. For our abstract definition of any aspect of a person would have to be subjected to a great and unspecified variety of revisions in order to apply adequately to the unique individuality which marks personal life. We may get some knowledge of the citizen or public official, the parent or child, the scholar or technician, but the living self pervades and exceeds and continually transforms these and all other partial definable aspects.

So here we should try to steer between two misleading extremes. The first, which has only been mentioned, is the error of vague mysticism. It rejects any degree of analysis or description or knowledge of the self. The second extreme, which we have been discussing, is the error of confusing our partial definitions of a person, in his various relations, with a thorough and exhaustive insight into the unique character of personality.

The lapse into the former error, that is, the failure to realize that a person is, in various respects, a certain kind of person and in those respects definable, perplexes the social relations of selves and confuses our expectations of each other. In each specific social relation a person is a certain kind of person to me, with whom I may have certain dealings but not others. While even here an abstract filing system of personal rights and expectations would scarcely suffice, we do perceive that within certain limits persons are classifiable. The statistical methods of psychologists and sociologists illustrate this approach to the study of persons, and it has great merits. Classifications and statistics have their merits, however, only so long as they do not lapse into the error of confusing the label with the living self. For is not this the deadly insult to a person, to regard or treat him merely as an abstract universal, as of a certain sort and nothing but that? That was the devil's view when Mephistopheles saw in Marguerite only the type of the seduced maiden, and dismissed her with his statistical report: "She is not the first one." William James's humane insight would not allow him to ignore the individuality even of a crab. We may define it as a crustacean, but James heard it protest: "I am no such thing! . . . I am *Myself, Myself* alone!" [21]

Individuality, identity, unity, all these characteristics of personality can be understood best in a dramatic perspective. We should remember that the Latin term *persona* signified the mask which an actor wore on the stage and through which the sound of his voice came to the audience, *per-sona*. In any specific relation a person is enacting a certain role. We know him in his part, but we recognize himself also, in his unique way of playing his various roles. He is Othello or Iago or Hamlet, but in each of these and beyond them all he is Henry Irving throughout. A person's career is a unity of diversities; in a variety of roles it manifests a unique achievement of character. It is dramatic in its tensions and in its continual development.

The uniqueness of a person does not signify merely that it is never quite duplicated. Any grain of sand is in a certain sense induplicable. We are told that no two identical leaves exist. But this sort of individual uniqueness is not the major aspect essential to our understanding of leaves. Botanists distinguish the various kinds of leaves, and they are thus definable as classes, and so in general is the structure and the function of a leaf. But in dealing with selves, while in each aspect or variety of relations some general definition may be available, what finally concerns us is the central characteristic of persons, that they comprehend and also transcend our formulas. More clearly than any other form of reality which we may consider, our understanding of a self demands our recognition of his dramatic self-manifestation, individual in and beyond his many roles, uniquely comprehending a variety of perspectives.

## 4. *The Creative Intelligence of Genius in Poetry and in Science*

The character of the self can be surmised even in its lowliest manifestations, in primitive life and in the experiences of the simplest folk. But it reveals its full range of capacity and achievement in the creative intelligence of genius. Without proposing here any formal and strict definition of genius, we may be justified in using the term to describe mental activity in its consummate plenitude and integrity. Genius in any field of experience is mind realizing its full range and summit: unique, creative, and thoroughly self-expressive. Unusually productive mental activity often seems to reach towards these heights of spiritual power. What distinguishes the mind of genius is an immensely greater and far steadier maintenance of altitude.

In my work, *The Ways of Genius,* I have endeavored to investigate in some detail the processes of creative mental activity: in the fine arts and especially in poetry and drama, in scientific thought and technical invention, in moral and social outlook, in philosophical insight and in religious vision. I began my inquiries without any definite preconceptions except that at first I shared the common tendency to distinguish sharply the free drive of the creative imagination in poetry and the fine arts from the rigorous intellectual activity in experimental and theoretical science. But I was gradually led to recognize certain revealing analogies of scientific and poetic genius. We may consider here briefly both the differences and the similarities in these two fields of mental activity.

The traditional distinction of scientific reason from the poetic imagination is significant and important. The scientist differs from the poet both in his methods and in his basic purpose. His aim is to understand nature: to formulate his knowledge of it demonstrably and systematically. Facts are to him evidences of some pattern or order, which he seeks to express in adequate theory and from which he draws inferences. The validity of these inferences he then tests by further experimental or logical inquiries. Scientific thought therefore emphasizes logical validity and coherence; it demands clarity and precision of statement; it uses words to report objectively its findings, the facts investigated, their relations, meanings, and implications.

Quite different is the poetic activity or the poet's purpose in

165

his use of ideas and words. A poem is not a proposed report of any facts or a description or explanation of anything beyond itself. It is an act of self-expression; it expresses itself. To be sure, it also has its data, its germinal idea or mood that aroused the poetic activity. But a poem is not a solution of the problem which its germinal idea or mood presented to the mind, nor a descriptive or explanatory analysis of them. The poet aims rather to possess his ideas and moods in the fullest possible expression. In the composition of a poem the creative imagination seeks to bring a mood or an idea to perfect fruition, contemplating them in some original setting, giving them freshness and intensity of living utterance. The poetic activity is the consummate expression of an experience, not the conclusive explanation of it.

This difference in the basic purpose of the poet and of the scientist may be noted also in their use of words. To the scientist, the words of daily discourse, like his technical symbols, are meant to convey certain definite meanings. In using them, he prizes accuracy and consistency of definition. But the poet's words are not terms, and they are not really definable. They may be in the dictionary, but not quite as he uses them in his poem. Vagueness or inconsistency in the use of words must be plainly admitted as a defect in a scientific statement. But such a charge would need much reconsideration when dealing with a poem. To be sure, a good poet is bound to respect the language which he uses, for it is his instrument and the condition of his being understood. Without it he could not share his experiences with his readers. But words are not to him molds of precise and fixed signification. They are no more set and established than he is himself, or his moods and ideas. He uses them to reveal new facets of meaning and moving power, in fresh glint and fusion. The old words come to new life in his poems. Thus unique and induplicable as he uses them, the poet's words do not have a strictly definite dictionary meaning. Their real significance is in the poet's lines. The direct perception of this significance by a sensitively responsive reader is one of the rare joys in reading great poetry.

The phrase "great poetry" should remind us of the wide disparity in mental powers and rank of poets, and likewise of scientists. Between Shakespeare and the usual versifiers the difference is surely as vital as between Newton and the routine labo-

166

ratory worker. If we may at this point anticipate our conclusion, we should state that alike in poetic and in scientific activity genius is marked by supreme manifestation of creative power of the integrative contemplation. This is shown characteristically by the capacity of genius to "glance from earth to heaven," as Shakespeare says, to perceive and express original kinships and analogies.

The presence and the absence of this decisive power were pointed out by Coleridge in his *Biographia Literaria* and by Wordsworth in the Preface to his *Lyrical Ballads*. Wordsworth especially distinguished Imagination from Fancy. In both of these poetic processes the mind evokes and expresses images and thoughts. But Fancy is engaged in the apt selection and assemblage of imagery; it "depends upon the rapidity and profusion with which she scatters her thoughts and images." [22] Fancy excels in the variety of its particular, delightful impressions; it leads the reader's mind from one enchanting detail to another. The poetic creative Imagination is another sort of power. It integrates its materials into a living and convincing unity. It reaches out across the whole span or abyss of experience to reveal unsuspected kinships, expressing a universal order and harmony of being. So we are reminded of the tragic outcry of Lear to callous Nature:

> I tax not you, you elements, with unkindness;
> I never gave you kingdom, called you children! [23]

The Imagination is not concerned with detailed, fanciful comparisons. A true imaginative utterance, as Wordsworth again writes, "grows — and continues to grow — upon the mind; the resemblance depending . . . less upon casual and outstanding, than upon inherent and internal, properties." [24] In our day Benedetto Croce made a similar comparison between the merely fanciful *immaginazione* and the creative and integrating imaginative power of *fantasia*, "the peculiarly artistic faculty." [25]

This distinction recalls a famous passage in Aristotle's *Poetics*: "The greatest thing by far is to be a master of metaphor. It is the one thing that cannot be learnt from others; and it is also a sign of genius, since a good metaphor implies an intuitive perception of similarity in dissimilars." [26] It is significant to note that these words have been quoted to describe the creative activity of genius, not only in poetry but also in scientific theory and in technical invention.

In scientific work we may trace a distinction analogous to that just noted in poetry between fancy and creative imagination. Science aims to achieve a systematic understanding of nature. This understanding includes the discovery of many particular facts and the ascertainment of numerous specific causal connections. The observation and the experimental testing of all these details occupy multitudes of scientists engaged in special research. These men have been called the "accumulators," and certainly the importance of their work should not be depreciated. But many of these special experts put a premium on detailed investigation and show no great capacity for or even interest in pursuing the larger patterns of understanding and scientific theory. In the field of scientific activity the work of these men corresponds to the accomplishments of fancy in poetry.

But in intellectual as in poetic construction the mind of genius manifests deeper insight and a more expansive view. These are the creative achievements of scientific theory. Beyond the accumulation of specific observations or the experimental ascertainment of particular causal connections, the great scientist seeks to grasp some cosmic pattern and to express the fundamental principles of order which bind together his entire field of study in a rational interpretation. In reaching towards his theoretical explanatory pattern, the scientific genius may often leap ahead of his specific evidence. But it is the gift and merit of genius that it knows how to leap in the right direction. Newton and Pasteur have stated the two parts in the true description of this achievement. Said Newton: "No great discovery was ever made without a bold guess." But, as Pasteur added, "chance only favors invention for minds that are prepared for discoveries by patient study and persevering efforts." [27] The so-called guess of hypothetical venture is one warranted by the evidence, but not directly provided by it. The genius in scientific theory brings to his specific data a mind stored with a rich treasure of complex and manifold evidence. Much of this evidence may seem, may only seem, unrelated to the facts now investigated. The mind of genius in exploring numerous channels of explanation is fertile in suggesting and tentatively contemplating various theoretical patterns. As Poincaré tells us, a great deal of this tentative sampling of fundamental principles is below the level of clear consciousness. But in the subconscious sorting of alternative ideas there is an activity similar to the creative imagination of the poet or the artist. He calls it "a feeling of mathematical beauty," [28] which enables the mind to select the most suitable and harmonious interpretation.

In framing his explanatory hypothesis the scientific genius seeks a contemplative grasp of his facts which relates them to the rest of nature; but he also recognizes their special characteristics. The mind searches for the link of kinship that both connects and distinguishes. Random surmises of comparison are of little avail here. It is the gift of genius to sift through an assortment of routine analogies so as to choose the one most appropriate and convincing. This is a sort of intellectual metaphor. It suddenly clarifies, in a theoretical pattern, the relation of a specific complex body of facts and processes to the larger cosmic order. If we may repeat Aristotle's words, it is, "an intuitive perception of similarity in dissimilars." The history of science records many of these metaphorical leaps in theoretical explanation. Here is Newton glancing from the fall of an apple in his garden to see its kinship to the courses of the stars in their orbits. Here is Darwin turning from Malthus's account of the limitation of population growth by the insufficient means of subsistence, to frame his own evolutionary theory of the survival of the fittest in the struggle for existence.

Intellectual mastery depends upon this power of theoretical synthesis. As Poincaré said: "Science is built up with facts as a house is with stones. But a collection of facts is no more a science than a heap of stones is a house." [29] The mind of genius brings to its scientific study of nature all its creative powers of understanding and expression, even as it brings them to its full poetic savor and expression of experience. We should go astray if we confused these two types of mental activity, but also if we divorced them. Like radii in the circle of intelligence, they show their differences along the periphery, but manifest also their kinship as they reach towards the center and summit of genius. The analogies which creative intelligence manifests in scientific and in poetic activity give us a revealing perspective of the spiritual aspect of reality.

## 5. *Tragedy and Comedy: the Pendulum of Dramatic Art*

The ultimate implications of Drama naturally point towards some form of philosophical activism. The plays on the Athenian stage were artistic reënactments of the old myths, in which the genius of Greek folklore expressed its dramatic view of life as an interplay and a struggle of contending roles, human and divine. The Greek anthropomorphic imagination personalized the counterplay of values even as it personalized, in its pantheon and mythology, the aspects and forces of nature and the various cosmic agencies.

Philosophical reflection outgrew mythology and anthropomorphism, but it was confronted in its turn by the problems which have never ceased to engross artistic, moral, and religious insight. These problems are of perennial interest for philosophy. The visions of poets and saints are themselves experiences which the philosopher must understand and integrate with the rest of his account of reality. A thorough philosophy must be one which comprehends poetry and religion as adequately as it comprehends the physical sciences. The philosophers and the dramatic poets of the classical Athenian period reveal and challenge each other. Matthew Arnold described the philosophic mind in a line about the dramatist Sophocles who "saw life steadily and saw it whole."

It has been said that poetic genius, as it reaches its greatest achievements, strikes the tragic note. For tragedy expresses most emphatically the struggle of values in which men's lives are embroiled. We have recognized that values are manifested in any situation or process when seen in a personal perspective, where desires or beliefs or ideals or wills are involved. Tragedy arises when a certain thought and temper are brought to bear on certain conditions and events. The crisis that eventuates may be a struggle of man's will with "something really wild in the universe," [30] or a clash with other wills that cross it, or it may be a tension in one's own thought and will, a personality self-rending in the tug of counter motives.

The ground note of tragedy has variable overtones in the different epochs of culture and in their respective dramas. While we should be wary of overstressing these differences, we should recognize the changing directions of emphasis. Greek tragedy portrayed the conflict between a will heroic but faulty in some

170

important respect, and the cosmic order of necessity or august right, Nemesis with her inevitable doom. The words of Aeschylus may be taken as almost the text of Greek tragedy: "The doer shall suffer." Modern tragedy has emphasized the crises in character itself, the wrenching of the will's career by callous circumstance, where one's purposes are flouted by one's desires, or spurned by a dull or hostile society. In all these cases tragedy has expressed the essentially dramatic character of value as a counteraction of alternatives, but it has expressed it in dark speech that leaves us baffled and dismayed.

The question has been raised if "real drama, whether in prose or verse, is not to be called poetry." [31] The apt medium of prose is some variety of reporting, narrative or expository. But drama shares with lyric poetry the quality of poetic utterance, the direct self-expression of experience, not a description or an explanation of it but utterance to the utmost. While a drama raises problems which demand a solution, and while it stimulates theories in our philosophy of life, it is not a proposed solution or a theory or a philosophy of life but the poetic self-revelation of ourselves and the issues in which we are embroiled. Indeed, whoever can interpret fully and truly the utterance of dramatic genius through the ages will perhaps give us the great words of a philosophy of life. Our discussion here can make no claim to fullness of interpretation, but we may raise several important points of inquiry.

Tragedy is man's most intense and insistent self-expression. In trying to understand the essence of the tragic principle in experience, we are bound to start with Aristotle's classical statement, but it will serve us only as a starting point. A good tragic plot, as Aristotle held, is one that involves "a man not preëminently virtuous and just, whose misfortune, however, is brought upon him not by vice and depravity but by some error of judgment." [32] This "error of judgment," this wrong choice and eventually ruinous action may seem to constitute in many cases, and perhaps usually, a moral downfall. But we do not sound the depths of tragedy if we reduce the tragic issue to the alternatives of explicit good and evil, nor if we confuse the tragic ruin with external disaster of whatever sort, defeat or suffering or death.

The essence of tragedy is not only, and perhaps not so much, in the moral misdirection of the will, as in the grim disclosure

**171**

of seemingly insoluble tensions in the moral scale itself. It is not merely that the tragic hero has done wrong, has gone wrong. The right way itself is not clear, and man is at the crossroad of alternative direful decisions. Whichever way he acts, or does not act, he is smitten with guilt. From Aeschylus and Sophocles to Shakespeare this seeming chaos of man's spiritual career dismays the tragic poet. Shall we call this the tragedy of conflicting duties, or the morally devastating quandary in the basic principle of duty and moral character? Antigone is crushed between the upper and the nether millstones of social obligations: "What law of heaven have I transgressed? . . . What ally should I invoke?"[33] Is there any real right, when one seems hopelessly hedged between counter wrongs? So Orestes has to choose between filial impiety in not avenging his father's murder—and, in avenging it, being stained with the guilt of matricide. "The divine law bids and forbids at the same time."[34] Hamlet similarly is torn between the decisions to act and not to act, both dire. His outcry expresses the tragical quandary of values:

> The time is out of joint;—O cursed spite,
> That ever I was born to set it right![35]

Even more devastating morally seems to be the tragedy of the self-undoing of virtue itself. Here is Euripides's pure Hippolytus, dedicated to his chaste goddess Artemis, resisting the morbidly passionate attachment of his stepmother Phedra. But his clean disdain of the lures of Aphrodite exacts its retribution and lays him low. So Shakespeare's Cordelia is the victim of her very virtues of integrity and candor. They earn her only her father's rancor and finally lead to her ruin as well as to Lear's.

In less dramatic ways this tragic dismay is often our common lot. Repeatedly we find ourselves in situations where if we tell the truth we are bound to hurt someone, and if we are not to hurt, we must perforce lie, or at any rate stain our own moral integrity by evasion and misdirection. We may either offend others by following our own convictions, or avoid giving offense, by some form of hypocrisy. This seeming instability of values in our unavoidable choice between alternatives is appalling morally. At this point one may seek refuge from pessimistic despair in the conviction of perplexity itself. Shelley held that even crime in Greek tragedy

172

was "disarmed of half its horror and all its contagion by being represented as the fatal consequence of the unfathomable agencies of nature." [36]

Can we say that tragedy, to remain tragic, must, of course, resist any easily pious or morally serene or complacent assurance; but that it must also not collapse in final negation? Tragedy expresses a morally baffling but not an utterly despairing view of life. Whether it concerns man's issues with men or women, or man's gage with fate, or his destiny with God, it discloses unsounded depths of cosmic involvement that leave our moral judgment reeling in dismay, but still not sunk in stark denial. The tragic view of life disillusions us about any clearcut and final tabulation of the moral scale of values or any ready solution of the moral problem. But the tragic view itself, the fact that it is tragic, rules out any moral nihilism. Ultimate pessimism is self-refuting. If our life were utterly depraved and chaotic, we should never be aware of its worthlessness. There is at least thus much consolation in the tragic sense of life.

In the dramatic gamut there are no pointer readings of neutral uncommitment. The pendulum sweeps the range to the right or to the left. From baffled dismay it may swing in genial or ironic mirth: from wail to laughter. The comic spirit of lenience, or relief, or buoyant self-maintenance, is even harder to comprehend in formal analysis than the tragic outlook on life. Its roots of motivation are as numerous as its ramified expressions, and the abstractions proposed to explain it provide at best only partial descriptions of some of its aspects. Horace Walpole's epigram comes to mind as a ready example: "The world is a comedy to those who think, a tragedy to those who feel." Alongside of this, consider Émile Faguet's two efforts at definition. After citing Walpole without naming him, he ventures to give his own revision: "The world is a comedy for the wicked, and a tragedy for the altruist." [37] But on his next page he takes another line: the same events and situations in life may be tragic or comic, depending upon the eventual consequences, whether they are terrible or of slight import. We are reminded of Whitehead's principle of importance. Our dramatic evaluation of an experience depends upon our judgment of how much it matters. These three statements have been cited because in the exploration of them we may recognize their respective limitations but also their expression of some significant phases of life in comical regard. So they will serve us well in our progressive understanding.

Faguet's first counter-epigram to Walpole's would mislead us as a definition, but if it does, we should be misled into some good company. For while the tragic note of life is not in the angelic choir, yet it is somehow on the side of the angels. We do speak of divine despair and tragic love: "The pity of it!" [38] But here we are told that the comic note is in an impish key; unlike tragedy which weeps for men and with men, comedy laughs at them:

What fools these mortals be! [39]

This view of comedy emphasizes its satirical aspect; it bespeaks the derision of the misanthrope: deriding, laughing down. Note its presumed superiority and its scornful mirth. Thomas Hobbes ascribed the comic mood to contemptuous "self-gloriation": "To see another fall, is disposition to laugh." [40] This sort of comic reaction cannot be gainsaid, but we may disavow it as discreditable. It is a fact that we laugh at the defects and clumsy mishaps of others. While the ridicule of a blind man's groping would be sure to arouse indignation, lesser defects have been ready occasions for vulgar amusement. The hunchback and the stammerer have been traditionally comic characters.

This sort of laughter may be distinctly malicious. The Germans have even a definite word for it, *Schadenfreude*. But more often it is an inoffensive but irresistible reaction towards the uncouth and defective. Protesting our good will and apologizing, we yet uncontrollably laugh. But we laugh only if it is no mortal matter. At the first sign of a grave mishap our mirth may subside and yield to distress and sympathy. We seem here to be turning towards the distinction between a comic and a tragic outlook as depending upon our judgment of relative importance. Whether malicious or genially humorous, the comic evaluation is depreciative. In comical regard values are laughed down as inconsiderable. They are nothing to weep about, and they are really funny withal!

How do we pass from a tragic to a comic response in our dramatic philosophy of life? Here is the tragedy of Othello, the more tragic because his wife whom he kills in jealous rage is spotless pure in her fidelity to him. But there is the whole gallery of

174

cuckolds in Restoration comedy, the more comical when they are ignorant of their betrayal. We have here clearly a contest of values or a dramatic swing in value perspective. A shifting context of evaluation turns our outlook from misery to mirth. What determines our eventual response? Walpole's epigram, if we take it for more than it probably is, a clever *bon mot*, would seem to trace comedy to reflection and tragedy to emotional mood. This is patently cynical, for it seems to say that if you really think about it, nothing in life is worth a tear. Aside from its cynicism, Walpole's wisdom is shallow in its sharp opposition of thought and feeling. Spinoza made it clear once for all that though we should distinguish these two aspects of our experience, we must not separate them. Every idea has some emotional tone, and precisely in dramatic regard these two are bound to be in active interplay.

Walpole's wit may prepare us for the keener insight of George Meredith, who speaks of high comedy as involving "thoughtful laughter." [41] Unlike rowdy farce, comedy aims its shafts at the head, where not many persons are vulnerable. If we study comedy as we study tragedy, at its highest, we should recognize and explore this thoughtful laughter. There is a comic feeling, but comedy expresses also a certain way of thought. We can only mention the various aspects of experience, the situations, characters, manners which arouse a comical reaction. What sort of value perspective provides a theme for comedy?

Comedy expresses a frustrating aspect in the process of valuation which is not altogether unlike the tragical but is different in tone. We recall the passage, at the close of the dialogue *Symposium*, in which Plato reports Socrates as urging the tragic poet Agathon and the comic poet Aristophanes "to acknowledge that the genius of comedy is the same as that of tragedy." The difference between the two forms of drama seems to be due largely to our different appraisal of the relative importance of the values with which they are concerned. Tragedy and comedy appear to operate at different levels of valuation. The crisis in a situation or character which may be judged as ruinous in tragical regard may in an altered outlook move us to irony or find its relief in disarming humor. Sometimes the borderline between the two reactions may be very slight. We laugh as it were in sheer futility, to avoid weeping. In the more explicitly comical experiences, the unsettlement of values appears more definitely as a basic confusion or

175

incongruity. It involves a sudden demand for our radical and humiliating readjustment in valuation. This is Kant's account of the ludicrous as "an affection arising from a strained expectation being suddenly reduced to nothing." [42]

This comical perception of incongruity may be also a self-exposure of incompetence in value-judgment. We have been convicted of irrelevance and inconsequence. Our reason, suddenly shocked at its confusion, finds its outlet in mirth. In this comic judgment one may be spectator and judge of the discomfiture of others, or one may laugh at one's own absurdity. But the basic reality of values and the final competence of spirit are not utterly negated by this comical disgrace any more than by tragical dismay. Though comedy shows us in our moments of clumsy futility in a topsy-turvy world, our intelligence and wit prevails over its gaucheries, perceives its incongruities, regains its balance, and moves on in gay laughter at itself or at others.

A distinction has been drawn between wit and humor: "Wit is the laughter of the ordinary man or of the intellectual man directed at others abnormal; humor is the laughter of the eccentric directed against himself." [43] But there is also sheer mirth irresistibly responding to a comical sally, even at one's own expense. Thus we are told that at the performance of Aristophanes's *Clouds*, where the opening scene showed Socrates suspended in a basket, the philosopher laughed freely with the audience.

We have noted here some of the occasions for the comic process and also some characteristics of the process itself. Comedy is our humorous perception and correction of our various incongruities. The term "incongruities" may admit of considerable extension to include whatever is unfit or misdirected in valuation: our empty vanities, our pretensions and pretenses, our rigid formalities of office or rank and status, our pedantries and sanctimony, our incompetence and awkwardness and ineptitude of whatever sort.

Bergson in his brilliant essay on *Laughter* proposed to explain comedy as resistance of the living spirit of man to any stiffening of mechanical and formal rigidity. What we demand in ourselves and in others is spiritual alertness; we object to mechanization and to any rigid snobbery and stolidity. Life and personal activity should be supple and resourceful. We do not want them brutalized and mechanized: we laugh that down. If a person is swallowed up in his office or his class or cast, so that mannerisms and ways of speech, uniforms and protocol regulations make him a certain sort rather than a certain one, this mechanizing, this insult to his own personality makes him ridiculous. How can he so far forget *himself*?

Bergson's theory has certain corollaries which may be considered more explicitly. The comical outlook and its expression in laughter have the definite social function of control by reproof. Even when it is not motivated maliciously it is derogatory in intention. This view of the comic spirit as the social censor in snubbing clumsiness or pretense or exorbitance or bigotry has been expressed with mastery by Meredith in the essay which we have cited on the idea of comedy and the uses of the comic spirit. From Lucknow in India the sociologist Radhakamal Mukerjee has maintained a similar interpretation of "laughter as the social gesture in valuation." This view emphasizes the sardonic note in comedy. Laughter is a regulator of social values; in Mukerjee's phrase, it is "the gay, alert constable of the community." [44] Meredith has expressed brilliantly the function of the comic spirit: it perceives the distortions of values in men's speech or manners or conduct, and it smartly nips any undue deviation or stupid disregard of reasonable social observance.

We have traced the pendular swing of dramatic art in its response to the range and the tensions of values. Tragedy and comedy both express a troubled sense of strain or incongruity in the texture of values. Whether we are moved to tragic dismay or to comic irony, in either case we are disabused of any rigid or too formal and confident valuations. Spirit thus stands corrected, but although corrected, it still stands. It does not renounce its problems nor despair of the reality of values. That is the note of prevailing sanity towards which it tends, the *catharsis* of great drama. Be it through the tragic reënactment of terror and pity or through the comical exposure of clumsiness and folly, the mind may be chastened and lifted to a purer and saner outlook on life.

## 6. *Moral Experience as the Drama of Values*

In our discussion so far the moral viewpoint has not been considered explicitly, but it must be clear that many of the conflicting alternatives which we have examined imply decidedly moral issues. The ethical outlook is a dramatic view of a man's life and of man's world. Our deliberation, our unsettled and then confirmed preference, our choice and action — the entire course of moral experience is concerned with alternative values, with rival desires or interests or purposes or ideals.

The moral crisis engages the self in contending directions. A man's eventual course and character are at issue, what he is to become. This complex interplay and reconstruction of personality is the drama of moral experience. Without it, we could hardly see how moral decisions would really matter. The serious view of morality signifies that a contest of real import is involved in each moral choice. The agent's own character and career, the well-being of society, and in more ultimate ramifications the whole system of values are concerned in every moral act. Religion and morality must share this vigilant mindfulness. Of course only a spiritual pedant would make a solemn ritual of his every step and turn, but only a vagrant soul would disavow its implicit duties and responsibilities. In his every moral choice a man may be affirming or denying, redeeming or betraying the higher values.

Moral activity here manifests the creative power of intelligence which is revealed also in poetic and in theoretical achievement. Morality is the field for the dramatic realization of values. In the words of Goethe's mystical heavenly choir,

> The Unattainable
> Here is achieved.[45]

Sociologists have traced some of this contention of ideas in the groping reflections of primitive individual and social experience. Descriptive ethics has traced the roots of morality in the evolution of custom, in two opposite reactions, both of them important. Patterns of conduct have been established by the tribesman's conformity to tradition. But critical moral judgment and the arousal of conscience have been the results of individual resistance to unquestioning submission. The role of taboos in primitive behavior illustrates both of these reactions. Taboos impose traditional prohibitory decisions in various circumstances or issues of daily behavior. But this very imposition tends to discredit itself when experience does not evince the dire consequences of transgression. Exposed as unsound in any one instance, it may be held suspect in others, perhaps in all. The riper judgment of men may then seek new standards in the review of its choice of alternatives. Thus moral advance proceeds from the level of custom to that of conscience.

## The Role of Conscience

The idea of conscience has signified reliable moral insight, a capacity to distinguish between right and wrong and an imperative charge to choose and do the right. Theological tradition has interpreted this moral capacity and demand as the voice of God in our souls. Secular ethics has alternated between two principal interpretations. The intuitionists have regarded the conviction of conscience as a direct imperative endowment of the moral self, a moral sense of an immediate emotional response or an incontestable rational insight. The empiricists, on the opposite, have treated conscience like all other mental responses, as the result of experience, varying with individual circumstances or social conditions and traditions, and subject to revision and recall.

Each of these three types of theories has its merits but is also defective in some respects. The theological doctrine expresses in religious supernatural terms a conviction of which we still need a reliable account in the language of direct human experience. The intuitionist shares with the theologian the moral claim that our recognition of right and wrong is universal and imperative. But both of these theories run against the factual variety of moral judgments, individual and social. The empiricist is more in accord with the historical evolution of morals, but he cannot get beyond variable tastes and habits and customs, to any convincingly fundamental convictions of conscience. We need an interpretation of our moral experience which can reveal the role of conscience in facing the issues of contending alternatives and choosing, and choosing rightly, between them. What takes place in the processes of moral deliberation and eventual choice?

The asking of this question emphasizes the dramatic character of moral activity. The problem of choice always involves an issue beween alternative sides or directions of one's character, conflicting interests or purposes or values. A man finds himself at

179

the crossroad of decision, to become one kind of personality or another kind by the very choice and action in which his deliberation eventuates. The conflict may be one between some fairly established customs or principles and some strong incursions of desires or passions of the moment. Or it may be a contest between duties and principles all of which command his regard and respect, but which cannot be reconciled and between which he has to choose his prevailing loyalty.

This contest and conflict may be important enough to merit careful reflection without involving any decisive gravity. Or it may be a tragic matter of moral life or death, such as those which we considered in the previous section. We noted there the searing of our moral consciousness and judgment by the sense of tragic dismay, by the baffling and seemingly insoluble problems of right choice, and the ruinous suspicion of a final moral chaos. But we also recognized in the very tragic character of this moral quandary and gloom the positive aspect of man's spirit striving towards the light.

Tragic dismay or serene conviction express opposite attitudes of conscience regarding the realization of its characteristic goal. But we should recognize more clearly this goal itself, what conscience aims to acknowledge and to achieve. Its basic character and purpose lead from partial and impulsive towards integral and imperative insight. Conscience is comprehensive knowledge, *con-science*. Its verdict is recognized as imperative just because it is meant to express our best judgment in the contest of values with which we are confronted. In this dramatic situation the loyalty of the moral will must be twofold. It must dutifully follow the best light it has, but to be really conscientious it must make sure that the light it does choose to follow is really the best light available. Our first duty in any situation is to see clearly what our chief duty really is. Our conscience should be loyal but not precipitate or bigoted and fanatical. More than firm resolution to play our role dutifully is required in the moral life. We need enlightenment to understand clearly what our own role is and what it demands. The critical interplay of intelligence and will may thus be seen as an essential factor in the drama of moral activity. In this drama the ideal of conscience expresses both the right acknowledgment and the loyal performance of each person's role in any situation calling for a choice of values.

*Freedom and Determinism*

The entire discussion of conscience implies a person's capacity to choose between contending values. But can we assume offhand such a capacity on our part in a world which is viewed as strictly determined in every detail?

Moral experience raises in a sharp manner a problem in our interpretation of personality which we have considered earlier in our general account of nature. It is the problem of the range or the limits of mechanism and causal necessity as categories of explanation. The traditional view of physical science has been deterministic. Every process of nature has been regarded as the necessary effect, and within the limits of available observation the predictable effect, of some specific antecedent conditions, and as having in its turn its specific necessary effect.

This view still prevails in dealing "statistically" with large-scale events, but with some very radical revisions in the more ultimate interpretations. As Eddington put it, "the entrenchment of determinism in physics was due to the fact that throughout the whole range of macroscopic phenomena the unpredictability is negligibly small, so that for all practical purposes a strictly causal scheme is the most obvious and simplest way of treating them." But this convenient procedure has become unavailable in dealing with minute particles. Their behavior, including both their velocity and their position at any instant, cannot be ascertained predictably. This principle of uncertainty or indeterminacy, with which the name of Heisenberg is especially joined, may be taken as indicating a limit of our ability to note causal determination, or in more ultimate regard it may imply a limit of causal necessity and a element of spontaneity in nature. Whichever way we interpret it, the radical shift in the scientific outlook becomes apparent. In Eddington's judgment, "Whether permanently or temporarily, determinism has disappeared altogether from modern physics."[46] Einstein's contrary view is an important exception.

The views of modern physical science on determinism and causal necessity have been cited here, because the principle of indeterminacy has been regarded by some thinkers as warranting the reaffirmation of genuine personal initiative and moral freedom. From the fact that an atomic particle behaves or does not behave in a certain way for no ascertainable cause, it has been inferred that man has an unpredictable and spontaneous freedom of choice and is therefore morally responsible for what he does. This surmise is very dubious. It is an inferential leap from the most elementary to the most complex processes in nature. But its main defect is that it misconceives the meaning of freedom in moral and in other activities of persons. The pseudo-scientific interpretation of a free moral choice as an unpredictable and decisive quantum jump misses the characteristic tenor of personal activity. Our deliberations and decisions are not analogous to minute atomic processes.

The unquestionable connection of moral freedom and responsibility indicates a recognition of a certain kind of determinateness in conduct as an essential element in the achievement of personal character. Consider the respective appraisal expressed in these two judgments of a man: "He is incapable of any such baseness," and "There is no telling what he may chance to do." Moral freedom of choice does not signify utter indeterminism. Some sort of determination operates in human affairs, else we could recognize no relation of present choice to past experience or to future expectations, no efficacy of education, or habits, or social medium. A consistent indeterminist could not take a single step that depended on promises or obligations or expectations. Our every moment of social existence proceeds on the assumption of some degree of reliable character in men's behavior. So our question about human freedom is: What sort of freedom do we have, with what sort of determination and responsibility?

Our answers to these questions must proceed from our acknowledgment of "a striving towards unity and coherence." [47] A motive, as a determinant in human conduct, should not be confused with any kind of a motor. We stray into confusion if we misinterpret moral deliberation and eventual choice as the counterplay of motives regarded as forces or mechanical factors. Such a phrase as "the equilibrium of motives" is misleading. Misleading also is the abstract listing of motives as A and B, between which the self presumably chooses. We recall the medieval conundrum of Buridan's ass, placed equidistantly between two bales of hay equally attractive, and so starving in its inability to proceed in either direction. We need not claim any familiarity with asinine predicaments, but we must disagree with Dante's well-known lines describing a similar quandary in human affairs.[48] If for no other reason, by the very slight margin of alternative attention, one motive or another is at each moment gaining or losing in its claim to be chosen. And each moment of deliberation is a stage in the ongoing revision or reconstitution of the self with regard to this or that motive. *A* and *B* in relation to each other do not remain self-identical. It is not a certain definite *A* which finally prevails over a certain definite *B*. The *A* as chosen in the end is not the *A* as initially considered; nor is the *B* as the original claimant identical with the *B* that is eventually set aside or rejected. Moral experience, in deliberation and choice and action, is the dramatic interplay of contending values; and the achievement of personality is the process in which eventually one kind or another kind of self-expression, one or another self, that had been only a possibility, becomes actually real.

In all our conduct we are bound to take account of a process of factual determination. A man's past experience has formed habits and tendencies which may seem to operate with almost causal necessity. Many of our reactions are matter-of-fact routine and foregone conclusions. But even habitual responses are not completely stereotyped. Personal determinateness is not to be understood as a mere resultant. It is ever impending and productive. It is a process of self-determination, self-expression, self-achievement. Its determinateness is real, but there are evident limits to the predictability of its course. This aspect of relative unpredictability is not due to its unascertainable minuteness of operation, nor on the other hand is it owing to its unmanageable complexity. Personality is an ever-active system of progressive redintegration, which is not wholly amenable to any abstract procedure of forecasting. At its summit of activity, personality manifests a creative *élan*, by which is meant nothing supernatural or mysterious but rather the fullness of nature in a personal value perspective, the achievement of consummate self-expression. The free self-determination involved in moral choice is thus a concrete manifestation of the creative strain in the world of values.

### Egoism and Altruism

The contest and conflict of values, which baffle and dismay the tragic will and which in more or less dramatic ways embroil but may also perfect the entire life of conscience, find a characteristic involvement in the social relations of persons. The alternatives between which we have to choose do not represent merely different sides of our nature. They also represent the issue between different persons. The moral question to be resolved is not only, What good are we to choose, but also, Whose good? This is the problem of egoism and altruism.

Without being dogmatic, we may recognize outright that, judged merely as a contest of individual wills, the perplexity in choosing between self-assertion and self-denial does not admit of clear resolution. Traditional moral profession has dignified benevolence; religious devotion has exalted the life of self-sacrifice. In the language of popular judgment the term "selfish" has been a ready synonym for "bad": "a selfish brute." But when convincing reasons have been asked for this denigration of the motive of self-regard, an adequate answer has not been forthcoming. Why, for instance, really why should I prefer promoting the happiness of others rather than my own? Is it because benevolent conduct will intensify my own happiness, or because it enhances the sum total of general satisfaction, or because I should promote the greater happiness impartially, my own or another's? Is it because my will and my welfare are affected by the fundamentally social character of personality, because my values are essentially social? But the individual will, without being willful, may well reply that these reasons are not always convincing. After all, if a certain will is to be subordinated and denied, why should it be my will? Can the moral life be interpreted convincingly in terms of self-denial, so that the individual would always feel duty-bound to step aside for others?

This quandary in which various ethical theories have been embroiled in their social applications is largely due to a confused interpretation of the self. As we have noted, a self is not rightly understood as any kind of a substance. It is not discretely out there alongside or over against other substantial selves. A self, a person is a more or less ordered system of activities. Its character and identity must be understood in terms of its course of prevailing or lapsing tendencies, its interests and purposes, the values which engage its concern, which it considers and chooses, neglects or outright rejects. As we have noted, every choice and eventual action involves a certain reaffirmation or else reconstitution of the self. Certain aspects or tendencies are emphasized, and others are negated. It is evidently confused, then, to speak of any action offhand as an action of self-assertion or an action of self-denial. We should rather consider the values which are affirmed or denied in a certain choice: how does that choice affect a person in his social relations to other persons?

In this reinterpretation of the entire problem of egoism and altruism, a guiding principle is offered in T. H. Green's doctrine of unshareable and shareable values, considered alongside the generally recognized distinction of the lower and the higher values in the moral scale. Typically selected situations from the gamut of human conduct will serve our present exposition. The pursuit of economic values or of any sort of material advantages is a pursuit of unshareable goods. Here one man's gain is apt to be another man's loss. The relations of individuals here is competitive, and any unusual subordination of one's interests to another's claim or need involves self-sacrifice. On the higher level of social-neighborly conduct of coöperation and friendliness, we pursue values that can be shared and that are not diminished in common participation: "the more, the merrier." But when we rise to the activities of our higher life — intellectual, aesthetic, religious — we are engaged in the choice and realization of values which are preëminently shareable, which must be shared to be fully achieved. Truth, beauty, spiritual perfection involve not the competition and conflict but the communion of selves. I cannot possibly gain spiritually at someone else's spiritual loss. Here, in the true words of Scripture, we are indeed "members one of another." [49]

The application of this insight to the problem of egoism and altruism is evident. What we condemn in the egoist is not his self-assertion, but the values which he asserts; we rebuke him as a selfish *brute*. Productive and achieving moral life in our relations to the lives of others is possible through the growing concentration on the pursuit of the higher values. The truth of this principle is manifest today on a world-wide scale in the field of international relations. In terms of economic or political dominance, — the control of coal or steel or oil or other material resources, naval or air bases, — the world crisis is one of conflicting power politics. World peace and coöperation can become possible only as men and nations gain a more active concern for the achievement of the higher values of culture and spiritual life, and work together for the general enlightenment and freedom and a more humane civilization, with decent living conditions for all.

## Contending Values in Justice [50]

The moral drama of values in the social order is manifested significantly in the problem of justice. Justice may be interpreted broadly as the moral principle of social order. In a still larger outlook, justice may be viewed as reasonable balance and right distribution of emphasis which is essential to moral fulfilment in any field of experience. The first of these meanings of justice expresses its more common usage. The second found its classical statement in Plato's ethics. Both meanings were recognized by Aristotle.

Social life, living socially, means living with others, and the others may be persons or things, conditions, which are either means or obstacles to the satisfaction of our needs and purposes. Putting it bluntly, on life's social journey everyone and every thing may be to me either a bridge or a barrier, and so am I a bridge or a barrier to others. There is a possible coöperation or available mutual dependence here, and there is likewise a liable obstruction and hostility. How are these opposite kinds of relations to find a reasonable settlement? This in the broadest terms is the practical problem of justice.

Any examination of justice is apt to start with the traditional formulation of it as *suum cuique,* giving everyone his own or his due. Presumably this statement will raise no objections, but the acceptance of it will not quite settle the matter. It may only serve to punctuate the discussion. For the formula seems to be somewhat tautologous: justice is giving everyone his due, that is his just claim. What is a man's due, to which he is entitled? By what principle is this to be adjudicated?

In speaking of a man's due we are relating but also distinguishing two meanings of justice or two fields in its range of application. This dual connotation is familiar to us all. It is recognized in the distinction between distributive and retributive justice. A just social order, we say, is one which safeguards duly the individual in the possession of what is his own, his property and other

186

rights, and which gives him his share of the common available products. A just social order, we also say, is one which imposes duly on the individual the penalties or the restraints demanded by his violation of the rights of others. In both statements, be it noted, the adverb "duly" has been inserted: duly safeguarding what is one's own, duly imposing penalties and restraints. That is to say, we still need to indicate the principle of justice in the appropriation and the infliction. So once again we ask: By what standard of evaluation are we to adjudge what man's due treatment is?

Let us consider first due restraints and penalties, punitive justice. This term should be preferred to the more common and traditional one, retributive justice; for retribution is only one of several available theories in penology. It is by a progressive criticism that we may be led to the basic principle and standard. The detailed appraisal of the alternative theories of punishment is precluded here, but it may be possible to point out some of their respective merits and defects. We ask: Why should the criminal be punished? The doctrine of retribution answers: Because a crime has been committed. Other theories reply: In order that other crimes may not be committed. But in both cases we may center our attention on the criminal act, or we may insist on considering also the personality of the criminal, the human being before us. There is the juridical framework, but there is also the moral perspective. The problem here is complex, for justice is almost impersonal in its declared fairness. In its court decisions it must abstract from the total moral situation, which is personal. Its verdicts can never express the full moral judgment, yet they should not be at total variance with it. The issue of contending demands must ever be kept in mind.

If we are concerned simply with the act, retributive justice may indicate its traditional derivation from revenge. Likewise in its specific relation to the persons involved in the crime, as offenders and victims, retributive justice is retaliatory, getting even: an eye for an eye and a tooth for a tooth, the murderer's life for the life of the murdered. That is what the ancient Pythagoreans had in mind when they regarded justice as the square deal and identified it with the number four, the first square: as we might say in English, a two for a two! Regarded as expressing the principle of vindictiveness, retaliation, or the satisfaction of the lust for revenge, retributive justice is unacceptable morally. A subtler version of it, that of Hegel, emphasized the solemn worth of the system of law which the criminal had violated. Retributive justice reaffirms the law and social order negated by the crime. In suffering his penalty, a criminal plays the only role which is still available to him in the social drama. The murderer has still a right, the right to be hanged!

If this analytic profundity seems to us morally astray, it is because on the one hand it exalts the human worth of the system of laws, but on the other hand disposes of the criminal's humanity abstractly, considering him merely as the agent of the crime. We cannot set aside a certain conviction and dismay that in this sort of legal abstraction which seems to be required by retributive justice in the punishment of a wrong, another wrong is being committed.

Several other theories of punitive justice, which in various ways appeal to the principle of prevention of crime, may be seen to suffer from a similiar moral defect. We say that a crime must be punished to prevent the criminal from further wrongdoing, or to deter others from criminal acts, or, more broadly, to protect society from more harm. This sort of restraining or preventive justice may require the isolation of the criminal from society, in prison, or even the complete elimination of him, in capital punishment. Now while in all these measures the social order may be protecting itself from the criminal's harmful acts, society itself is suffering a moral harm if it neglects its further personal relations to the criminal which have not been wholly nullified by his crime and which should be duly respected.

Full justice here requires not only the prevention of the criminal's destructiveness but also the reformation of his lawless and hostile spirit. For all his wrongdoing, he is still not a mad dog, to be locked up or killed; he is a person to be reclaimed into the social order. We are thus led imperatively towards some variety of the reformatory doctrine as the only alternative in punitive justice which is acceptable morally.

We may see, then, under what conditions the imposition of penalties and restraints by the social order on the individual is in accord with the full moral principle of justice. Punitive measures are ethically defensible when society does not ignore its thorough concern with the criminal, who despite his crime is still a person, a member of the society to which he is a problem, as it also is a problem to him. Penalties are moral and just, first, when they are motivated by respect for the personal rights or social values that have been violated by the crime; but second, when they do not ignore the problem of somehow safeguarding the criminal's own major right in the emergency, though he may himself be unaware of it, his right to reclamation into the social order of law-abiding life. It is clear that the demands of justice here seem to operate in a dual perspective.

At this point we may note a fundamental meaning of our principle, which should be stated explicitly. Justice expresses the moral demand for thorough and balanced recognition of all the personal factors and values involved in a complex social situation. Full justice is thus opposed to any abstract rigidity or onesidedness in dealing with acts that involve conflicts of personal rights, individual or social.

This same principle of respect for the moral dignity of every man and for his rights and duties in his relations to others, which we have had to recognize the hard way in dealing with punitive justice, may be vindicated even more clearly in dealing with distributive justice. We declare that in a moral society each person is to get his due portion of the available goods, his just share to which he is entitled. But directly we are bound to ask: what is this just and due portion? By what standard is it to be established that a person is entitled to this but not to that share of the goods in the social economy?

The readiest standard may seem to be that of equal distribution: everyone to count as one, and nobody as more than one. This would be an offhand distributive application of the principle that all persons should be equal before the law. But do we really mean that all are to have the same share irrespective of individual performance? The socially available goods that are to be distributed are in considerable part produced by the labors and services of men. The formula of justice, *suum cuique*: due or right distribution, implies the formula, *quid pro quo*, fair compensation. Fair distribution presupposes that all who are to share in the produced goods have had some share in the production of them.

We recognize readily the first clause or premise in the various proposed statements of fair distribution: "From everyone according to his abilities," according to what his capacities and work have produced. What is the right completion of this prescription of justice: "to everyone equally," or "to everyone according to his needs," or "to everyone according to his services"? The comparison and the eventual choice in dealing with these alternative standards mark contending programs of social order. They are cited here in order to point out without too extended argument that each one of them has its limits of convincing worth as an expression of distributive justice.

Distribution according to bare equality seems indiscriminate and really negates the expectations aroused in the clause, "from everyone according to his abilities," which implies a variety of capacities and output, and so, we judge, a variety in just distribution. Where capacities or performances differ, mere equality of apportionment would not be equal in real experience. That is why we need a standard of fair distribution. On the other hand, compensation according to needs, or according to actual services rendered, both suffer from the difficulties of reliable appraisal. Furthermore, they both seem to set aside the counter demand for a certain degree of basic equality of treatment despite differences of capacities or needs or services.

Once more we see justice operating on a dual level. The social conscience seeks a balance between a fair equality of consideration for all and a reasonable discrimination of different claims and deserts. There is the right demand for a fair recognition of distinguished achievement, and there is also the concern not to dismiss the decent regard which we owe to any man whatever. Just treatment is equal treatment, but equally fair, not indifferently equal and identical. So we say that everyone is to be equal before the law, but not that everyone will fare alike. The equality expressed in justice is basic fairness in situations of variable capacities and needs and services. Justice does not preclude distinctions; what it does preclude is prejudice and favoritism. Everyone, the greatest and the least, the best and the worst, is to be recognized and treated justly, namely, as he is. The scales of Themis are fair not in that they register everyone's weight the same, but in that they are not loaded.

This basic impartiality at the core of justice involves in practice an endeavor to balance or harmonize contending considerations in dealing with the different abilities and needs and services of various persons. Outstanding service may get distinguished compensation irrespective of need; or crying need may gain recognition despite inadequate performance; or a least share of social benefits may be accorded even to utter incapacity, as in the case of the so-called "vagabond wage," the minimum subsistence which a decent society, in justice to its own humane self-respect, cannot refuse to any of its members however unproductive. The principle of equality in justice operates so as to maintain a fair balance in a variety of contexts.

We have spread too cursorily perhaps over a very broad field. We should reaffirm, in dealing with distributive justice as previously with punitive justice, the same fundamental characteristic of our principle. Here as before, justice is disclosed as the principle of thorough and balanced recognition of all the factors and values involved in a complex social situation of contending individual rights, as opposed to any abstractly rigid or onesided adjudication.

This essential character of justice may be traced in a more extensive moral reference. We can only glance briefly towards a still larger range of meaning in which justice expresses basic rightness or balance in various interests and social relations. In that vaster prospect, as Plato first of all taught us, justice is a fair synonym for virtue, virtue *par excellence*.

Regarded thus more broadly or perhaps more fundamentally, the specific virtues may be treated as manifold phases of the well-ordered and reasonable life, especially in the various social relations in which we are active. Justice in any social situation would then express the response or treatment which a fair-minded person should accord to others. This would make justice in connotation the essential principle of moral worth. The specific virtues would then be instances of justice in various social relations: loyalty and fidelity, honesty, fulfillment of promises, truthfulness, gratitude, courtesy, fair play, tolerance, generosity. In this wide prospect the principle of justice brings out the Platonic kinships of the Aristotelian standard of the Golden Mean. A number of modern versions of this fundamental idea come to mind. Samuel Clarke proposed it as a universal principle, to match in ethics Newton's law of gravitation. His term for it, righteousness, was appropriate in his philosophical theology.

Shaftesbury gave us a statement of it in an emotional perspective: the good life is a life in which our affections are rightly, that is justly, balanced and moderated.

This historical rehearsal cannot be pursued here. We should be warned that it is apt to be misleading. Justice expanded or inflated in meaning so as to embrace piety in religion, temperance or courage in personal reactions, and rational balance in intellectual activities, is liable to lose its characteristic significance in ambiguity. We should be aware of this hazard, but still it is of advantage to keep in mind these broadly ramified implications of the principle of justice. In the exploration of them we may perceive the integral structure of the moral life. We may thus see justice as the basic ethical principle of the right, that is the balanced, fair-minded, and reasonable organization of values.

### 7. The Dramatic Principle in Religion. The Problem of Evil and the Ideal of Divine Perfection

We should remember that tragedy was religious in its ancient motives, and in its modern themes also the religious strain has persisted in some forms. The Greek tragedies were reënactments of the traditional myths. Aeschylus, Sophocles, and Euripides all three rewove the plot of Orestes. What most concerned the Athenian audience was the way in which a dramatist retold the old tales of the treatment of men by the gods. The action on the stage echoed and evoked the dramatic crises in men's own religious ideas.

Religion throughout history has expressed men's conviction of the supreme reality of the highest values. This vision of the highest has varied with men's spiritual range. Growing maturity has opened new vistas but has also left men perplexed about their earlier sanctities and confused regarding any final devotion. On one side was the higher aspiration, as in the great Chorus in the *Agamemnon* praising Zeus as the cosmic power of justice and perfection.[51] But against those new sublime visions were the myths of the old tradition, undivine fables that shocked men's riper thought of the nature of Deity. The crisis in religious convictions which was the ground note in Greek tragedy may be traced in its various expressions throughout the prophetic reform of the popular cults of Israel, and likewise in other cultures. But religious crises have not been merely struggles of man's growing spirit with his superstitious traditions. At its higher levels also, faith has had to face spiritually baffling actualities. Against its sublime ideals of the highest and holy, religion has also centered its attention on the callous, the corrupt, and the hostile, on evil powers and principalities, sinful in men's lives, titanic or satanic in the cosmic scheme. This is the abysmal problem of evil which has divided philosophies and religions, with their rival solutions and their common quandaries.

The significance of Drama as a basic view of reality is shown by the tendency of both theology and philosophy to give their spiritual commitments a metaphysical connotation. The supreme in values has been viewed as the most real, the first principle and the finally prevailing. The history of thought records the mind's resolution to make the idea of God signify the metaphysical ultimate: the Pure Form, the First Cause, the World Soul, the Alone, the Uncreated Creative Nature, the Supreme Being, the Absolute, Ultimate Reality.

Religious reflection may well protest that these metaphysical substitutes for God do not qualify religiously. Who ever worshipped "the Absolute"? The right spiritual advance, we are told, cannot be from theology to metaphysics but from metaphysics to theology: not by learnedly interpreting God as the Absolute but by devoutly acknowledging the Absolute as God. Proceeding on a principle analogous to Kant's "Primacy of Practical Reason," religious thought has insisted on giving its metaphysical finalities an unmistakable value connotation. The Ultimate is the Supreme; the Absolute is the Perfect.

The ascendency of value judgments in modern theology has been credited mainly to the influence of Kant's moral argument for God. It has much earlier origins. Suffice it to mention the theological connotation of Plato's Idea of Good or principle of value and prevailing perfection. Plato's view of ultimate cosmic order was thoroughly teleological and evaluative. We should remember his decisive question regarding the nature of anything. It was not "What caused it?" but "Is it for the best?" [52] This view was shared by Aristotle, who conceived of the Divine principle as the primal value dynamic in the world, which "produces motion by being loved, and by that which it moves, it moves all other things.." [53] This vision of the Divine motive power was expressed with poetic mastery by Dante in the last line of the *Divine Comedy*:

> The Love which moves the sun and the other stars.
> *L'Amor che muove il sole e l'altre stelle.*

At the dawn of modern thought, Nicholas of Cusa contemplated God as the Value of values, *valor valorum*.[54] This idea of Deity is central in modern idealism; in the words of Sorley, "God must . . . be conceived as the final home of values, the Supreme Worth." [55]

This emphasis on value brings out the dramatic character of the religious outlook on reality. The adoration of the Highest has always been countered by a grievous sense of the low and the corrupt with which we are all tainted. The conception of religion as "the conservation of values" [56] expresses its positive note of final assurance, but the assured note is a hope ever in crisis. The belief in God is itself a conviction of tragic sublimity. It expresses the refusal of man's spirit to resign itself utterly to its own finite inconclusiveness and futility. Somehow, ultimately, despite all the drag of lower drives, the urge for the higher will prevail, in the world and also in us. The Great Perhaps surely cannot prove illusory in the end. So Baillie has interpreted religion as "a moral trust in reality." [57]

In a striking phrase Samuel Alexander described God as "himself the theatre of the contest between value and unvalue." [58] In a pessimistic temper this idea may signify that the tragic issue is rooted deep in the essence of Deity itself, with precarious prospects at best and with a distressing thought of final defeat and ruin. To more buoyant spirits, Alexander's thought may connote the arduous but finally productive and prevailing Good. It need not mean that there is any dark streak in the Divine Light itself. Plato rejected as utterly untenable the suggestion that God is in any sense the author of evil. In the dramatic contest between value and unvalue, the divine must surely be viewed as the upward dynamic. So Matthew Arnold spoke of God as "the enduring power not ourselves, which makes for righteousness." [59]

Are we not confronted here by some sort of cosmic value dualism, explicit or incipient? No great religion has proceeded from its trust in the sublime and ultimately prevailing Good to a complacent notion about the gravity of evil. But the religious spirit has also resisted final doubt and despair. Between these two extremes religion has sought some ground sufficiently firm for hope. Agreeing in their worship of God as unflecked purity of perfection, religions have differed in their views of the villain in the cosmic drama.

Philosophy, committed to the pursuit of truth, has recognized the villain on its own stage, as error. This contrast in theory of knowledge and its metaphysical corollary of reality and mere appearance, both have religious implications. Spinoza, "the God-intoxicated man," in his doctrine of "God or Nature" also wrote of "God or Truth." Plato contrasted the supreme reality of the Idea of Good, or the principle of value, with matter as the realm of error and phenomena, mere seemings, and also as the field of corruption and evil. This triple derogation of matter has found its religious parallels in the various forms of ascetic scorn of the carnal and mortification of the flesh. In Christian tradition, it has had both orthodox and heretical versions.

The most explicit moral-religious dualism and cosmic strife of good and evil was presented in Zoroastrianism, and in one respect it was almost unique. Many philosophical theologies, in their apotheoses of the Supreme Value as the Supreme Reality, have denied ultimate metaphysical rank to the corrupt world of sense. So Plato, while grievously aware of the actuality of matter, yet called it "non-being." This view of inconclusive dualism raised difficulties of final explanation of evil and corrupt matter, for if the Supreme Being is thoroughly rational and perfect, and, as Plato held, if God could nowise be the author of evil, then how could the actual existence of corrupt material "non-being" be explained? Brahmanic pantheism faced the same perplexity: How or why did the Infinite Brahman become manifested in this world of Maya, with its illusions and confusions and evils?

Zoroastrianism took a radically different position, different at least in its initial view. It was not concerned so much to maintain the metaphysical supremacy of Deity as to reaffirm and champion God's moral perfection. It set aside monism with its ultimate moral and religious perplexities and started with an unambiguous dualism, a drama of worldwide strife. The first principle of Zoroastrianism was the irreducible antithesis of good

195

and evil. Good and evil are both underivable realities in this world. They are radically opposite in nature and action, and they cannot possibly have the same source. Therefore there must be, not one but two creative agencies in existence, and these two in universal conflict with each other. The God Ahura-Mazda is perfect unmixed good and the creator of good only. Against him is the evil creative power of Angra-Mainyu or Ahriman. The whole world course to its least detail is a battle between Ahura-Mazda with his blessed host and Ahriman with his evil cohorts. Everywhere light is contending with darkness, health with disease, cereals and fruits with weeds and brambles,—and in man's soul truth is resisting error and deceit, and righteousness is assailed by depravity. Religion is loyal and ceaseless co-warriorship with Ahura-Mazda all along the farflung battle line: not in prayers and sacrifices and temple worship only, but also in every detail of the farmer's and artisan's and the housewife's daily activity.

Even in this most emphatically dualistic religion, however, the dualism is not unqualified. In cosmology, the eternity of Ahriman is ambiguous. To the question, When did Ahriman start his evil work? the Zoroastrian replied: As soon as Ahura-Mazda began his creation. In subtle metaphysics, this answer might have implied a concession to monism, a Brahmanic correlation of evil with finitude or with the Platonic world of material phenomena. But to the moral and religious spirit it signified that corruption and iniquity were nothing recent or accidental; they were as old as creation, warping the very texture of existence. In his distant prospect, however, the Zoroastrian refused to admit the eternity of his cosmic dualism. The cosmic drama was bound to have its climax. A day of final decision is coming, when the hosts of Ahura-Mazda, led by the blessed leader Saoshyant, will rout completely Ahriman's wicked might. The evils of the whole world will then be consumed in a cosmic conflagration, and universal purity and perfection will thenceforward flourish forever under the blessed sway of Ahura-Mazda.

The influence of both Platonic and Zoroastrian dualism may be traced in the course of early Christian tradition, both on heretical teachings and on orthodox doctrine. During the Patristic period Gnosticism drew a pessimistic inference from the dualism of God and matter. The corrupt nature of material existence implied a tainted strain in Deity itself. The basic taint was in the tendency of the Infinite to assume finite manifestations. This tendency, or as we might say, the desire of the star for the moth, drags Divine Perfection all the way down the scale of being, towards and finally to the low level of bodily existence with all its depravity.

Against this doctrine of cosmic degradation, the Neoplatonism of Plotinus was a protest buoyant in spirit but ambiguous in argument. In the Plotinian philosophy of emanation, Deity was conceived as infinitely active, radiating its perfection in outflowing zones of existence: rationality, soul, matter. Each of these zones or levels of reality manifests the divine nature in its characteristic way and order. If we may use a crude example and not press it unduly, we could speak of an original typescript and a number of carbon copies. The copies are legible to a lesser and lesser degree, but in each of them the original text is recorded in some measure. So we must regard the process of emanation as hierarchical, but not draw any pessimistic inferences. If there is to be a finite manifestation of Divine Reality at all, there is bound to be a type of nature which, being a manifestation, must be in some respect or degree less than the radiating Deity itself. And so in the outermost zone of emanation there is necessarily a least manifestation of Deity. This "least" of Divine Light is matter. The Neoplatonists cited the words of the Fourth Gospel and declared that they should be engraved in gold: "The light shineth in the darkness, and the darkness apprehended or overcame it not."

There is a continual ambiguous redistribution of emphasis here; we shall note it also in St. Augustine. On the one hand, the imperfection of material existence is regarded as its characteristic level of perfection in the process of emanation, and therefore it is declared to imply no fundamental taint in the nature of Deity. The radiating center is absolutely perfect light. On the other hand, the corruptions of matter are not only recognized but are also accentuated. If we read the texts fairly, we should say that the Neoplatonic verdict is intended to incline finally towards a positive cosmic valuation.

A parallel to the Neoplatonic critique of Gnosticism, with its alternating emphases, may be noted in the controversies of St. Augustine with two opposite extremes which he condemned as heretical: Manicheanism and Pelagianism. The Manicheans re-

newed the Gnostic polemic of cosmic pessimism by their combination of the Greek dualism of God and matter with the
Zoroastrian dualism of good and evil. Evil, they said, is as it
were organic in the very constitution of reality, in the material
strain of existence, which always opposes the spiritual perfection
of God. Manicheanism flourished especially during the fourth
century both as a religious rival of Christianity and as a heretical
movement in the Christian churches. Augustine was attached to
this doctrine for some ten years. Upon his conversion to Christianity he became the chief critic of the Manichean heresy and its
basic fallacy of cosmic dualism. He declared: There is one and
only one creative agency, God; matter can nowise be regarded as
a fundamental evil nature staining the absolute perfection of
the Creator. Evil is the privation of good and a misdirection of
an essentially good nature. It is due to the perverse choice of
man's will.

The sturdy British monk Pelagius reaffirmed man's moral
capacity and consequent responsibility. The evil influence of
Adam's and Eve's original sin is countered by the blessed influence of Christ's life and death. A Christian is an active con-
tributor to his own salvation. By free choice he can obey and
fulfill God's laws; if he does not, he is justly liable to God's
punishment. St. Augustine denounced Pelagianism as heretical.
True Christianity teaches the salvation of man's utterly helpless
and undeserving soul by God in Christ. The contending interpretations of the doctrine of Divine Grace are spread across the
pages of Christian theologies through the centuries. Calvinism
and Jansenism represent early modern instances of this perennial
issue in Christian thought, Protestant and Roman Catholic.

An extended historical examination of the various interpretations of the nature of evil is obviously beyond the province of
this work. It has been undertaken in my book *The Nature of
Evil*. Our brief discussion here should lead us to avoid some of
the quandaries of theodicy, by developing further a gradational
principle of value recognized by St. Augustine, and before him
by Plato and Plotinus. A main principle of Platonic rationalism
is its aristocratic emphasis, both in valuation and in basic conception of nature. Plato viewed reality as a hierarchical scale of
Ideas, and the truest expression of reality for him was the highest
Idea, the principle of value. Aristocracy signified "dominance of

the best"; it pointed to a dramatic moral issue between alternatives, calling for a wise distribution of emphasis. Aristocracy was also a leading principle in Platonic cosmology. So at the summit of the Platonic scale was the Idea of Good, and at the other end, unstable and corrupt matter, "non-being."

We may return a moment to the Neoplatonic philosophy of emanation, to note the religious intensity with which it expresses the drama of man's moral career. The cosmology of Plotinus presents a moral and spiritual challenge. In the hierarchy of emanations the soul's activity points in two directions. On the one side it aspires towards rationality and the higher reaches of spirit. On the other, it has a carnal inclination to the lures of sensuality. In our every act or word or thought or feeling we are either rising Godward or else are "deserting towards the abyss." The soul's character and destiny are decided by that choice of direction. The soul that grows in perfection may lift even bodily life to higher worth: "The material thing becomes beautiful—by communicating in the thought that flows from the Divine." [60] But if the soul is misdirected by lower desires, its thoughts and feelings themselves may become tainted with bodily corruption.

These principles and ideals point towards a theodicy which found its great utterance in a golden passage in St. Augustine's *City of God:* "When the will abandons the higher and turns to what is lower, it becomes evil—not because that is evil to which it turns, but because the turning itself is perverse." [61] This has been called "the gradational view of value." [62] It proceeds from the recognition of the basic characteristic of values which we have just noted in Plato and Plotinus. Values in any field are never merely similar or different. Their order is hierarchical; they are related to each other as higher and lower. We do not describe or explain them in a neutral way. They engage us in a preferential choice. That is their dramatic character.

This fundamental insight into the nature of values should clarify some traditional confusions which have perplexed theodicy in its treatment of the problem of evil. Evil and good are misunderstood when they are regarded offhand as certain things or conditions. There are no sheep and goats in the fold of values. Good and evil must always be considered in relation to the contending alternatives which engage the will in any situation. They are directional. A choice is good or evil depending upon what is preferred—to what. On the ladder of personal activity, be it intellectual, aesthetic, or moral, any action may be seen either as a step upward or as a decline. And approval or disapproval of it, as good or evil, must always depend upon the level of previous attainment and the expectations which that level of realization justifies. This is Gospel wisdom: "To whom much is given, of him will much be required." [63] Every university man knows that the standard of judging intellectual performance is progressively more exacting. The finest undergraduate quality of work may not meet graduate requirements. The correct execution of finger exercises which we may commend in a musical beginner would be absurdly irrelevant in a professed virtuoso. So in moral and other spiritual activities. In the evaluation of our action, as good or evil, the important thing is not so much where we are but rather this, whence and whither we are going.

The application of dramatic activism to the problem of evil is thus evident and significant. Activism generally considered advances from the view of nature as a system of substances to a recognition of the central importance of processes or activities. In a value perspective these activities must be acknowledged as hierarchical, as higher or lower, as contending alternatives involving us in judgments of choice.

This directional or gradational view does not, in the manner of Leibniz, reduce the value alternative, good-evil, to a metaphysical statement in which perfection and imperfection are ambiguously equated with infinite and finite. It points furthermore to a theodicy which avoids the two extreme alternatives of placid piety or final pessimism. On this position we cannot argue that evil is merely a privation, only finite appearance, somehow absorbed ultimately in infinite pure good. Our view shares Plato's forthright recognition that "evils can never pass away; for there must always remain something which is antagonistic to good." [64] But this reflection is nowise dismal. It springs from an insight into the essential character of values.

The higher is higher only in distinction from what is lower in the scale. And there must always be a lower, for the active, maturing character of any value is itself continually relegating its former summits to a lower status. The entire range of activities of our higher life is a portrayal of this principle. The progressive self-reconstitution of scientific truth is the readiest instance that comes to mind. Perfection is an ongoing process which is ever outreaching its former activities. Any supposed finality of perfection bodes stagnation and in its further context, evil. So Mohammed's institution of polygamy was a good reform of the Arabian promiscuity with which he had to contend. But it did not lead the world of Islam to the still higher stage of monogamy, and in a more mature social and moral outlook it stands condemned.

It should be repeated that there is nothing complacent in the gradational view of evil. We should not say that evil is merely relative to good, that their antithesis is merely one of direction. This extenuating connotation of the term "merely" is wholly unwarranted. There is no opposition more radical than that of direction. Evil is not "somehow good" either for us or for God, any more than sinking is somehow rising. The ignoring of this basic choice between the higher and the lower is the cankered core of spiritual ruin. The dismissal of it is the devil's cunning of sophistry. Throughout history it has undermined the moral life, and in our own day it is undertaking in various ways to dismiss the element of validity in ethical judgments. This is the screech of the witches in *Macbeth*:

> Fair is foul, and foul is fair.[65]

This is the wile of Mephistopheles:

> Step up. I might have said: Step down—
> 'T were all the same.[66]

Precisely between these opposite directions of higher and lower values is the choice of moral life or death. So Hamlet dooms it tragically to his adulterous mother:

> Have you eyes? . . . What judgment
> Would step from this, to this? [67]

We may see, then, that the gradational view of values does not in any way ignore the gravity of moral choice or the tragic element in spiritual activity. But, on the other hand, it does not proceed to dismal negation. We may restate our conclusion with a redistribution of accent. The gradational view nowise explains evil away as merely finite, but on the other hand it does not

201

regard any good as final. The dramatic activism which we are advocating rules out absolutism at any stage of the hierarchy of values. To Plato's profound words that "evils can never pass away," we should now add that no good is ever static; real good will never be brought to a standstill. Our theodicy has neither ignored the fundamental reality of evil nor has it regarded its reality as a stain on God's perfection. We have seen the essentially contending relation of good and evil in the basic nature of value activity. But the gradational view of value demands a reinterpretation of our ideal of perfection, human or divine. And our conclusion may well be stated plainly here. Perfection, finite or infinite, is perfectibility.

The traditional idea of perfection has emphasized the note of finality. This strain of absolutism may be traced in the languages of various religions. The Buddhist term *an-uttara,* meaning "the Beyondless," connoted a conclusive fulfilment without any further problem or prospect. The Greek *teleios* signified full and final attainment of the goal, *telos.* The Latin participle which gives us our word, perfect, expressed the complete working out, the consummation of an activity.

The ideal of absolute finality of perfection, and the needed revision of it in the spirit of genuine dramatic activism, may both be traced in our experience of values. Two aspects may be distinguished in that experience: what we aspire to achieve, and what we actually find in the process of achieving. An ideal goal is, by intention and intension, by purpose and meaning, the expected solution of our problem, the satisfaction of our need, the fulfilment of our hope: our conclusion and destination and arrival. We contemplate our goal *as* final: therein do we acknowledge it as the ideal. If we were regarding it as only on our way to a further goal, then our aspiration would fix its sight on that further goal as the ideal. This demand for finality, which may be noted in every pursuit of value, should enable us to appreciate the religious mind's vision of absolute divine perfection. Eternal finality of value fulfilment is precisely what traditional religions have worshipped in their ideals of God.

But the demand for finality is not the only essential aspect of our experience of value. The ever active, ongoing character of that experience is also fundamental. Do we ever find in any fulfilment of purpose a cessation of the value activity? Quite the contrary: real achievement, or rather achieving, becomes directly an expansion of prospect, a reconstitution of the activity. Were the experience no longer ongoing, its alleged realization would have proved self-defeating. In science every experimental or theoretical conclusion seems to deepen our insight and expand our outlook towards some further and more perfect truth. So in morals, as Royce taught us, "the best world for a moral agent is one that needs him to make it better." [68] Likewise the whole history of philosophy has been regarded, in continual solutions, as an unending problem. And does religion ever record the life of any saint who deemed himself holy? Even Jesus, when addressed as "good Master," asked: "Why do you call me good? No one is good but God alone." [69]

"But God alone": here is our problem. Do we have to accept this as the supreme divine exception, in the sense of static absolutism in perfection, with all the difficulties which it involves in theology and theodicy? Or can we recognize this solely divine perfect Good as the expression of an ideal demand for an ever infinite overplus of value? Or shall we follow further some essential implications of this second idea and, by respecting more fully all the fundamental characteristics of spiritual values, proceed to a thorough recognition of infinitely active perfection, unterminated, inexhaustible, and never static?

We cannot accept the first of those three alternatives just mentioned, for only ambiguity in its exposition can fail to expose the perplexities in which it is involved. If divine perfection differs from ours in that it is without prospects or problems, who would trade places with God? And can the religious mind really think of Deity in terms of thoroughly static perfection? God is surely a problem to me: am I not also a problem to Him? Consider a moral crisis seriously, all the way through. Doesn't my deliberation and eventual choice somehow ultimately matter to God? Happiness or misery, my own or another's, advance or defeat of justice or other social values, a better or a worse world somewhere along the line: unless I recognized some or all of these impending values as involved in the crisis which confronts me, what could duty or conscience or moral activity possibly mean? The whole experience is surely a problem to me and to others. The theologian may appeal to divine omniscience and foreknowledge and hold that my choice and eventual action are never a problem to Deity. But

203

to hold that they are of no concern to God's absolute perfection is a view that may well drive man's spirit to moral atheism.

The traditional theologians might reply to these objections and perplexities with the question: Will you then advocate belief in a finite God, and what kind of God will that be? The idea of a finite deity has been advanced by John Stuart Mill and others, and in our day it has been advocated as a sort of theistic consolation prize, as the best that we can expect. But the apologetic tone in which it is often presented, whether intended or unwitting, may lead us to reconsider its adequacy, which is very dubious. A finite or a limited God, if regarded as in any respect deficient, simply cannot qualify religiously. This view of divine perfection seems to go astray in the opposite direction from that of the traditional theologian.

The true alternative to absolutism in theology is not in the idea of finite or limited divine perfection but in a truer interpretation of real infinitude in value, really infinite perfection. We must first grasp and hold firmly the truth of dramatic activism in the reality of values. Value activity along its boundless range is always aiming at a finality of achievement which it continually finds to be ongoing and inexhaustible. Every realization has two aspects: its base and background, and its expanded outlook, prospect, and problem. The rise in the hierarchy of perfection is marked by expansion in both respects. The expert or the genius in any field of activity differs from the beginner not only in having more answers and conclusions but also in facing a vaster outlook, with more problems, deeper issues. Expand this familiar comparison on a boundless scale: gain the vision of Infinite Creative Spiritual Reality, all-comprehending in resources, in active concern, in pervading creative power, in spiritual reach and prospect. Where else does our dramatic activism manifest its significance better than in leading us to this deeper spiritual insight? And we cannot find a better religious statement of our truth than the words ascribed to Jesus in the Fourth Gospel: "My Father worketh hitherto, and I work." [70]

## 8. Philosophy as the Correlation of Perspectives

This study has taken us over several main fields of our experience of nature and human nature. We should now try to elicit some reasonable implications concerning the province and the outlook of philosophy.

Science in its broad and basic character is an integrative activity. By careful observation it ascertains specific data, but always seeks in them the marks of some dependence or other significant relation and the evidence of some general character which it can express in universal terms. It moves from its complex of theories to consider certain new data or instances; it contemplates these instances in some familiar or new hypothetical pattern; it aims to formulate its description and explanation of them in a law. In the field of relevance outlined by its specific postulates, each science exhibits this integrating procedure, which is an essential activity of intelligence.

The first principles and postulates of a science represent its characteristic slant or window on nature. They determine its chosen approach to inquiry and what is relevant to it. We have called this characteristic outlook the perspective of a science or of a type of investigation. This perspective determines the kind or the degree of abstraction which is appropriate to a certain field of research. So plain geometry is concerned with the world of space in two dimensions; and biology, with the varieties, conditions, and evolution of living beings. In each case the perspective serves to outline and delimit relevant inquiry.

This systematic-integrative operation which marks each science in its own field impels the mind to seek some extension of its theoretical patterns across the boundaries of its own investigation. Alongside of the special laws and problems of physics, chemistry, and biology, of each in its own field, these sciences involve problems for each other. They have borderlands of shared interests where their postulates seem to overlap. They lead to intermediate inquiries, like physical chemistry or biochemistry. In all this interplay of various scientific researches, each science would hold firm in its commitment to its own postulated framework of reference. Thus arise issues between the special sciences, where their respective postulates seem to contend in undetermined emphasis and priority. This contention and basic indeterminateness, as we shall presently note, is especially evident in biological theory. But these strains do not disrupt the scientific alliance. The physical scientist, whatever his special field and whatever the reactions and tensions of his science *vis-à-vis* other specialties, is convinced of the basic soundness of the general scientific position. There is no fundamental discord in the ground-note of the various laboratories. Whatever it be that a physicist, a chemist, and a biologist may be saying to each other around the luncheon table at the faculty club, they are sure to blend voices when a historian or a moralist joins the discussion.

This final insistence on definite special postulates, which narrows the range or the thoroughness of intellectual integration, is not limited to the physical sciences. We may note it also in the various humanities. Here likewise there are borderlands of inquiries in which the data and the methods or principles of specialized research combine and contend for choice and emphasis. We have economic history and histories of art and of literature. Art and literature and economics, however, are still distinguishable from history, and so on the borderland of discussion we may note again the issue of prevailing emphasis. Which of the related inquiries is to color and prevail over the other? Will economic theory yield to historical exposition, or will historical research be directed by economic postulates? Yet despite these humanistic strains, the "liberal arts" do not fail to present a fairly common front to any untoward physical scientific incursion.

In two widely remote fields we have noted the finally unavailing intellectual integration of specialists. The specialist's reach towards integration expresses the normal drive of intelligence. For thorough thinking cannot remain narrowly specialized. It cannot be provincial; it must point to some commonwealth of correlated insight. In the first sentence of his *Metaphysics* Aristotle recognized that "all men by nature desire to know," — to know, if possible, all the way through. This demand for some ultimate integration is the philosophical note in human reflection. It may be recognized in the thought of deeply searching minds in various fields of investigation. Some of the most fruitful contributions to philosophical understanding in our time have been made by scientists working down at the roots or else on the outermost range of their own fields of research, where their special explorations touch other related inquiries. But it should be noted that these philosophical ventures on the part of specialists have not always proceeded to fully philosophical integration. The reason for this, as has been mentioned already, is that the philosophical turn in the thinking of a specialist is likely to proceed from his own set of postulates. The specialist recognizes the larger problems and issues that are raised by his particular investigations or are involved in his theories. He undertakes an integration of ideas, and his coördination is philosophical in its expanding glance towards the whole circle of reality. But it is not fully philosophic, for it still proceeds from his own special radius. Every specialized investigation, when its inferences are pursued critically, raises problems that concern its relation to other specialties. These problems are of philosophical import, and they are major contributions to philosophical reflection. But philosophy cannot realize its full character unless it undertakes the systematic correlation of the various perspectives.

We are now in a position to recognize more clearly the role of a philosophy that understands its true function in the life of intelligence. Philosophy has no special postulates, nor any special territory in the realm of knowledge. It is not a paradox but the plain truth to state that philosophy specializes in not being special. Its specialty is unspecialized integration. It is not rightly engaged in pursuing any particular kind of knowledge, but in exploring the possible organization of the various special "knowledges" into some reasonable system.

We do not develop philosophical insight by any kind of rigid exclusiveness in our reflection. Philosophy cannot be defined by any abstract formula. It expresses not the delimiting but the expansive activity of intelligence. It is not a fence but a vista. Did not William James say of his summer house by Chocorua that it had ever so many doors, all opening outwards? A philosophic house indeed!

To be sure, philosophy also asks particular questions — logical, aesthetic, ethical — but always in the systematic pursuit of rational synthesis. Unless we keep this guiding emphasis on integration, we miss our essential task in philosophic thinking. We may note several instances of such misleading specialization in philosophical inquiry.

Philosophy is bound to be a criticism of abstractions, and so it must be critical of its terms and beware of foggy verbiage. Modern logical analysis has exposed the confused thinking in many of our ideas and beliefs and problems. It has perfected our use of language as the instrument of understanding and communication. This has been great gain for philosophy, provided we do not mistake our basic purpose. Philosophy cannot be too rigorous in its conceptual analysis, but it cannot be merely an elaboration of grammar or a logical syntax. Sharpening and polishing and oiling the tools of thought are all very important: not as the end and aim of philosophical reflection, but as means to the more adequate mastery of the philosophical problems. We need the right words, rightly understood, in their right order,—for the sake of saying the right thing.

Likewise, in recognizing the role of philosophy as a correlation of the special sciences, what is required is more than a recapitulation or a syllabus of the laws and theories of physics or biology. A philosopher may be only presumptuous if he proposes to correct the conclusions of the scientists; but he fails even to undertake his task if he merely reports them. He must endeavor to interpret their bearings on each other and also on other basic ideas of a humanistic order.

Once more, philosophy is not, or at any rate cannot remain, an ivory tower of cold reason. It is analytic and factual, but it is also a practical engagement; it must concern itself with the tensions and crises in men's lives. Aristotle who defined man as a rational animal called him also a political animal, a social being. On the other hand, while philosophical reflection is involved in practical issues, it must resist the lure of partisanship. Engrossed though it be in social-political problems, philosophy should not become merely the lofty platform of a democratic social order, much less a communist or a fascist manifesto. It should not be a preachment or propaganda of any sort. Novalis said that philosophy bakes no bread but can give us God, freedom, and immortality. More truly understood, it may neither give us nor deny us any of these boons, but it may enable us to understand better the motives and the grounds of our quest for them.

We have noted that we get both help and hindrance, both enlightenment and a constriction of outlook from the philosophical reflection of specialists. But again we should state plainly that we are not thinking only of scientific specialists, or of humanistic specialists, but also of onesided philosophers. All the way through, as we consider various exclusive emphases in philosophical reflection, we find them unavailing. Philosophy is concerned with them all in one way or another, in various degrees; but it cannot be limited to any one of them. Philosophy is the thorough and balanced inquiry into the nature of existence and into the meaning and values of human life.

This basic principle is so important that it can scarcely suffer by elaboration. It is made manifest by the historical development of philosophical ideas. Our Western civilization records two major instances of over-specialized or over-simplified cosmic emphasis, each of them deeply significant in its own way, but each one also tending to mislead us unless it is amplified and rounded out by more integral philosophical reflection.

The medieval Scholastic doctors at their best, in the thirteenth century, contemplated the course of existence, in its cosmic range and in the least detail, as the field of operation of Divine Providence. Theory of knowledge, cosmology, ethics, social principles, all were slanted in a theological perspective. This theological outlook and direction of thought basically subordinated human experience and knowledge to supernatural revelation. It sought both certitude and sanction in dogmatic authoritarianism. Our modern age is apt to dismiss this scholastic commitment too summarily. We should be balanced in our criticism of it. Scholasticism was keen and profound in its spiritual insight. Its consecration to the Christian values and the Christian vision yielded the penetration and the ecstasies of saintliness, which we may not ignore if we are to do justice to the creative intelligence of genius. But in their preoccupation with the ways of Divine Providence the medieval doctors neglected the factual ways of existence; they did not investigate thoroughly the mechanics of nature. Instances to the contrary can be cited, like the statement of Albert the Great that for the study of botany he must go to the fields, or much more to the same effect in Roger Bacon. But the scholastic point in these instances is their exceptional character. Modern scientific research and scientific advance became possible, not through the scholastic philosophy, but outside of it and in direct opposition to it, in the Renaissance.

Our modern scientific outlook may be described and appraised in just the converse terms. And here it will be well to keep in mind an important distinction. Modern physical science is at least four centuries old, going back to Copernicus and Vesalius in 1543, two years before the Council of Trent. But the acknowledged dominance of the principles of physical science, and the resolute reliance on them for men's view of their own nature and range and destiny, which is called "scientism," is a comparatively recent philosophical outlook. Even toward the middle of the nineteenth century, when young Helmholtz was deciding on his university specialty, his family and friends could not see how such a brilliant young man could think of making a career in physics! It was only about that time that a chemist, Dr. Eliot, could become president of Harvard. The monumental spread of scientific laboratories and scientific research, in universities and other institutions of private endowment or governmental administration, is a chapter of definitely contemporary history.

Just as in appraising the scholasticism of the medieval doctors we are critical of the adequacy of their strictly theological philosophy rather than of their Christian piety, so here we are concerned not so much with modern science but with contemporary "scientism." It is a certain kind of philosophy; it expresses a view and estimate of science and scientific principles. As to physical science itself, how can it need any recommendation of ours? It has revealed to us with superlative mastery the factual details of the cosmic mechanism; it has formulated its laws and principles and framed its theoretical patterns. And where unresolved problems have confronted it, or limits to likely or to possible deeper insight, it is science itself which has discovered and forthrightly acknowledged them. Its practical achievements have been as epoch-making as its theoretical mastery.

How natural it is that our age should look to science for its new gospel and its new dispensation! But this contemporary "scientism" has its serious qualms. Science has indeed split the atom, but can it also bind men to live together? The new nuclear mastery before us may transform and incredibly perfect our whole civilization, but again, it may blow us all to pieces. The concentration on the physical mechanism of existence has not enabled us to understand or express men's rational activities or the values of human experience. The rejoinder would be readily forthcoming: "That is not the task of physical science." Precisely; for then, if we are to have an adequate philosophy of life, we need the acknowledgment and the inclusion of other perspectives of thought, to supplement the scientific outlook. And not only to supplement the scientific outlook, but to do full justice to the scientists themselves. What other class in our society express more thoroughly the spirit of intellectual integrity, unwavering devotion to the pursuit of truth? The scientist himself is a living evidence of the reality of intellectual values. And his science, which deals with the physical mechanics of nature, is itself not a physical matter but a rational system. Can the Quantum Theory itself be regarded merely as a quantum jerk?

Here is a contention of onesided perspectives, each of which concentrates on a major important aspect of reality, but exposes its abstractness and insufficiency in failing to do justice to its needed significant completion by the other. How many professed philosophers proceed on the mistaken assumption that they can reach the full truth simply by exchanging the spiritual for the materialistic perspective! But each one of these is a particular view which requires further integration. If you replace the august authority of theology by the august authority of physical science, you may only be exchanging one partial view for another. We cannot correct the onesidedness of a scholastic theological philosophy by adopting finally a physical mechanistic position. What is onesided in each of them is the presumption, from its own particular viewpoint, to speak integrally and authoritatively for the whole. And that is neither good science nor good religion, and it cannot lead to a good philosophy.

This contention cannot be settled by the simple device of subordinating one of these perspectives to the other. For the subordination cannot be applied all the way through. The postulates of each perspective, in its own respective scope and relevance, are decisive. The merit of physics, as physics, is in its consistently mechanistic outlook; and likewise, but contrariwise, with the postulates of history and political theory. We need integration but not a confusion of basic principles. The proposal of subordination which looks toward some one finally prevailing specialty is unavailing.

One side of this debate may be summed up by citing Samuel Butler, who remarked somewhere that religion tells many little lies in order to express one great final truth, whereas science tells many little truths in order to conclude with one big lie. One might counteract this epigram with one equally witty; but neither would avail to meet the demands of a truly cosmic integration.

The fundamental philosophical requirement of a correlation of perspectives, which is expressed strikingly in considering the

211

contrast of medieval scholasticism and contemporary "scientism," may be noted also by considering some of the problems which confront the biological evolutionary outlook and the two definitely humanistic perspectives, the historical and the dramatic.

Evolutionary biology expresses the conviction that there is no abyss in nature separating the world of physics and chemistry from the world of living beings. The great achievement of Darwin was that he allied biological method with the method of the physical sciences, by accounting for the origin and the evolution of species in causal terms, without any appeal to providential or other design. The factual explanation of the origin of species, as due to the fortuitous variations making possible the survival of the fittest, that is, the species best adapted to certain environments, did not require any reference to mind or purpose as determining factors in the process of evolution. But while Darwin thus did not need mind or purpose to explain the origin and evolution of species, he did require something in his theory to explain mind, boundless range of mental activity. With his characteristic candor of genius, Darwin did recognize the radical difficulty of this problem of "mental powers and the moral sense." In his *Descent of Man* (1871) he endeavored to trace possible lines of development from animal reactions to human responses, but he did not propose a solution of the problem of the first origin of mind, and he was cautious in his speculations about the explanation of its development in strictly evolutionary terms.

The basic philosophical problem of evolutionism here is not only that of explaining the emergence of mind. It is the problem of doing full justice to the higher stages of rational intelligence, with its principles and values, in terms coherent with the evolutionary biology of the *Origin of Species*. As we have tried to point out in an earlier chapter, the evolutionary perspective, at one end of the stream of life, is sustained by abundant evidence which integrates biology with the physical sciences. That is its great merit. But at the other end, at the higher reaches of human life and experience, evolutionism is confronted by insuperable evidence of its insufficiency. It raises the problem of its supplementation by the acknowledgment of other, unambiguously humane and rational perspectives. And this is a still greater merit of evolutionism, that its far-flung evidence, from the paleontological record of geological strata to the individual and social history of human lives, may lead our philosophy from the knowledge of mechanical process to the wisdom of recognizing personal and historical values.

The true conclusion of a thoroughgoing evolutionary philosophy, it seems clear to say, cannot sustain either rigid materialism or an inexorably spiritual conception of nature. Our integral view here must mediate between physics and physiology on one side and history and the other humanities on the other. The historical perspective, in its turn, has likewise a dual correlation. Its characteristic outlook must not be mistaken: its concern with the development and interplay and contest of social values. While the higher ranges of the historical development cannot be interpreted rightly without the acknowledgment of distinctively human-spiritual energies and ideals, its lower processes and more primitive origins cannot be understood without the recognition of various material factors. And indeed all along the line history moves in a natural setting and is affected by natural conditions and changes. Browning's poetic wisdom should save both scientist and philosopher from onesidedness in dealing with the historical life of men:

Nor soul helps flesh more, now, than flesh helps soul![71]

This needed balance in our philosophical interpretation of the historical perspective should save us from onesided philosophies of history. The idealist Hegel contemplated the history of the world as the world's court of judgment, as the progressive realization of the capitalized Idea of Freedom. To Schopenhauer's pessimistic view, on the contrary, history was a futile and wretched succession of cat-fights. In the dialectical materialism of Karl Marx and the Communists, the course of history, with its succession of ideologies, is caused by the operation of economic and other material factors in the environment. A plausible case for each of these theories may be made by the citation of considerable evidence, for the historical data are vast and complex. But all three theories, and others that may be cited, fail of conclusiveness through their onesidedness. Man is a social and a rational animal. Neither the noun nor the adjectives in this statement should be neglected.

The view of the World as Drama is the most characteristic

**213**

outlook on the Reality of Values. Here man's intelligence—reason and feeling and spiritual vision—contemplates its own creative activity up to the verge and summit of genius. Corresponding to the factual interplay of causes and urges and reasons and purposes across the vast span of cosmic perspectives which we have been endeavoring to understand, the dramatic outlook reveals the strains in the life of spiritual aspiration, the counterplay of ideals in the pursuit of perfection and in the struggle with evil.

The perspective of the world as process at this distinctively spiritual level manifests a dynamic of values. The world as drama is a gradation of higher and lower satisfactions and purposes and ideals. Value is never simply there, to be described or explained. It enters the stage of possible realization as a challenge and an aspiration, or as a menace or an insidious lure. The entire realm of values is one of striving or relapse, achievement or frustration, perfection or degradation. For here on the highest reaches of reality, man is ever resisting the drags of his lower nature or yielding to them. In social activities progress appears dubious when so often man's reason itself is bedeviled to serve lower impulses, to make him "beastlier than any beast," in the words of Goethe's Mephistopheles. Artistic creation is so often checked or misdirected by confusion or vulgarity. The moral life is itself a dramatic contest of values and purposes, arduous in the struggle between aspiration and appetite, baffling in the tragic choice between counter-evils. These are gray and grim aspects of the spiritual life, and religion has expressed them in its emphasis on man's sinfulness and his utter need of redemption. The religious gospel of salvation is a gospel of hope, hope to contrite man. The parable of the Prodigal Son evidences this dual conviction. The prodigal son is the son of his Father—but a prodigal son.

Have we presented the dramatic perspective of the world of values in a dour pessimistic regard? It has also its vistas of more positive and sublime achievement. In our other views of the world—as cosmic mechanism, or evolution or history—we have been considering the varieties and the complexity and the limits of available knowledge. Now we contemplate man's paths towards wisdom, so frequently uncertain, unmarked and untrodden, so limitless in their forward reach, onward and upward. Here man's creative spirit surpasses itself, so often by not being subservient to cautious reason, but not by an initial dismissal of reason. How wisely St. Thomas Aquinas counselled his theological doctors: Go with reason as far as it takes you, in its right direction; faith will then take you the rest of the way. In many fields of spiritual activity this same basic wisdom has been expressed. So Pasteur affirmed that the great creative ideas come to minds that have been prepared for them by thorough inquiry. And Poincaré: After having tried really hard, stop trying, and it will achieve itself. From scaling the ideal heights, will some of my readers turn to plain mountain climbing? On the slippery trails inexperienced foolhardiness may prove fatal. But repeatedly the seasoned climber comes to a step of precarious outcome, where only a resolute leap can sway the possible odds between success and disaster. The lower ramparts of achievement may be reduced by plodding reflection, but eventually genius must storm the citadels of perfection. The fuller truth, however, requires that we write this last sentence also in the reverse order, so as to include the recognition of the superlative capacity for hard work.

In our insistence on the true character of philosophy as the correlation of perspectives, it should be made clear that we are not advocating any indefinite eclecticism. What we are trying to emphasize is the philosophical importance of approaching every particular problem with a full awareness of its implications for the whole, the importance of synthesis and integration in all philosophical reflection.

The integration or correlation of perspectives should not be the expression of an initial commitment to some one general principle of synthesis or organization, be that principle idealistic or materialistic, formal logical or pragmatic. The direction and the form of the truly philosophical synthesis must be one which has issued from the thorough exploration of the problems themselves.

Our modern specialized and often onesided thinking has found expression in the over-departmentalized organization of our universities. We need greater integration in our programs of higher education. Any real basic problem is bound to lead our research beyond our departmental bailiwick. In my own experience, at least, I have found that this is especially true in philosophy. In studying the belief in immortality, the problem of evil, the ways of genius, I was again and again led from "straight philosophy" into religion, into history and literature, psychology and other sciences. Real problems pay no attention to departmental fences; they go their ways, and in following their various courses one may learn the importance of integrative thinking.

Our philosophy should not be the philosophy of a school. It must not be dictated by conformity to any preconceived formula, but must itself be the integration of various evidence and inference that leads to the confirmation or to the revision of traditional and provisional formulae. For this is always the advantage of sound philosophical interpretation, that in its critical integrating outlook many special ideas reveal significant aspects or inferences which they do not manifest when regarded solely in their special provinces. Ideas become more cultivated; their meaning expands and mellows when they enter into the stimulating society of more thorough and balanced reflection.

We have been endeavoring here in various ways, even at the risk of some repetition, to express and emphasize a principle which is fundamental in philosophy. May we in conclusion mention some practical applications of this principle of philosophical method? Philosophers should be loyal to their own task and not seek to pattern their work on some chosen special form of inquiry. We do not become scientific philosophers by peppering our pages with equations or with physical and chemical verbiage. To be truly scientific, that is, to yield knowledge and insight, philosophy must deal critically and thoroughly with its characteristic problems, which include but also exceed the problems of the physical sciences. But on the other hand, we do not achieve a truly spiritual philosophy and an insight into the reality of values, at the expense of critical objectivity, by disdain of factual knowledge and rigorous logic and by surrender to mystical vision or existentialist ardor.

Philosophical reflection, just as all systematic thinking, should consider each idea, each problem, in its appropriate context. Thus a certain element or degree of abstraction is essential to all intellectual activity. But philosophical thought must reveal a keen sense of the correlation of various abstractions and the need of a clearly integrative direction.

# NOTES

## CHAPTER I. THE TRADITIONAL WORLD OF BODIES AND MINDS

1. Goethe, "*Gott und Welt: Atmosphäre.*"
2. Plato, *Phaedo*, 99.
3. L. Feuerbach, *Werke*, ed. Bolin and Jodl, Vol. X, p. 22; J. Moleschott, *Lehre der Nahrungsmittel*, 3. ed., p. 110.
4. T. H. Huxley, *Methods and Results: Essays*, ed. of 1917, p. 95.
5. Berkeley, *Principles of Human Knowledge*, I: 1, 3.
6. Spinoza, *Ethics*, II: vii.
7. H. Driesch, *Mind and Body*, 1927, p. 23.
8. *Cf.* the passage quoted from Richard Avenarius by A. E. Taylor, *Elements of Metaphysics*, 1903, p. 315, Note.
9. Goethe, "*Gingo biloba,*" in *West-Östlicher Divan.*

## CHAPTER II. THE WORLD OF CAUSAL MECHANISM

1. *Cf.* S. Alexander, *Spinoza and Time*, 1921, p. 36.
2. A. N. Whitehead, *Modes of Thought*, 1938, p. 174.
3. Jeans, *The Mysterious Universe*, ed. of 1932, p. 95.
4. *Cf.* Philipp Frank, *Philosophy of Science*, 1957, p. 244.
5. Jeans, *Op. cit.*, pp. 46, 94.
6. Eddington, *The Philosophy of Physical Science*, 1939, p. 110.
7. Bergson, *Creative Evolution*, transl. by Arthur Mitchell, 1922, p. 261.
8. H. A. Wilson, *The Mysteries of the Atom*, 1934, p. 109.
9. Jeans, *The Mysterious Universe*, p. 23.
10. *Cf. Cratylus*, 440.
11. Leibniz, *Theodicy*, transl. by E. M. Huggard, 1952, p. 147.
12. Kant, *Prolegomena to Any Future Metaphysics*, Introduction.
13. Ph. Frank, *Modern Science and Its Philosophy*, 1949, p. 115.
14. W. Heisenberg, "The Development of the Interpretation of the

Quantum Theory," in *Niels Bohr and the Development of Physics*, ed. by W. Pauli, 1955, p. 28; *cf. also The Physicist's Conception of Nature* by Heisenberg, transl. by A. J. Pomerans, 1958, pp. 14, 15.

15. Heisenberg, *Nuclear Physics*, Engl. transl., 1953, p. 30.
16. Erwin Schrödinger, *Science and Humanism*, 1951, p. 50.
17. Louis de Broglie, *The Revolution in Physics*, 1953, p. 216.
18. Bohr, "Biology and Atomic Physics," 1937, published in his *Atomic Physics and Human Knowledge*, 1958, p. 19.
19. Bohr, "Unity of Knowledge," 1954, in *Atomic Physics and Human Knowledge*, p. 72.
20. Eddington, *The Nature of the Physical World*, 1928, p. 309.
21. Eddington, *The Philosophy of Physical Science*, 1939, p. 63.
22. *The Mysterious Universe*, pp. 165, 186.
23. *The Philosophy of Physical Science*, p. 137.
24. H. A. Wilson, *The Mysteries of the Atom*, p. 111.
25. Planck, *Scientific Autobiography and Other Papers*, 1949, p. 122.
26. *Op. cit.*, p. 124.
27. *Ibid.*, p. 149.
28. H. A. Wilson, *Op. cit.*, p. 110.
29. *Cf.* Voltaire, *Oeuvres complètes*, ed. Moland, Vol. XVII, p. 584.
30. *Cf.* LaMettrie, *Traité de l'Ame*, in *Oeuvres philosophiques*, 1796, Vol. I, pp. 206 ff.; Watson, *Behaviorism*, 1930, p. 238; *The Battle of Behaviorism*, 1928, pp. 34 ff.
31. *Behaviorism*, p. 238.
32. Whitehead, *Modes of Thought*, 1938, p. 32.
33. Emerson, "Brahma."
34. *Creative Evolution*, p. 41.
35. *Cf.* Lloyd Morgan, *Mind at the Crossways*, 1929, p. viii.
36. *The Mysterious Universe*, pp. 150 f.
37. Margenau, "Advantages and Disadvantages of Various Interpretations of the Quantum Theory," in *Physics Today*, Oct., 1954, pp. 6-13.

## CHAPTER III.  THE WORLD OF EVOLUTION

1. *Cf. The Early Philosophers of Greece*, ed. by M. T. McClure, 1935, p. 72.
2. Aristotle, *De Partibus Animalium*, in *Works*, Oxford edition, Vol. V, translated by William Ogle, 1912, p. 640-a.
3. "Autobiography," *Life and Letters of Charles Darwin*, ed. by Francis Darwin, 2. ed., Vol. III, 1887, p. 252.

4. H. F. Osborn, *From the Greeks to Darwin,* ed. of 1913, p. 20.
5. *Kant's Critique of Judgment,* transl. by J. H. Bernard, 2. ed., 1914, pp. 312 f.
6. Erasmus Darwin, *Zoonomia,* 1801, Vol. II, p. 237.
7. Osborn, *Op. cit.,* p. 141, Note.
8. Lamarck, *Philosophie zoologique,* ed. of 1873, Vol. I, p. 38; *cf.* pp. 67 f.
9. *Philos. zool.,* Vol. I, pp. 235 f.
10. For a vigorous statement of the Neo-Lamarckian position, *cf.* F. le Dantec's work, *Les Limites du Connaissable,* 1904, Introduction, and the same author's more detailed treatment in *Lamarckiens et Darwiniens,* 1899.
11. Wm. McDougall, *The British Journal of Psychology,* Vol. XX, p. 218; *cf.,* Vol. XVII, pp. 270 ff.
12. *Cf.* Lloyd Morgan, *Life, Mind, and Spirit,* 1925, pp. 122 ff.
13. Darwin, *Life and Letters,* Vol. II, p. 215.
14. *Ibid.,* p. 23.
15. Darwin, *Origin of Species,* New York ed. of 1897, Vol. I, pp. 12, 167, 309 f.
16. Darwin, *The Descent of Man,* New York ed. of 1896, p. 565.
17. *Ibid.,* p. 33.
18. *Origin of Species,* Vol. I, p. 6; Vol. II, p. 293.
19. *Ibid.,* Vol. I, p. 5.
20. *Ibid.,* Vol. I, p. 5.
21. *Life and Letters,* Vol. I, p. 83.
22. *Loc. cit.*
23. *Origin of Species,* Vol. I., p. 365.
24. *Origin of Species,* Vol. I, p. 163.
25. *Op. cit.,* Vol. II, pp. 267 f.
26. *Cf.* Osborn, *Op. cit.,* pp. 244 f.
27. *Origin of Species,* Vol. I, p. 207.
28. *Op. cit.,* Vol. II, p. 275.
29. *Op. cit.,* Vol. I, p. 319.
30. *The Descent of Man,* p. 97.
31. *Ibid.,* p. 66; *cf.* p. 126.
32. *Ibid.,* p. 67.
33. *Cf. ibid.,* p. 126.
34. *Ibid.,* p. 619.
35. *Origin of Species,* Vol. I, p. 99.
36. *Ibid.,* p. 102; *cf.* p. 103.
37. *Op. cit.,* Vol. II, p. 305.
38. *Cf.* Haeckel, *The Riddle of the Universe,* transl. by Joseph McCabe, 1900, pp. 215 f., 179, 225.

39. *Ibid.*, p. 81.
40. *Cf.* Darwin, *The Variation of Animals and Plants under Domestication,* Chap. XXVII; *cf.* Haeckel, *Gemeinverständliche Werke,* Vol. I, pp. 224 f.
41. Hugo de Vries, "Mutations in Heredity," in *The Rice Institute Pamphlet,* Vol. I, No. 4, p. 347.
42. Schrödinger, *What is Life?* 1954, p. 34.
43. Morgan, *Regeneration,* 1901, p. 109.
44. Morgan, *Evolution and Adaptation,* ed. of 1928, pp. ix f.
45. *Ibid.*, p. 462; *cf.* p. 23.
46. Driesch, *The Science and Philosophy of the Organism,* Vol. II, ed. of 1908, p. 80.
47. J. S. Haldane, *The Philosophical Basis of Biology,* 1931, p. 157; *Materialism,* 1932, p. 123.
48. Quoted by Haldane in his *Materialism,* p. 177.
49. Haldane, *Mechanism, Life, and Personality,* ed. of 1914, p. 104; *cf.* his *Philosophical Basis of Biology,* p. 38.
50. Smuts, *Holism and Evolution,* ed. of 1927, p. 326.
51. "Integrative Levels in Biology," in *Philosophy for the Future,* ed. by R. W. Sellars, V. G. McGill, and M. Farber, 1949, p. 231.
52. H. S. Jennings, *Behavior of the Lower Organisms,* 1915, p. 316.
53. Cannon, *The Wisdom of the Body,* 2. ed., 1939, p. 24.
54. *Ibid.*, p. 38.
55. Haeckel, *The Riddle of the Universe,* p. 256; *cf.* pp. 254 ff.; *The Wonders of Life,* transl. by J. McCabe, 1904, Chap. XV, pp. 350-373.
56. Alexander, *Space, Time, and Deity,* ed. of 1920, Vol. II, p. 46.
57. *Ibid.*, p. 45.
58. *Cf.* J. B.Watson, *Psychology from the Standpoint of a Behaviorist,* 2. ed., p. 2, Note; cited by C. Lloyd Morgan, *Life, Mind, and Spirit,* 1925, p. 47.
59. *Space, Time, and Deity,* Vol. I, p. 180.
60. *Op. cit.,* Vol. I, p. 3.
61. *Cf. Op. cit.,* Vol. II, p. 63.
62. *Ibid.*, p. 38.
63. *Life, Mind, and Spirit,* pp. 140 f.
64. *Space, Time, and Deity,* Vol. II, p. 245.
65. Green, *Prolegomena to Ethics,* Section 184.
66. C. Judson Herrick, *The Evolution of Human Nature,* 1956, p. 138.
67. Lloyd Morgan, *Mind at the Crossways,* p. 235.
68. J. S. Mill, *An Examination of Sir William Hamilton's Philosophy,* 2. ed., 1865, p. 198.

69. *Space, Time, and Deity,* Vol. II, p. 309. *Cf. also* Alexander's *Philosophical and Literary Pieces,* 1939, p. 286.
70. *Space, Time, and Deity,* Vol. II, p. 413.
71. *Cf. Ibid.,* pp. 416, 409.
72. *Ibid.,* pp. 362, 428.
73. *Life, Mind, and Spirit,* p. 313.
74. Bergson, *Creative Evolution,* transl. by Arthur Mitchell, ed. of 1922, p. 5.
75. *Ibid.,* p. 8.
76. *Ibid.,* p. 261.
77. *Ibid.,* p. 252.
78. *Ibid.,* p. 174.
79. *Ibid.,* p. 262.
80. *Ibid.,* p. 144.
81. *Ibid.,* p. 142.
82. *Ibid.,* p. 159.
83. Bergson, *The Two Sources of Morality and Religion,* transl. by R. A. Audra and C. Brereton, 1935, p. 188.
84. *Creative Evolution,* p. 265.
85. *Ibid.,* pp. 189, 250.
86. *Ibid.,* pp. 191, 259.
87. *Ibid.,* p. 192.
88. *Ibid.,* p. 267; *cf.* pp. 125 ff.
89. *Ibid.,* p. 120.
90. *Ibid.,* p. 391.
91. J. S. Haldane, *The Philosophical Basis of Biology,* pp. 20, 21.
92. Köhler, *The Mentality of Apes,* transl. by Ella Water, ed. of 1948, pp. 11 ff., 25 ff., 101, 119 f., 128 f., 167 ff., 276.
93. *Cf. Progress and History,* ed. by F. S. Marvin, 1921, p. 262.

## CHAPTER IV. THE WORLD AS HISTORY

1. Dewey, *Experience and Nature,* 1925, p. 163.
2. *Cf.* R. G. Collingwood, *The Idea of History,* 1946, p. 114.
3. *Cf.* Bury, *Selected Essays,* ed. by Harold Temperley, 1930, p. 10.
4. J. Burckhardt, *Force and Freedom,* ed. by J. H. Nichols, 1943, p. 53.
5. Tolstoy, *What Is To Be Done?* Chap. xxxiv; Harrison, *The Meaning of History,* p. 11.
6. Bury, *Op. cit.,* p. 46.
7. *Cf.* Emery Neff, *The Poetry of History,* 1947, title-page.
8. Cited by A. Nevins, *Gateway to History,* 1938, p. 351.

9. *Cf.* Herbert Butterfield, *History and Human Relations,* 1952, p. 228.
10. Gentile, *The Theory of Mind as Pure Act,* transl. by H. Wildon Carr, 1922, p. 213.
11. *Cf.* Rudolf Eucken, in *Kultur der Gegenwart,* I, vi: *Systematische Philosophie,* 1921, pp. 224 f.
12. *Cf.* Hilda Oakeley, *History and the Self,* 1934, p. 93.
13. *Cf.* Croce, *On History,* transl. by D. Ainslie, 1923, p. 272.
14. *Cf.* Cassirer, *The Problem of Knowledge,* transl. by W. H. Woglom and C. W. Hendel, 1950, p. 235.
15. Cf. Oakeley, *Op. cit.,* p. 235.
16. Eucken, *Main Currents of Modern Thought,* transl. by Meyrick Booth, ed. of 1913, p. 324.
17. F. Max Müller, *Natural Religion,* ed. of 1907, p. 199.
18. *Philosophy and History,* Cassirer volume, ed. by Raymond Klibansky and H. J. Paton, 1936, p. 313.
19. Bury, *Selected Essays,* p. 23.
20. Croce, *On History,* p. 135.
21. Bergson, *Creative Evolution,* transl. by Arthur Mitchell, ed. of 1922, *cf.* pp. 7, 9, 31, 38 f.
22. *Philosophy and History,* Cassirer volume, p. 195.
23. *Cf.* Karl Löwith, *Understanding History,* 1949, p. 53.
24. H. Taine, *Ancien Régime,* transl. by John Durand, ed. of 1913, Preface; *History of English Literature,* transl. by H. van Laun, 1907, Vol. I, p. 11.
25. LaMettrie, *Oeuvres,* 1775, Vol. III, p. 27.
26. Feuerbach, *Werke,* ed. by Bolin and Jodl, Vol. X, p. 23; *cf.* Vol. I, pp. 55, 134.
27. Marx, *Das Kapital,* ed. by Karl Kautsky, Vol. I, 1928, p. xlvii.
28. The translation of this passage is by Karl Löwith in his *Meaning in History,* pp. 40, 45.
29. *Cf.* E. R. A. Seligman, *The Economic Interpretation of History,* 1924, pp. 31 f., Note.
30. *Cf.* R. A. Tsanoff, *The Problem of Immortality: Studies in Personality and Value,* 1924, Chapter v.
31. Hume, *Dialogues Concerning Natural Religion,* Part I, ed. by C. W. Hendel, in *Hume, Selections,* 1927, p. 292.
32. Lucretius, *On the Nature of Things,* III: 945.
33. Shelley, "Hellas."
34. Marcus Aurelius, *Thoughts,* transl. by George Long, ed. of 1891, xi: 1.
35. St. Augustine, *The City of God,* XII: 17, 20; transl. by Marcus Dods, Vol. I, pp. 506, 511.

36. Eucken, *Main Currents of Modern Thought*, p. 246.
37. Spencer, *First Principles*, Amer. ed. of 1896, p. 550.
38. Nietzsche, *Works*, Vol. XVI, transl. by A. M. Ludovici, 1911, p. 250.
39. Nietzsche, *Works*, Vol. X, transl. by Thomas Common, 1910, pp. 270 f.
40. Nietzsche, *Gesammelte Briefe*, Vol. IV, p. 70.
41. Nietzsche, *Werke*, Vol. XII, ed. of 1919, p. 370.
42. Nietzsche, *Works*, Vol. XVI, p. 245.
43. Hegel, *Lectures on the Philosophy of History*, transl. by J. Sibree, 1914, p. 476; *Philosophy of Right*, transl. by S. W. Dyde, Sect. 340; Schiller, "Resignation," penultimate stanza.
44. Comte, *Système de politique positive*, "Appendice général"; cited here from Cassirer, *The Problem of Knowledge*, p. 246.
45. *Cf.* G. H. Mead, *Movements of Thought in the Nineteenth Century*, 1950, p. 116.
46. *Cf.* Alexander, *Space, Time, and Deity*, 1920, Vol. II, pp. 309, 413.
47. Smuts, *Holism and Evolution*, p. 340.
48. Lucretius, *On the Nature of Things*, transl. by W. H. D. Rouse, Book V, Lines 1448 ff.
49. Bury, *The Idea of Progress*, ed. of 1924, pp. 21 f.
50. Reinhold Niebuhr, *Faith and History*, 1949, p. 70.
51. S. J. Case, *The Christian Philosophy of History*, 1943, pp. 96, 98.
52. Bury, *The Idea of Progress*, p. 344.
53. Rousseau, *Oeuvres complètes*, 1836, Vol. IV, p. 246.

## CHAPTER V.  THE WORLD AS DRAMA

1. C. Lloyd Morgan, *Mind at the Crossways*, 1929, p. 270.
2. N. Berdyaev, *The Meaning of History*, transl. by George Reavey, 1936, p. 28; *cf.* p. 42.
3. M. R. Cohen, *The Meaning of Human History*, 1947, pp. 273, 295.
4. Rudolf Eucken, in *Die Kultur der Gegenwart*, I: vi, *Systematische Philosophie*, 1921, p. 208.
5. Antonio Labriola, *Essays on the Materialistic Interpretation of History*, transl. by Charles H. Kerr, 1908, pp. 232, 233.
6. Hegel, *Philosophy of Right*, transl. by S. W. Dyde, 1896, Sect. 340; *cf.* Schiller's poem "Resignation."
7. James, *The Will to Believe*, ed. of 1912, p. 61.
8. *The Philosophical Review*, XXXIX, 2; republished in Alexander, *God and Man's Destiny*; C. Lloyd Morgan, *Mind at the Crossways*, Chapter XII.

9. A. N. Whitehead, *Science and the Modern World,* 1927, p. 90; *Modes of Thought,* 1938, pp. 191, 201.
10. Whitehead, *Science and the Modern World,* p. 99; *The Function of Reason,* 1929, p. 22; *Process and Reality,* 1929, p. 11.
11. Whitehead, *Modes of Thought,* pp. 5, 159.
12. Whitehead, *The Aims of Education and Other Essays,* 1929, pp. 62 f.
13. Whitehead, *The Function of Reason,* p. 11.
14. *The Function of Reason,* p. 12.
15. *Ibid.,* p. 11.
16. Whitehead, *Adventures of Ideas,* 1933, p. 249.
17. *Science and the Modern World,* pp. 10, 12, 174.
18. *Process and Reality,* p. 129.
19. St. Augustine, *Confessions,* XI: xiv: 17.
20. Royce, *The Conception of Immortality,* 1900, pp. 16 ff.
21. James, *The Varieties of Religious Experience,* ed. of 1915, p. 9.
22. Wordsworth, Preface to *Lyrical Ballads,* 1815.
23. Shakespeare, *King Lear,* III: ii.
24. Wordsworth, *loc. cit.*
25. Croce, *Breviario di estetica,* 3. ed., 1925, p. 31.
26. Aristotle, *Poetics,* transl. by Ingram Bywater, Chap. 22.
27. *Cf.* W. D. Bancroft, "The Methods of Research," in *The Rice Institute Pamphlet,* 1928, pp. 171, 179; J. M. Montmasson, *Invention and the Unconscious,* transl by H. S. Hatfield, 1932, p. 139.
28. Henri Poincaré, *Science and Method,* transl. by G. B. Halstead in *Foundations of Science,* ed. of 1929, p. 391.
29. Poincaré, *Op. cit.,* p. 127.
30. James, *The Will to Believe,* p. 61.
31. *Cf.* S. Alexander, *Beauty and Other Forms of Value,* 1933, p. 87.
32. Aristotle, *Poetics,* 1453$^a$, *Bywater's* translation.
33. Sophocles, *Antigone,* Lines 920 ff.; Jebb's translation.
34. Laura Jepsen, *Ethical Aspects of Tragedy,* 1953, p. 13.
35. Shakespeare, *Hamlet,* I: v.
36. *Cf.* W. M. Dixon, *Tragedy,* 1929, p. 42.
37. Émile Faguet, *Drame ancien, drame moderne,* ed. of 1898, pp. 5 f.
38. Shakespeare, *Othello,* IV: i: 206.
39. Shakespeare, *A Midsummer Night's Dream,* III: ii: 115.
40. Hobbes, *Human Nature, English Works,* ed. Molesworth, Vol. IV, 1840, p. 53.
41. George Meredith, *An Essay on Comedy,* ed. of 1913, p. 82.
42. Kant, *Critique of Aesthetic Judgment,* transl. by J. C. Meredith, 1911, p. 199.
43. Allardyce Nicoll, *The Theory of Drama,* 1931, p. 199.

44. R. Mukerjee, *The Social Structure of Values*, n.d., Chap. vi, p. 174.
45. Goethe, *Faust*, Part II, last page.
46. A. S. Eddington, in *Aristotelian Society Proceedings*, Supplem. Vol. X, 1931, pp. 162, 181.
47. B. Bosanquet, *The Principle of Individuality and Value*, 1912, p. 335.
48. Dante, *Divine Comedy, Paradise*, IV; 1-3.
49. *Ephesians*, iv; 25.
50. Part of a Symposium; cf. *Ethics*, LXVII, 1956, pp. 12-16.
51. Aeschylus, *Agamemmon*, Lines 170 ff.
52. *Cf.* W. R. McKenzie, *Ultimate Values*, 1924, p. 170.
53. Aristotle, *Metaphysics*, transl. by W. D. Ross, XII: vii: 1072$^b$
54. *Cf.* W. R. Inge, *The Eternal Values*, 1933, p. 5.
55. W. R. Sorley, *Moral Values and the Idea of God*, 2. ed., p. 467.
56. *Cf.* Harald Höffding, *Philosophy of Religion*, transl. by B. E. Meyer, 1914, pp. 209 ff.
57. *Cf.* A. C. Garnett, *Reality and Value*, 1937, p. 312.
58. Alexander, *Space, Time, and Deity*, 1920, Vol. II, p. 421.
59. M. Arnold, *Literature and Dogma*, Chap. I, ed. of 1900, p. 43.
60. Plotinus, *Enneads*, I: vi: 2, 3; cf. Grace H. Turnbull, ed., *The Essence of Plotinus*, 1934, p. 43.
61. St. Augustine, *The City of God*, XII: 6.
62. *Cf.* R. A. Tsanoff, *The Nature of Evil*, last chapter.
63. *Luke*, xii: 48.
64. Plato, *Theaetetus*, 176.
65. Shakespeare, *Macbeth*, I: i.
66. Goethe, *Faust*, Part II; *Finstere Galerie*.
67. *Shakespeare*, Hamlet, III: iv.
68. Royce, *The World and the Individual*, Vol. II, ed. of 1901, p. 340.
69. *Luke*, xviii: 19.
70. *John*, v: 17.
71. Robert Browning, "*Rabbi Ben Ezra*," xii.

# INDEX

# INDEX